THE CONDENSED GOSPEL OF SRI RAMAKRISHNA

MAHENDRANATH GUPTA

GYAN

Published by

Gyan Publishing House
5, Ansari Road
Daryaganj, New Delhi-110002
Phone: 011-47034999, 9811692060
E-mail: books@gyanbooks.com

Distribution Network
gyanbooks.com
India, USA, Canada, UK, Australia

ISBN: 978-93-6920-051-1 (HB)

First Published, 1911

2nd Impression 2025

Printed at: Gyan Press, Delhi.

THE CONDENSED GOSPEL OF SRI RAMAKRISHNA
Author: MAHENDRANATH GUPTA

CONDENSED GOSPEL OF SRI RAMAKRISHNA

(M's own English Version)

CONDENSED GOSPEL OF SRI RAMAKRISHNA

(According to M., a son of the Lord and disciple)

SRI RAMAKRISHNA MATH
MYLAPORE, MADRAS.

PREFACE TO THE SECOND EDITION

This volume contains the inspired words of the great divine world Teacher of this age, Sri Ramakrishna Paramahamsa, the Guru of Swami Vivekananda and his brothers. It is a series of conversations in which the highest spiritual truths were expounded by the Master in simple language with homely illustrations to disciples like Swami Vivekananda and men like Keshab Chandra Sen, Dr. Sirkar and others. These conversations were carefully recorded and preserved by an earnest and faithful house-holder disciple, M. and translated by himself into English. It received the hearty commendation of Swami Vivekananda.

The first edition of this book was published by the Brahmavadin office, Madras. As the teachings contained therein offer a complete and profound exposition of the universal religion and philosophy of Vedanta in all its aspects, as there is no metaphysical problem or practical spiritual difficulty that is not brought up and solved in these pages, and as the lofty message given by the Great Master is especially suited for the present age, the demand for copies of the book has been steadily on the increase. To meet that, the task of publishing a second edition completely revised by the author was entrusted to the Ramakrishna Math of Madras and they have great pleasure in presenting this volume to the earnest and thoughtful public.

Madras, PUBLISHERS
1st December 1911.

PREFACE TO THE THIRD EDITION

With the efflux of time there is coming a wider recognition of the spiritual profundity of Sri Ramakrishna's life and teachings, in both the Eastern and Western countries. The wonderful spirit of harmony his utterances breathe, their naive simplicity, and the vast ground of spiritual life they cover,—all these prove peculiar points of fascination to all who come into contact with his teachings. And we may say, they are affording the celestial manna to many a hungry soul. It is manifest from the ever-increasing circle of his followers and admirers all the world over, and an ever-growing thirst to know more about him. So we offer our humble service to the Master and his followers by bringing out the 3rd edition of this precious book.

Owing to the exorbitant increase in the cost of printing and paper we have been compelled to raise slightly the price of the book.

SRI RAMAKRISHNA MATH
Mylapore, Madras.

PUBLISHERS

LETTERS ON THE

GOSPEL OF SRI RAMAKRISHNA

FROM

SWAMI VIVEKANANDA

I

Dear M.,

C'est mon ami—now you are doing just the thing. Come out man. No sleeping all life; time is flying: Bravo! That is the way.

Many many thanks for your publication—only I am afraid it will not pay its way in pamphlet form *** Never mind: pay or no pay let it see the blaze of daylight. You will have many blessings on you and many more curses—but

वैसाहि सब काल बनता सहेब ![1]

This is the time.

Yours in the Lord,
VIVEKANANDA.

October 1897, c/o Lala Hansraj, Rawalpindi.

---

[1] That is always the way of the world!'

II

DEHRA DUN,
24th November, 1897.

My Dear M.,

Many many many many thanks for your second leaflet. It is indeed wonderful. The move is quite original, and never was the life of a great Teacher brought before the public untarnished by the writer's mind as you are doing.

The language also is beyond all praise, so fresh, so pointed, and withal so plain and easy.

I cannot express in adequate terms how I have enjoyed them. I am really in a transport when I read them. Strange, isn't it? Our Teacher and Lord was so original, and each one of us will have to be original or nothing. I now understand why none of us attempted His life before. It has been reserved for you, this great work. He is with you evidently.

With all love and namaskar,

VIVEKANANDA.

(*P.S.*) Socratic dialogues are Plato all over—you are entirely hidden. Moreover, the dramatic part is infinitely beautiful. Everybody likes it—here or in the West.

V.

THE HOLY MOTHER'S LETTER TO 'M'.

Jayarambati,
21st Ashad 1304
(4th July 1897)

Dear Child,

Whatever you had heard from Him is nothing but the Truth. You need not feel any diffidence about it. At one time it was He who had placed those words in your custody. And it is He who is now bringing them to the light of the day according to the needs of the times. Know it for certain that unless those words are brought out, man will not have his consciousness awakened. All the words of His that you have with you — every one of them is true. One day when you read them out to me I felt as if it was He who was speaking.

INTRODUCTION TO THE 1978 EDITION OF THE CONDENSED GOSPEL

HISTORY OF THE GOSPEL LITERATURE

M's own condensed English version of The Gospel of Sri Ramakrishna is reappearing before the public in 1978 after a period of about thirty six years' hibernation. When Swami Nikhilananda's full English translation of M's Bengali Sri Ramakrishna Kathamrita came out under the name The Gospel of Sri Ramakrishna in 1942, this valuable volume, which was the sole authentic work that spread the Great Master's teachings till then among the English reading public was withdrawn from circulation. But even now, many devotees of the Great Master, who by chance happen to go through the pages of this old publication, are thrilled by this, M's own English version; for unlike Swami Nikhilananda's, it is no sentence by sentence translation but 'M's own rendering of his thoughts, rather than language, directly into English with many elaborations and elucidating repetitions. A persistent demand for its republication therefore has been coming from the English reading public both in India and abroad. As an earnest of their deep interest in the work, the public have responded liberally to our appeal for funds for a subsidised edition of this work. The book is now, therefore, appearing in a twin form — an economical subsidised edition and a more expensive deluxe edition.

The present work '*The Condensed Gospel of Sri Ramakrishna,*' has got a historical importance in the development of the Gospel literature, besides its inherent spiritual appeal and its thrilling capacity to enliven the dead past. M. or Mahendra Nath Gupta, known also as Master Mahashay, was, as it were, brought by Providence to record the Great Master's conversations and transmit them to posterity. As Swami Sivananda, a direct disciple of the Master and the second president of the Ramakrishna Math, has remarked: "Whenever there was an interesting talk, the Master drew his attention to the holy words spoken. We did not then know why the Master did do. Now we can realise that this action of the Master had an important significance; for it was reserved for Master Mahashay to give to the world at large the sayings of the Master".

While commissioning M in this way, the Great Master, who shunned publicity and lionising, had also prohibited this disciple from writing about him in papers as Keshab had been doing, and this precious diary of conversations therefore remained unknown to, and unread by, any one till 1897. The diary was with 'M' during all those years — for him to read and go back on the wings of imagination, to relive those old ecstatic days and experiences he had during the Master's lifetime.

It was only in October and November 1897, more than ten years after Sri Ramakrishna's demise in 1886, that some important parts of this diary appeared for the first time in print as two pamphlets under the name '*The Gospel of Ramakrishna*' — and that in English, the world language of our times, a fact which all English-knowing people should take note of. Again it was in appreciation and authentication of these two pamphlets that Swami Vivekananda wrote those short but memorable letters published on pp7 & 8. It was, perhaps, also the great Swami who prompted him to bring out all his diary in book form for the good of humanity, and thus mankind has got today this incomparable scripture, the Gospel of Ramakrishna. It came out in instalments in five volumes in Bengali in 1902, 1905, 1907, 1910, and 1932 respectively. Swami Vivekananda had not perhaps seen the Bengali Gospel, as he died in July 1902, and the first volume in Bengali came out sometime that year only. In Swamiji's life we get no reference to his having seen it. Hence the first instalment of the English version, which elicited Swamiji's unstinted praise and approval, assumes tremendous importance from the historical perspective of the Gospel literature. It has, however, to be admitted that no copy of these first two early pamphlets of 1897 is to be had anywhere today in spite of vigorous search. But we can with certainty surmise that M must have incorporated them in his own English version, which he must have been contemplating and which came to be first published in 1907, five years after the first book in Bengali came out.

It is this 1907 publication that is now brought out as M's own condensed English version of the Gospel — a book that is not a translation in a literal sense but an independent writing by M himself on the same theme based on his diary. This first edition of 1907 was brought out by the Brahmavadin office, Madras, and its second edition, revised by the author himself and freed from its Biblical turns of expression, was published by Ramakrishna Math, Madras in 1911. Subsequently several editions of it were published by the Madras Math, and it was in circulation till 1942 when the full English translation of the Gospel by Swami Nikhilananda came out. But this M's English version is too precious and authentic a book to be thrown into the limbo and forgotten by humanity, and so we are re-publishing it as a condensed edition of the Gospel. Some of its chapters (cf. II) have tremendous doctrinal importance, throwing light on Sri Ramakrishna's sayings: "My realisations go beyond the Vedas and the Vedanta."

We are not attempting in this short Introduction any survey of the great teachings contained in the book. But we feel that for preventing misunderstanding, especially among Western readers, an expression that is used so often by the Master in these teachings and translated here as 'Woman and Gold', requires an explanation. The original Indian expression of Sanskritic origin, '*Kamini Kanchana*' is translated as 'Woman and Gold'. It is a very imperfect translation, and it would have been better to translate it as 'lust and lucre'; but 'Woman and Gold' has now become an established usage in the Gospel literature and it is now difficult to correct it. It will however be a great injustice to the Great Master, who looked upon all women as manifestations of the Divine Mother, if any critical reader interprets the expression as that of a woman-hater. Sanskrit is a wonderful language with several synonyms for the same idea with subtle differences of meaning, and the Sanskrit word '*Kamini*' does not actually mean 'woman', but a 'sexually inclined or exciting female'. So wherever the Master inveighs against 'woman and gold' in this text, it must be understood only as warning against 'sexuality and greed', or 'lust and lucre', which are the greatest obstacles in man's spiritual progress.

ABOUT THE AUTHOR HIMSELF

It is natural for the reader of such a precious volume as this, to feel an urge to know more details about the life and personality of its great author, but considerations of space compel us to refer such earnest seekers to the very elaborate account we have given in the complete translation of the Gospel under the caption 'The Recorder of the Gospel, Mahendranath Gupta'. Suffice it to say here that he was as unique as his book itself. A learned professor in oriental and occidental arts and sciences, he felt life in his joint family so unhappy and wretched to put up with that he walked away one midnight with the idea of committing suicide. But early next morning a divine destiny, which we ordinarily call chance, directed him unknowingly into the Dakshineswar Temple-garden and into the divine presence of our Great Master. What followed during the succeeding few moments — so momentous in the spiritual history of mankind — the reader will find in the opening pages of this great scripture. Literally, the man who went to die, remained to pass through a spiritual ascension without physical death. He now found the real vocation of his life, the true purpose of his earthly sojourn. Mahendra Nath, the Professor of Sciences and Arts, and the teacher of college students, now became the Recorder of the Gospel of Ramakrishna and the anonymous spiritual teacher of mankind, even as the great Vyasa in olden times reached the peak of his spiritual ministry when he took to recording the life and teachings of Sri Krishna.

During the last twentyseven years of his life, he retired from his professorial works, and lived the life of a veritable sage in a room on the third floor of his Morton Institution — a room which he converted literally into a modern Naimisaranya, resounding all the hours of the day, and sometimes of the night too, with the words of God coming from his Rishi-like face, addressed to the earnest group of God-lovers sitting round him. And at other times, perhaps at midnight often, calling on an attendant devotee-disciple he would say, "Let us listen to the words of the Great Master in the depths of the night as he explains the truth of the Pranava." And to such devotee-amanuenses he would dictate, stirring the depths of his stupendous memory with the help of his diary and deep meditation, and reliving those blessed days he spent with the Master, what he had then heard with vivid and detailed description of the scenic contexts in which they were delivered. Thus has mankind got for the first time in history something that is very near to what an Incarnation of God spoke.

Here we have to draw the reader's attention to the brief remark of Swami Vivekananda at the end of the second of his letters: 'You will have many blessings on you and many more curses — that is always the way of the world, Sir'. This remark of the Swami has proved prophetic; for this great work has had hostile criticism from different sources from different points of view. Some with their fanatical slant to pure Advaitam and a supercilious contempt and patronising attitude towards the conception of a Personal God and practice of devotion to Him, have the habit of dubbing the *Gospel* as a mere Sunday report of M, and that the Great Master had many great and superior teachings which he did not reveal to M. But they, however, never reveal their authority for upholding this claim. — a claim that falsifies the certification by Swami Vivekananda and the Holy Mother.

It is, however, reasonable to concede that the Gospel does not contain all that the Master taught during a decade or more of his ministry, or record all the instructions he gave to individuals specially for their practice. But this is far different from questioning the representative character of the Gospel as the Master's message to mankind, as certified by Swami Vivekananda and the Holy Mother.

There are some others, especially among Christian ministers, who want to downgrade this book on the ground that its contents are all M's thoughts, foisted on Sri Ramakrishna who was quite an unlearned rustic. Such critics forget that if by such argument these conversations recorded by so learned and talented a contemporary, a close and keen observer, and a devoted disciple like M could be set aside, the same logic would utterly devastate the credibility of their own scriptures—the Bibles, the Kurans, the Tripitakas and all other scriptural texts supposed to be the utterances of great men, but neither recorded during their lifetime, nor authenticated by any one whose intellectual and spiritual competence to preserve them correctly can be proved. They are all mostly traditions which have been handed down by later generations of disciples and have taken shape in some cases more than a century after the original teachers had passed away. Under the circumstances, they are most unreliable and if there is in the world any one text that comes very near the original teaching of a God-man, it is the record of M and M alone.

The five Bengali volumes of the Gospel were brought out one after another by M, until before the midnight of 3rd June 1932, the Phalaharini-Kali Pooja day, he had finished reading the proof of the last book of the Gospel. He had now finished his mission in life, and lo! his chronic neuralgic pain suddenly became severe that night; and in the early hours of 4th June 1932, he left his mortal coil, chanting the prayer; "O Master! O Mother! Take me in Your arms!"

Ramakrishna Math
Madras. 1.1.'78

SWAMI TAPASYANANDA

CONTENTS

SECTION		PAGE NO
	INTRODUCTION	1
I	Sri Ramakrishna at Dakshineswar	25
II	A Visit to Pandit Iswara Chandra Vidyasagar	57
III	Sri Ramakrishna at the Temple of Dakshineswar with Narendra, Rakhal, M. and other Disciples.	93
IV	Steamer Trip with Keshab Chandra Sen	111
V	Sri Ramakrishna with Keshab Chandra Sen at Lily Cottage	140
VI	A Day with Sri Ramakrishna at the Temple of Dakshineswar	155
VII	Visit to Surendra's Garden	167
VIII	Visit to a Hindu Pandit and Preacher.	183
IX	Sri Ramakrishna at the Temple of Dakshineswar	198
X	Sri Ramakrishna at the Temple of Dakshineswar with Narendra and other Disciples.	223
XI	Sri Ramakrishna at the house of Balaram, a Disciple, with Narendra, Girish, Balaram, Chunilall, Latu, M., Narayan and others.	238
XII	Sri Ramakrishna at Syampukur (Calcutta) with the Disciples, and Ishan, Dr. Sarkar and others.	266
XIII	The Master at Syampukur, Calcutta, with his Disciples.	283

XIV	Sri Ramakrishna at Cossipore Garden with Narendra, Rakhal, M., Girish and other Disciples.	302
	INDEX	315

CONDENSED GOSPEL OF SRI RAMAKRISHNA

INTRODUCTION

SRI RAMAKRISHNA — A short sketch of his life

Birth of Sri Ramakrishna—his father Khudiram and mother Chandramani—the primary school—his daily worship of Raghuvir, his household God—mixing with holy men—listening to the recital of Sacred Books—beholds a miraculous Light or Glory—comes down to Calcutta—sees God at the temple of the Universal Mother at Dakshineswar—'Like one mad'—thrown into the company of holy men in the temple—listens to the recital of the Vedanta by Tota Puri—practises austerities according to the Sacred Books—talking with the Mother of the Universe—his chosen disciples—his devotees—Ramakrishna and the Brahmo Samaj—reconciliation of all Religions—his female devotees—the Communion of Devotees.

Sri Ramakrishna was born in a village called Kamarpukur in the district of Hugli (Bengal) on Wednesday, the 18th of February 1836, or the 10th of Falgun 1757 Saka, the second lunar day of the light fortnight. He came of a highly respected, though poor, Brahmin family. The village of Kamarpukur is about eight miles west of the sub-division Arambag, formerly called Jehanabad, and about 26 miles south of Burdwan.

Sri Ramakrishna's father, Khudiram Chatterjee, was a great devotee. His mother Chandramani Devi was the personification of kindness. In her there was no guile. The family used formerly to live in a neighbouring village called Deray, three miles from Kamarpukur. Khudiram with the independence of a cultured Brahmin declined to appear before a law-court and give evidence in favour of the local magnate, the landlord of the village. This man made the place too hot for Khudiram, and he left Deray with his family and settled in Kamarpukur.

Sri Ramakrishna was called Gadadhar in his childhood. He received some lessons in reading, writing and arithmetic at the village primary school. Subhankar, the well-known Mathematician whose arithmetic is widely read in Bengal, simply threw his head into confusion, as he used to say.

After leaving the village school, the boy was not allowed to sit idle at home. His next duty was to attend to the daily worship of his household God Raghuvir. Every morning he chanted the name of the Lord, put on a holy garment, and gathered flowers. After ablutions, prayers[1] and meditation on the Supreme Being,[2] the One and Indivisible God, he worshipped Raghuvir, also called Rama, one of the Incarnations of the Supreme Being, and the Hero of the well-known epic, the Ramayana. He could sing divinely. The songs that he heard during theatrical performances,[3] he could recite from beginning to end. From a boy, he was always happy. Men, women and children—everybody loved him.

Holy men used to visit the guest-house of his neighbours, the Lahas of Kamarpukur. Gadadhar, as Sri Ramakrishna was then called, would go amongst these holy men and try his best to minister to them with the devotion of a disciple.

Brahmin scholars were often, as is the practice amongst the Hindus, engaged to read from the Sacred Books about the Life and Teachings of the various Incarnations of God, and sing and narrate the incidents in the vernacular. Sri Ramakrishna would listen to these men with rapt attention. In this way he mastered the Ramayana, the Mahabharata and the Bhagavata—all religious epics relating to Rama and Krishna who are both regarded by the Hindus as Incarnations of God.

When eleven years old, Sri Ramakrishna was one day going through the corn-fields to Anur, a village near Kamarpukur. As he told his disciples afterwards, he suddenly

[1]Gayatri [2]Brahman. [3]Jatras.

saw a Vision of Glory and lost all sense-consciousness. People said, it was a fainting fit; but it was really that calm and serene mood, that superconscious state, called Samadhi, brought on by God-vision.

After the death of his father, Sri Ramakrishna, then seventeen or eighteen years old, went with his elder brother to Calcutta. The brothers came down to Calcutta with an intention of seeking their fortune. They spent some days at Nathair Bagan; thence they shifted their lodgings to Govinda Chatterjee's house at Jhamapukur. Sri Ramakrishna was employed by Govinda to officiate as an assistant priest under him. In this capacity he came in contact with the Mitras and other respectable families of Jhamapukur, who entrusted to him the daily worship of their household Gods.

Rani Rashmani, a rich and pious Bengali lady, built the well-known temple at Dakshineswar, a village about four miles from Calcutta, in the summer of the Bengali year 1262, Thursday, 31st May 1855 A.D.,-the day of the full-moon, the 18th of Jaistha. The eldest brother of Sri Ramakrishna, Pandit Ram Kumar, was appointed the chief priest of the temple.

Sri Ramakrishna used often to come to the temple to see his brother. Within a few days he was himself employed as an assistant priest. His second brother, Rameswar, also officiated as a priest from time to time. He has left two sons, Ramlal and Sivaram, and one daughter, Lakshmi Devi.

In the course of a few days a change came over Sri Ramakrishna. He was found sitting along for long hours before the Image of the Mother[1]. Evidently his mind was drawn away from things of this world. It was in quest of some Object not sought by men of the world.

His people shortly arranged his marriage. They hoped that marriage would turn his mind away from his Ideal

[1]Kali or Consort of the Lord of Eternity.

World. His newly married bride Sri Sri Saradamani Devi was the daughter of Ram Chandra Mukhopadhyaya of Joyrambati, a village only four miles from Kamarpukur. She was only six years old at the time of her marriage (1859) while her husband was twenty three.

After his marriage Sri Ramakrishna returned to the temple-garden at Dakshineswar. This was the turning point of his godly life. In a few days, while worshipping the Mother, he saw strange Visions of Divine Forms. During the evening service his duty amongst other things was to wave the lights[1], holy water, flowers, etc., before the Sacred Image. But filled with the Divine Idea as he was, he would begin the ceremony but very often forget to bring it to a close! Indeed, he did not stop until his attention was drawn by the Temple people to the strangeness of his conduct. On other occasions, he would sit down to worship the Mother; but very often it was noticed that he was not going to stop at all! Stranger still, he would place on his own head the flowers intended as offerings to the Mother of the Universe!

It was soon found by the temple authorities that Sri Ramakrishna was, in the present state of his religious feelings, incapable of doing the duty of a priest any longer. Indeed, in the present state of those feelings, he went about like a man who was not in the right state of mind. Rani Rashmani's son-in-law, Mathoor, however, looked upon him in a different light. He called him a prophet sent by God for the salvation of mankind. As for the daily worship of the Mother, Mathoor had another priest appointed to do the duty.

Thus it came about that Sri Ramakrishna could not go on with his work as a priest. Nor could he go on doing his duties as a householder.

The marriage had been only in name. He said 'Mother, O! Mother!' night and day. Now he was like a stock or stone, or a figure made of wood! Now he was found behaving

[1]Aratrika.

like a person of unsound mind. At another time he behaved like a child! He hid himself from the sight of worldly minded men! He did not like those who did not love the Lord, nor did he listen to any words except those of God! He cried without ceasing, 'Mother O! my Divine Mother!'

There was a guest-house in the Temple-garden. Holy men who had given up the world used to come there as guests. Tota Puri, a holy man, stayed there as a guest for eleven months. He it was who expounded to Sri Ramakrishna, the Vedanta philosophy. During the exposition Tota observed that his disciple was no ordinary man, and that he frequently went into a state of Divine Ecstasy[1] in which the finite ego goes out of sight and becomes one with God, the Universal Ego!

A Brahmin lady who had also given up the world came as a guest to the Temple a little before Tota Puri. She it was who helped Sri Ramakrishna to go through the practices enjoined by the Scriptures called the Tantras. She looked upon him as the incarnation[2] of Chaitanya, the God-man of Nadia, and read before him the Sacred Books[3] relating to his life and teachings.

Vaishnav Charan, a well-known Pandit amongst the Vaishnavas at the time, used often to come and see Sri Ramakrishna. Once he took him to Colootola, a district in Calcutta, to witness the proceedings of a religious assembly.[4] The people there were a little shocked at the sight of Sri Ramakrishna, then in a state of God-consciousness, stepping up to take the seat set apart for Chaitanya, the Divine Incarnation whom they all worshipped. Vaishnav Charan was the president of this religious assembly.

Vaishnav Charan once said to Mathoor, son-in-law of Rashmani, then manager of the Temple,—'The madness of this young man is not of the ordinary kind. He is mad after the Lord!' Both Vaishnav Charan and the Brahmani[5] found out that Sri Ramakrishna was filled with the 'Great

[1]Samadhi. [2]Avatar. [3]Charitamrita, etc. [4]Chaitanya Sabha. [5]The Brahmin lady.

Idea'—the Divine Idea. Like Chaitanya he used to pass through three different states of religious consciousness *viz.*, the purely Internal or Super-conscious State, in which there can be no outward consciousness; the Half-conscious State in which outward perception is not entirely lost; and the Conscious State in which it is possible for one to chant the holy name of the Lord. With 'Mother, O! Mother!' ever on his lips, he would talk to the Divine Mother without cessation. He would ask Her to teach him. He would often say, 'O Mother, I know not the Sacred Books[1]; nor have I anything to do with the Pandits well versed in them. It is Thou alone whose words I shall hear. Teach Thou and let me learn.'

The sweet name of Mother, Sri Ramakrishna applied to the Supreme Being, God the Absolute, who transcends all thought, all time and space. The Divine Mother once said to him, 'Thou and I are one. Let the end of Thy life in this world be deep devotion[2] to Me. Do thou pass some days in this world for the good of mankind. And there shall come to thee many worshippers. Then thou shalt be pleased to see that there are in the world not only the worldly-minded but also those that are pure and free from worldly desires, loving Me alone, their Divine Mother.'

In the evening at the time of divine service[3] Sri Ramakrishna would, amidst the sounds of bells, cymbals and drums, cry out from the terrace of the Kuthi, saying, 'Come ye that love God and tarry not; O! how I long to see you all! Come, my own; or else my life shall quit my body!'

Keshab Sen saw Sri Ramakrishna about the year 1875. Keshab was then staying with his disciples in a garden at Belgaria about three miles from the Temple-garden at Dakshineswar. With Sri Ramakrishna was his nephew Hridoy.

Viswanath Upadhyaya, usually known as Captain, visited Sri Ramakrishna about this time. He was the re-

[1] Shastras. [2] Bhakti. [3] Aratrika.

presentative of the Nepal Government at Calcutta. Mahimacharan met him shortly after.

His disciples, some of those that were near and dear to him, first met him between 1879 and 1882. He had then passed the stage of 'madness for the Lord.' He was like a child, gentle and full of joy and gladness. Only he was, as a rule, in a state of intense God-consciousness[1]. Coming down from this plane he used to move about in his Ideal World. Verily he behaved like a child five years old,—with 'Mother! O Mother' always on his lips!

About the end of 1879 came Ram and Manamohun. Kedar, Surendra came next; Chuni, Latoo, Nritya Gopal, Tarak also came about that time. Towards the end of 1881 and the beginning of 1882 came Narendra (Vivekananda), Rakhal, Bhabanath, Baburam, Balaram, Niranjan, M., Jogin. In 1883, 1884, the following disciples came and met Sri Ramakrishna:—Kishori, Adhar, Nitai, Gopal of Sinthi, Gopal (junior), Tarak of Belgharia, Sarat. Sasi, Subodh, Sanyal, Gangadhar, Kali; Girish, Devendra, Sarada, Kalipada (Ghosh), Upendra, Dwija, Hari; Narendra (junior), Paltu (Pramatha), Purna, Narayan, Tej Chandra, Haripada; Haramohan, Jojneswar, Khirode, Hajra, Jogin and Kishori of Krishnanagar, Manindra (Khoka); Bhupati, Akshoy, Navagopal, Govinda of Belgharia, Ashu, Girindra, Atul, Durgacharan, Suresh, Prankrishna, Nabai Chaitanya, Hariprasanna, Mahendra (Mukherjee), Preo (Mukherjee), the Saint Manmatha, Binode, Tulsi, Daksha; Harish (Mustafi), Basak, Kathak Thakur, Sasi Brahmachari of Bally, Nritya Gopal Goswami, Bepin of Konnagar, Dhiren, Rakhal (Haldar) and others.

The following also saw Sri Ramakrishna—many of them men of light and leading:- Pandit Iswar Chandra Vidyasagar, Pandit Sasadhar, Doctor Rajendra, Doctor Sarkar, Doctor Bhaduri, Bankim (Chatterjee), Mr. Cook of the United States, Mr. Williams, Mr. Missir, Michael

[1]Samadhi.

Madhu Sudan (the poet), Krishna Das Pal, Pandit Dinabandhu, Pandit Syamapada, Doctor Ram Narayan, Doctor Durga Charan; Nilkantha, Trailanga Swami, the great Saint of Benares. Ganga Mata of Brindavan also met him when he was with Mathoor during his pilgrimage to Brindavan. Ganga Mata regarded him as Radha, the Incarnation[1] of Divine Love. She was therefore unwilling to part from him.

Before his immediate disciples ever met him, other well-known devotees had been to the Temple-garden to see Sri Ramakrishna. Thus he came to know Krishna Kishore, the venerable old Brahmin of Ariadah, Mathoor, Sambhu Mallik, an English-educated wealthy citizen of Calcutta, Narain Sastri, a Sanskrit scholar who read logic[2] at one of the colleges at Nadia, Gouri Pandit of Indesh near Hugli, Achalananda, Chandra, Padmalochan, the court Pandit of a former Maharaja of Burdwan, Dayananda, the founder of Arya Samaj, and many others. It is needless to add that the inhabitants of Kamarpukur, his native village, and those of Seore and Syambazar, etc., many of them intensely devoted to God, were amongst those who used often to meet him.

The leaders of the Brahmo Samaj with their disciples often came in contact with him. Keshab Sen, Bijoy, Kali Bose, Pratap, Sivanath, Amrita, Troilokya, Krishna Bihary, Manilal, Umesh, amongst the older members,—Hirananda, Bhawani, Nandalal, Benoy, Pramatha, Mohit, and many others amongst the younger members of the Brahmo Samaj, often met him. He too would often go to them. During the lifetime of Mathoor, Sri Ramakrishna saw Devendra Tagore, leader of the Adi Brahmo Samaj; and he once paid a visit to that Samaj during Divine service. He paid a similiar visit to Keshab's church when Divine service was being conducted by Keshab; and to the church of the Sadharan

[1]Avatar. [2]Nyaya.

Samaj, one of the many sects into which the Society[1] of the Brahmos has been split up.

Sri Ramakrishna often visited Keshab at his house and rejoiced in his company and that of his followers. Keshab also, sometimes alone and sometimes with his disciples, often came to the Temple-garden at Dakshineswar to see him. At these meetings Sri Ramakrishna spoke for long hours about the Lord, and as he spoke, his audience listened with rapt attention to the words of wisdom that fell from his lips. Like an inspired prophet he spoke, and very often he was thrown into a state of Divine Ecstasy! His corporeal frame would become motionless; his respiration stop; his eyes move not! All sense-consciousness would leave him, and he became filled with God-consciousness instead.

At Kalna near Burdwan he met Bhagvandas Babaji, a Vaishnava saint. The Babaji observed his unique state of Divine Ecstasy and said, 'Verily Thou art an Incarnation of God, eminently fit to take the seat set apart for Chaitanya.'

Besides teaching the fact that *God may be seen*, his great object was to point out the harmony amongst all religions. He realised, on the one hand, the Ideal set up by each of the various sects of the Hindu religion, and on the other, the Ideal of Islam and that of Christianity. He recited in solitude the name of Allah and meditated upon Jesus Christ. In a vision he saw Jesus in his glory. In his chamber he made room for the pictures not only of Hindu Gods and Goddesses including Buddha, but also for that of Jesus. In that picture Jesus is represented as delivering Peter who is about to be drowned, and as stilling the storm that is raised. The picture of Jesus is still seen in his chamber. English and American men and women may be found to-day squatting on the bare floor of that room, meditating upon God and upon Sri Ramakrishna.

One day he said to the Divine Mother, 'O Mother,

[1]Brahmo Samaj.

I long to see how Thy Christian devotees pray to Thee. May it please Thee to take me to a place where they come together for Divine service.' Some days after, he was found standing at the entrance of a Christian church in Calcutta, looking in and watching the Divine service held within. Upon his return to the Temple-garden he said to his disciples, 'I went to the church but did not get in, lest the steward of the Temple should not suffer me to enter the Sanctuary and worship the Mother.'

Sri Ramakrishna had devotees also amongst women. He would give joy to Gopal's Mother by calling her by the sweet name 'Ma'. He looked upon all women as Incarnations of the Divine Mother and he worshipped them as such. Only he would warn men not to come in contact with women until they had realised them as such Incarnations, and until they had learnt to have pure love for God. Indeed, he enforced this rule even in connection with women well known for their purity, piety, and deep devotion to God. To the Divine Mother he once said, 'O Mother, I will run a knife across my throat if any impure lustful thought arises in my mind!'

The number of his followers is large. Some of them are known and some unknown. It is impossible to name all. In this Gospel the names of many will be found mentioned. The following names may be added, of those who visited him during their boyhood: Ramakrista, Putto, Tulsi, Sasi, Bepin, Nagendra, Upendra, Surendra (Gupta), Suren, Santi, etc. Many girls also saw him. All these are at present his devoted followers.

Many are those who have become and are becoming his followers to-day. Madras, Ceylon, the United Provinces, Kumaun, Nepal, Bombay, Rajputana, the Punjab, Japan, all contain men and women who aspire to follow in his footsteps. Nay, the family of his disciples lies scattered to-day not only in Asia but also in America and Europe, and notably in the United States and in England.

THE TEMPLE-GARDEN—A short description

THE MASTER TEACHING IN THE TEMPLE:—It is Sunday. The devotees are free from work, and they have come in numbers to the Temple-garden to see Sri Ramakrishna. His door is open to every-body. The Master freely talks with all men regardless of creed or colour, sect or age. Holy men, be they novices or those who have attained the highest stages of spirituality; orthodox Hindus, Christians and members of the Brahmo Samaj; Hindus who worship God as the Primal Divine Energy[1] as well as those[2] who worship Him as the Preserver (Vishnu); men and women; all alike are coming to see the Master. Blessed art thou, O Rani Rashmani, for it is thy religious merit that has caused this beautiful Temple to be raised up! To thee also is due that we are able to meet and worship this Prince amongst men, this Holy Image of the Divinity, which unlike marble or clay does move about to the delight of all who love the Lord.

2. THE PORCH AND THE TWELVE TEMPLES OF GOD THE FATHER:—The Temple-garden is situated about four miles north of Calcutta on the banks of the holy river Ganges. Going there by boat one lands on the broad brick-built steps of the ghat leading to the Temple. Sri Ramakrishna used to bathe at this ghat. East of the landing is the Chandni or the Porch. Its roof resembles an awning supported on pillars. The Chandni is especially used at night by the Temple watchmen on duty. Their chests of mango-wood and one or two water vessels or *lotas*, made of brass, are often found there lying about. The gentlemen of the neighbourhood often come here and take their seats before stepping down to bathe in the Holy Waters. They amuse themselves with gossip as they rub themselves with oil. Many holy men and women belonging to various sects of the Hindus come to the Temple and wait here until the hour for morning

[1]Shakti. [2]Vaishnava.

offerings to the Gods is over and they have partaken of the accepted offerings—the consecrated food[1]. Not infrequently a woman worshipper[2] of the Mother will be found sitting here. She has given up the world, is dressed in ochre-coloured clothes and holds in her hands the trident, the symbol of her order. She, too, will come into the guest-house and wait until the morning offerings have been presented.

The Chandni is exactly in the middle of a long row of Temples, dedicated to Siva who symbolizes God the Father. These Temples are twelve in number, six of them being to the north of the porch and the remaining six to the south. People passing in boats on the river point out to one another the Twelve Temples, saying 'Look! yonder is the Temple-garden of Rani Rashmani!'

3. THE TEMPLE OF GOD AS LOVE INCARNATE :—Eastwards within this row of Temples and the Chandni is the courtyard. The yard is paved with tiles set in concrete. In the middle are two Temples, one facing west and the other south.

The first is situated northwards and is dedicated to Radha and Krishna—God manifesting Himself as the Incarnation of Divine Love. The two Images stand with their faces to the west. Steps lead from the courtyard into the Sanctuary. Its floor is paved with marble. Chandeliers hang from the ceiling of the verandah, they are protected by red linen, except when uncovered on festive occasions. In front of the verandah is a row of columns. At the entrance to the passage between two of these columns is seated a solitary porter keeping watch. In the afternoon the direct rays of the setting sun would find their way into the Sanctuary, and for this reason canvas screens have been provided to place between the columns. They are intended for the passages left open between the columns. In the south-east corner of the erandah is a great jar containing holy water

[1]Prasad. [2]Bhairavi.

from the Ganges. Close to the threshold of the door leading into the Sanctuary is a small brass vessel containing the 'Nectar of the Feet of the Lord.' The devotees come, bow down before the Images of the Gods, receive some drops of this sacred water on the palm of their right hand and drink it with the greatest reverence.

Inside the sanctuary are the Holy Images of Radha and Krishna.

4. THE TEMPLE OF GOD THE MOTHER:—In the southern temple is the beautiful image of the Divine Mother. She is called here the Saviour of the World.[1] The floor of the temple is paved with marble. The image stands on a dais of stone with steps to the south. The stone platform has upon it a silver 'lotus of a thousand petals.' On this lotus lies Siva, the Symbol of the Absolute, with His head to the south and His feet to the north. This Image is made of white marble. Upon Him stands the Mother of the Universe with one foot on His breast and the other on His thigh. She is apparelled in a gorgeous Benares *sari*[2] and Her Person is decorated with jewels of many kinds. On Her lotus feet are, amongst others, the tinkling anklets called *nupur* and the scarlet *jaba* with fresh leaves of the *bael* tree fragrant with sandal paste. One of these anklets is the *panjeb* used by our up-country women. This ornament was procured by Mathoor, son-in-law of the foundress Rani Rashmani, at the special desire of Sri Ramakrishna. The Mother's arms are adorned with various ornaments made of gold set with jewels; the lower arm, with the bracelets known as the 'cocoanut flowers', *paińcha, bauti,* and *bala*; the upper with the armlets called *tarr, tabiz, baju*, the last with a pendant attached to it. Round Her neck She wears the golden *cheke*, a pearl necklace of seven strings, a golden necklace of thirty-two strings, a 'chain of stars' (*tara har*) and—a garland made of human skulls. On Her head She wears a crown of gold

[1]Bhavatarini. [2]Cloth for ladies.

and Her ears are adorned with *kanbala* and *kanpash*; and with golden earrings that look like flowers; and *chaudani* and the 'golden fish.'

The beauty of Her aquiline nose is set off by a golden nose-ring with a pearl-drop attached to it. She has three eyes, the third being the Eye of Divine Vision. She has four arms. In one of the two left hands She holds a freshly severed human head and in the other a sword. With one of Her right hands She offers boons to Her devotees, and with the other—the uplifted one—She says 'Fear not.' The head and the sword symbolize Death and the terrible side of the Divinity, even as Her offer of boons and Her assurance of help to Her devotees bring out the loving side and put them in mind of Her boundless Love and Mercy.

Round Her waist She wears a terrible garland made of human arms and also golden waist-chains called *neem fruit* and *komarpata*.

In the north-east corner of the shrine is a bed on which the Mother takes Her rest. Near this hangs on the wall a *chamar*, made of the white hairs from the tail of the deer called *chamari*, used for fanning the Mother. Many a time has Sri Ramakrishna himself fanned Her with this *chamar*. On the steps stand vessels which hold Her drinking-water. On the silver lotus is a small image of a lion made of the eight metals, an image of the guana and a trident. At the south-western corner of the dais stands the image of a she-fox. To the south is that of a black bull and to the north-east that of a goose. On one of the steps of the dais the image of Narayana or God the Preserver is installed on a small silver throne. By His side is the image of Ramlala or Ramachandra, God Incarnate, obtained by Sri Ramakrishna from a holy man. Close to Ramlala on the same step is a small emblem of Siva called Baneswar and also the images of various other manifestations of God. The Divine Mother stands with Her face to the south.

Within the shrine and close to the northern wall is the sacred pitcher made of copper, filled with the holy water of the Ganges for the Mother to wash Her face with. Above the Holy Image is a beautiful canopy, and the background is a piece of Benares silk embroidered with flowers of many colours. The canopy adds greatly to the beauty of the Image. Twelve columns, inner and outer, made apparently of silver, stand at the corners of the dais round about the Holy Image.

The entrance to this shrine is by a pillared verandah and is protected by strong doors. The guard sits near one of the passages. Close to the threshold again, as in the case of the other shrine, is a small cylindrical brass vessel containing the Nectar of the Mother's Feet. The top of the temple is adorned with nine pinnacles.

5. THE THEATRE-HALL[1]:—In front of the temple and exactly to the south of it is the spacious Theatre hall[1]. It is rectangular and the splendid terrace is supported by both inner and outer rows of columns. Theatrical performances[2] etc., take place here on special occasions, especially on the day of the festival[3] held in honour of the Mother.

6. THE GUEST-HOUSE[4]:—To the west of the courtyard is the row of twelve temples of the Father already mentioned. On the three other sides are sets of rooms with corridors leading to them. The rooms to the east are the store-room, the room[5] for keeping *loochis* and sweetmeats, the room for cooking the food offerings for Vishnu who does not accept any fish or meat offerings, the room for getting ready fruits and other offerings, and the room for cooking the offerings for the Divine Mother. Lastly, there are the corridors used for feeding the guests including holy men, Brahmins, beggars etc. These, if they do not sit at meals in the Guest-house must proceed to the Office of the steward of the Temple-garden and apply for their doles of rice and *dal* and other necessaries. The steward bids the officer in charge of the stores give what they want.

7. To the south of the Theatre hall, is the place of sacrifice.

[1]Nat-Mandir. [2]Jatras. [3]Kali-puja. [4]Atithi-sala. [5]Noochi-ghar.

8. No fish or meat is offered to Vishnu, God the Preserver, who is worshipped here under the name of Radhakanta or the Lord of Radha. The food-offerings for the Mother include fish and meat. On days of lunar conjunction,—on the dark night[1] of the month—goats are sacrificed. The worship at the temples is completed before 12 o'clock noon, by which time rice and the various dishes that are prepared in the kitchen are offered. In the meantime the Guest-house is filled with holy men, poor men, women and other guests.

The Brahmins have a separate corner allotted to them during dinner. The officers of the Temple who happen to be Brahmins dine with the other Brahmins.

The steward has his food[2] carried to him into his own room. The Babus of Janbazar, the descendants of the foundress Rani Rashmani, pay occasional visits to the Temple, when they put up in the two-storied building outside the temple courtyard called the Kuthi. They too have their food[3] carried to them at the Kuthi.

9. THE STEWARD[4] AND THE OFFICE ROOMS:— In the rooms lying south of the courtyard are the quarters set apart for the officers of the Temple and also the office rooms[5]. Here the steward and the clerk are always present; the store-keeper, the maid-servants, men-servants, priests, Brahmin-cooks, and porters are always found walking in and out. Some of these rooms are kept under lock and key. They contain the sacred utensils, the furniture of the Temple-garden, carpets, awnings for the courtyard, etc. Some of these rooms were used as store-rooms on the occasions of the great Birthday Festival formerly held here in honour of Sri Ramakrishna. The cooking for this great festival used to be done on the adjoining grounds lying south of this set of rooms.

There is a gate north of the courtyard and leading into it. Porters are stationed here as well as in the Chandni.

[1]Amavasya. [2]Prasada. [3]Prasada. [4]Khajanchi. [5]Daftarkhana.

The votaries who desire to worship God in the temples must leave their shoes behind at the gate.

10. THE MASTER'S CHAMBER:—In the north-west corner of the courtyard and immediately to the north row of twelve temples dedicated to Siva is the well-known chamber in which Sri Ramakrishna used to pass his days in communion with God. Next to it and situated to the west is a semi-circular verandah with a roof also semi-circular, supported partially by columns. It looks out on the Ganges as she flows past the terrace of the Temple-garden running along her bank. Sri Ramakrishna often watched from this place the sacred waters with his face to the west, looking upon the holy river all the time as a manifestation of the Deity. To the west of the balcony is a narrow garden-path running from north to south. To the west of this path is a flower garden. Next to the garden is the terrace along the side of which flows the Ganga with sweet melodious murmurs.

11. THE CONCERT-ROOM[1]:—The Master's chamber is bounded by a rectangular verandah on the north. Next to this room and the verandah is another garden path going west to east. This path again has a flower-garden next to it lying north. North of the flower garden is the concert-room. The revered mother of the Master, now in Heaven, passed her last days in a small chamber just under the concert-room.

Next to this building are the Bakultala or the 'Foot of the Bakul' trees, and the riverghat which leads to it. The women folk of the neighbourhood bathe at this ghat. A pious and devout Brahmin lady as she was, the dying mother of Sri Ramakrishna was removed to this ghat, and she breathed her last in the presence of her weeping son—with the lower half of her body immersed, after the manner of the Hindus, in the holy waters of the Ganges.

There is a second concert-room in the south-west corner of the Temple-garden, close to the office-rooms.

[1]Nahabatkhana.

12. The Panchabati:—The Panchabati is situated a little north of the Bakul trees. It is a 'collection of five trees,' *viz.*, Bata (the Indian fig), the Peepul, the Neem, the Amlaki and the Bael tree. They were planted at the desire of Sri Ramakrishna. It was at the foot of the Panchabati that he went through various religious practices.[1] Latterly he used often to walk about this place, sometimes alone, sometimes with his disciples. Coming back from Brindavan, he caused to be scattered about this place, the holy dust that had been brought from that place of pilgrimage.

Close to the Panchabati and situated east was a thatched hut (now turned into a brick-built room), in which Sri Ramakrishna practised many religious austerities and with a single-minded devotion meditated upon God.

In this place there is a second Banyan[2] tree, with a terraced seat built round at its foot. It is an ancient tree, and joined with it grows another, *viz.*, a Peepul[3] tree. This ancient tree has many hollows within. It has become the home of birds and other animals.

The terraced seat is circular in form. It is provided with steps at two different points—the south and the north. It is used by people who visit the Temple garden and specially by those who wish to retire into solitude and meditate upon God, with the holy Ganges flowing past before them. Seated here with his face to the west, many a day did Sri Ramakrishna pass in the midst of his devotional exercises. In those days he would call to the Mother of the Universe with a yearning which only equalled that of the cow crying for her calf! Across that hallowed seat to-day there has fallen a branch of the Peepul tree, the comrade of the Banyan. This branch has not been completely severed from the parent tree, but continues partially to adhere to it. It seems as though the God-man who is worthy to take that seat where God has been realised, has not come into the world yet.

13. Jhautala and Baeltala:—Going a little north

[1]Sadhana. [2]Bata. [3]Aswatha.

of the Panchabati one reaches a railing made of iron wire. On the other side of the railing is the Jhautala, a collection of five trees known as the Bengali pine or singing tree (*casuarina*). Devout worshippers of God rejoice to see them from the bank of the Ganges at Baghbazar, Calcutta, where they may have come for purposes of ablution.

Going a little east from the Jhautala is Baeltala or the 'Foot of the *Bael* tree.' Sitting at the foot of this tree Sri Ramakrishna went through various religious austerities.

Beyond the Jhautala and the Baeltala is the wall that separates the Temple-garden from the Government Magazine.

14. THE KUTHI:—Getting out of the northern passage at the entrance of the courtyard, one comes across a two-storied house called the Kuthi. Whenever Rani Rashmani or her son-in-law Mathoor visited the Temple, they used to put up at the Kuthi. During their life-time the Master used to pass his days in a chamber there on the ground-floor, facing the Ganges. A splendid view of the holy river can be had from this room. A straight path from the Kuthi, running from east to west, leads to the river ghat at the foot of the Bakul tree.

15. THE GAZITALA, THE MAIN GATE, AND THE BACK GATE:—Going towards due east from the northern entrance of the courtyard in the direction of the eastern gate, we have on our right a fine tank called Gazi-pukur, having two *pucca ghats* one to the north and the other to the west of the tank. The western *ghat* is used for the purpose of washing the sacred utensils, and is called *Plate-washing ghat*. A little to the north-east of the *ghat* is an old tree and the foot of this tree is called Gazitala. This is the place where an old Mohammedan Said used to live long ago and pass his days in the contemplation of God. His departed Spirit is worshipped even to-day by the poor people, both Hindu and Mohammedan, who live in the vicinity of the Temple.

The eastern gate of the Temple-garden, which is the main gate, is a little to the east of Gazitala. People who come from Alambazar or Calcutta enter into the Temple through this gate. The people of Dakshineswar come in through the back gate or the north-eastern gate. When the Master used to come back from Calcutta into the Temple, sometimes at midnight, the cab which brought him would be stopped at the main gate. The porter then would be waked up and asked to unlock the gate. Sri Ramakrishna would ask him to come with him to his chamber in the Temple and he would see him rewarded with sweet-meats, which the Temple people would send him every evening out of the sanctified offerings made to the Deity.

16. THE HANSPUKUR AND THE COW-HOUSE:—There is another tank called the Goose-tank to the east of the *Panchabati*. To the north-east of this tank are the stables and the cow-house. To the east there is the back gate or north-eastern gate. Through this gate the people of Dakshineswar come into the Temple. This gate is also used by the officers of the Temple who live in this village with their families. Those without families have their rooms within the Temple.

There is a straight narrow path-way running from the southern extremity of the Temple-garden to the Panchabati. This path runs from south to north along the bank of the Ganges and is lined with flower plants on both sides. Passing on its way between the Chandni and the southern ghat of the river, it comes to the 'Foot of the Bakul trees,' just leaving the northern ghat on its left, and at last comes up to the Panchabati.

The garden path which runs from the west to the east and is situated to the south of the Concert-room[1] and the Kuthi, goes past the Gazitala as far as the eastern gate. This too has flower plants on both sides. In the same way the path leading from the south to the north on the eastern side of the Kuthi runs past the Hanspukur until it reaches the cow-house. The garden to the east of this path contains many flower plants and fruit trees and also a tank.

[1]Nahabatkhana.

17. THE FLOWER-GARDEN:—Just before the break of day the sweet sound of bells comes from the Temple to the ear of the devotee. They herald the morning service with the Waving of Lights,[1] which brings the tidings of Love and Joy to all God's creatures; for the Mother of the Universe is up again and will continue to bless Her own, her beloved children. The morning tunes are played on the flageolet[2] to the accompaniment of drums and cymbals and come to the ear from the Concert-room. It is not as yet red in the east—for the day-star is not up yet to give light and life to this world of ours. At such an early hour they are plucking flowers in the Temple-garden to be offered during morning service to God.

On the bank of the holy river and just to the west of the Panchabati are the *bael* tree and sweet-scented milk-white *gulchi* flower. Close to them is the mango-creeper.[3] Sri Ramakrishna had a great liking for the flower-plant *mallika* (the tulip), the mango-creeper so dear to Sri Radhika, and for the *gulchi* flower. He had the mango-creeper brought down with him from Brindavan whither he had gone with Mathoor on pilgrimage, and planted it at the Panchabati.

The part of the Temple-garden to the east of the path running towards the cow-house above mentioned contains many flower plants. Amongst others there are the fragrant *champak*, the five-faced *jaba*, the *jaba* pendant like ear-rings, the rose and the gold-flower.[4] On the hedges grows the creeper amaranth, called *aparajita* or 'the unvanquished', with blue flowers used for the worship of the Divine Mother. Very close to these are the *jui* (jasmine) and the *shefalika* flower.

Alongside the long line of the twelve temples of Siva and situated just to the west of them are also many flower plants—the white oleander[5], the red oleander, the rose, the jasmine,[6] the large double jasmine[7]. There is also the

[1] Aratrika. [2] Rasunchouki [3] Madhabi. [4] Kanchan.
[5] Kirva. [6] Jui. [7] Bel.

thorn apple[1], especially used for the worship of Siva. At intervals there is the sacred basil[2] plant growing on brick-built platforms.

To the south of the Concert-room are the double jasmine, the single jasmine, ' the king of scents' and the rose—all sweet-scented flowers. Within a short distance of the southern river-ghat are two flower-plants with beautiful fragrant flowers,—one called the lotus oleander and the other the cuckoo-eyed. The colour of the latter resembles that of the eyes of the cuckoo.

Near the Master's room and growing west of it are a couple of plants with flowers called the Krishna-crest (the cox-comb flower) resembling the crest adorning the head of Sri Krishna, the Incarnation of Divine Love; also the double jasmine, the jasmine, the king of scents, the rose, the tulip, the *jaba*, the white oleander, the red oleander, the five faced *jaba*, the china-rose, etc.

Sri Ramakrishna too used formerly to gather flowers for Divine worship. On one occasion he was plucking the leaves of the *bael* tree near the Panchabati when a portion of the bark came off. It seemed to him as if the Divinity that was within him and manifest in all things without had received a severe wound. He *felt* this in his very soul, and thence-forward ceased plucking the leaves of the *bael* tree. On another occasion he was walking about, gathering flowers for the worship of the Mother. Suddenly it flashed on his soul that the various flower-plants before him were but so many nosegays—things of beauty decorating the macrocosm,—bouquests adorning the outward manifested form of the Absolute. Sri Ramakrishna perceived in his soul that the worship of God was thus being celebrated night and day without cessation. Henceforward he ceased to pluck flowers any more for the purpose of worship.

18. THE LOBBIES AND THE BALCONY:—There is a lobby running east to west leading to the Master's room. It is

[1] Dhutura. [2] Tulasi.

two-winged; one wing facing the courtyard to the south, the other facing north and commanding a view of the Kuthi and the garden paths round about. The Master used often to be seated in the southern lobby with his disciples, talking about God or singing with them the Name of the Lord. In the northern wing there used sometimes to be celebrated the festival in honour of his birthday. There with disciples and other devotees, he would sit at meals and partake of the accepted offerings[1] amidst the joy and excitement of the festive occasion. Very often at the head of his disciples Keshab Sen would come to see Sri Ramakrishna and meet him in this very verandah, listen to the words of wisdom that proceeded out of his mouth and watch the state of Divine Ecstasy into which he was frequently thrown. Here it was that Keshab and his disciples were entertained with popped[2] rice, cocoanut, luchi, and sweets. It was here again that the Master was once put in a state of Samadhi at the sight of Narendra (Vivekananda).

19. THE ABODE OF JOY AND GLADNESS:—The Temple-garden has become an abode of joy and gladness. The Deity is worshipped night and day in His various aspects as Father[3]; as the Incarnation of Divine Love[4]; and again as the Mother[5] of the Universe, Saviour of the world. The offerings regularly made during Divine worship every day are many and various. The Guest house which accords welcome to holy men and mendicants is an institution connected with the Temple, highly valued by those that resort to it. The view of the sacred river flowing past the Temple-garden calls up thoughts that appeal to the highest nature of man. No less inspiring is the garden within the Temple compound, with flowers of variegated hues which charm the devout lovers of God with their fragrance, beauty and sanctity. What gives the finishing touch to this fascinating picture of the Temple garden is the saintly figure of the God-man intoxicated night and day with the joy of the Lord.

[1]Prasad. [2]Muri. [3]Siva. [4]Krishna. [5]Kali.

Verily here goes on a perennial festival in honour of the Ever-joyful Mother. The music from the Concert-room celebrates this never-ending festival, pouring out melodies that send a thrill of joy through the soul of the lover of God and very often put him in a state of ecstasy. The sacred music never tires of proclaiming night and day to the world the glad tidings of joy that our Mother has not only created us but always looks after us, Her own children. It begins the song at early dawn, repeats it at about nine in the morning at the time of Divine worship, and again at about noon when the Deity retires to rest. The song is again taken up at about four in the afternoon when the Mother rises once more, sits in state, and is ready to receive the worship offered by Her devotees. The festive song is yet once more repeated at candle-light when it calls upon the world to be ready for evening worship. The closing strains of this soul-stirring music reach the ear at about 9 o'clock at night, when the Mother retires to rest—music sweet in the solemn stillness that reigns in the Temple-garden at that solemn hour—in the midst of the gathering Darkness,—the garment which the Mother now puts on to remind her children of the eternity when nothing was,—neither Man nor Woman, neither the Sun nor the Moon, neither the Earth nor the Starry Firmament!

CONDENSED GOSPEL OF SRI RAMAKRISHNA

SECTION I

SRI RAMAKRISHNA AT DAKSHINESWAR

1882

CHAPTER I

The First Meeting With the Master

It is the spring of 1882, the season of flowers and of the sweet southern breeze. The sun is about to set on the Temple of the Mother of the Universe one pleasant day in the month of March. All nature smiles and rejoices. At such a time came about M.'s first vision of the God-man.

The Temple of the Mother where Sri Ramakrishna has made his abode for years is on the eastern bank of the Ganges in the village of Dakshineswar, about four miles north of Calcutta.

He is sitting on the lounge (the smaller of the two bedsteads[1]), in his own chamber which looks out on the sacred waters of the Holy Stream (the Ganges) as it flows past. The disciples and other devotees are seated on the floor. They look on his benign and smiling face and drink the nectar of the living words that fall from his hallowed lips.

Facing the east and smiling, the Master talks of the Lord.

M. looks in and stands speechless; M. wonders if It is Sukadeva[2] before him that talks of the Lord? M. feels as if he were standing on a spot to which have come together the various holy places of pilgrimage to hear the Divine

[1]Taktaposh. [2] The holy sage who loved the Lord from his childhood.

Preacher that is seated before him. It might have been the Lord Gouranga Deva (Chaitanya) seated before him with Ramananda, Swarup and other beloved disciples in the Holy Land of Puri[1], singing forth the sacred name of the Beloved Lord and His glorious works.

Renunciation of work for the Lord.

Sri Ramakrishna speaks, saying: Suppose at the Name[2] of the Lord your hair stands on end or tears of joy start from your eyes; verily I say unto you the term is over of your 'work for the Lord'; for instance, the daily service[3], morning, noon and evening, laid down for the twice-born. Then and not till then have you the right to give up work[4]; then indeed work will drop off of itself. When this state of the soul is reached, the devotee need only repeat the name of the Lord (Rama, Hari or simply the symbol Om). That will suffice; no other work need be done.

Again says the Master: Sandhya ends in Gayatri;[5] Gayatri, in the simple symbol Om.[6]

M. is staying at Barahanagar (near Dakshineswar). He has come with Sidhu, a friend, to the Temple-garden in the course of an evening walk. It is Sunday and M. is free from work.

In the course of his walk M. had first visited the garden-house of P. Banerjee. There Sidhu had said to him, "There is a beautiful garden on the bank of the Ganges. Let us go there. A holy man dwells there called the Paramahamsa."

M. stands speechless! He thinks within himself: How charming is this place! What a man! How sweet and charming are his words! The very idea of leaving this place troubles the soul. But let me first look about and form a clear idea of the Temple. I will then come back and sit at his feet.

[1]Puri, in Orissa, contains the temple of Jagannath. Gouranga (Chaitanya) was here for about the last twenty-four years of his life.

[2]Hari or Rama. [3]Sandhya. [4]Karma.

[5]Gayatri, the Vedic Mantra (sacred text) which the Brahmin and other twice-born Hindus repeat every day while meditating upon the Supreme Being.

[6] Om, Vedic symbol for the Supreme Being. This is the sacred unspoken syllable of the Hindus.

M. comes out of the room into the quadrangle. He begins to visit the temples of God the Father,[1] of God Incarnate as Love[2] and lastly, that of God the Mother[3].

It is just evening—the time of Divine Service. The priests are waving the lights before the sacred Images to the accompaniment of bells, cymbals and drums. From the southern end of the Temple-garden is wafted upon the soft southern breeze, sweet music, melody after melody played by the temple orchestra upon flageolets and other instruments. That music is carried far over the bosom of the Ganges until it is lost in the distant Immensity! The breeze that blows from the south, how gentle and fragrant with the sweet fragrance that comes from many a flower! The moon is just up and the temple and the garden are soon bathed in the soft silvery light. It seems as if Nature and Man both rejoice and hold themselves in readiness for the evening service.

M.'s joy is full at the blessed sight. Sidhu speaks to M., saying: This is Rashmani's temple. Here the Gods are ministered unto from day to day—from morning till night. Here too holy men and the poor are daily fed out of the offerings made to the Deity.

The two friends wend their way through the grand quadrangle back towards Sri Ramakrishna's chamber. Coming up to the door of the room they notice that it is closed. M. has learnt English etiquette and thinks it will be rude to try to enter without leave.

The incense has burnt a little while before.

At the door stands Brinda, the maid-servant. M. talks to her.

M.: Well, my good woman, is he in—the holy man?

Brinda: Yes, he is inside this room.

M.: How long has he made his abode here?

Brinda: O, many many years.

[1]Siva. [2]Radhakanta.

[3]Kali—God in His relations to the conditioned and the finite, as distinguished from Brahman or God the Absolute.

M.: I suppose he has many books to read and study.

Brinda: O dear, no; not a single one. His tongue talks everything—even the highest truth! His words come from above.

M. is fresh from college. He is told the Master is not a scholar! At this he stands aghast—speechless with surprise!

M.: Very well. Is he now going on with his evening worship[1]? May we come in? Will you be so kind as to tell him that we are anxious to see him?

Brinda: Why, you may go in, my children; do go, and take your seats before him.

Thereupon they enter the room. No other people are there. The Master is seated alone on the smaller of the two bedsteads. Incense is burning and the doors are closed. M. salutes with folded hands. A mat is spread on the floor. At his word, M. and Sidhu take their seats.

The Master makes many kind enquiries: What is your name? Where do you live? What are you? What has brought you to Barahanagar? etc., are some of the questions put to M. M. answers all these; but he notices that even as he speaks, Sri Ramakrishna gives his mind to some other subject on which he appears to be meditating.

Is this God-consciousness? It calls up to M.'s mind the image of a man sitting, rod in hand, on the edge of a lake. The float trembles just as the fish bites at the bait. Eagerly the man looks at the float. He grasps the rod with all his mind and strength. He talks to no one but is all-attention.

M. heard later on that he was put into a peculiar state of God-consciousness[2] several times every day, when he lost all sense of the external world.

M. (to Sri Ramakrishna): I am afraid, Sir, you will have still to go through your evening worship[3]. In that case we must not trouble you any more to-night, but call at another time.

[1]Sandhya. [2]Samadhi. [3]Sandhya.

Sri Ramakrishna: No, no, you need not be in a hurry.

He is silent again for a time. When at last he does open his lips, he says in a dreamy tone, 'Evening worship? No, no, it is not that.'

A short while after, M. salutes the Master. He bids him good-bye, saying: Come again.

On his way back to Barahanagar, M. says to himself: Who may this God-man be? How is it that my soul longs to see him again? Is it possible that a man may be great and yet not a scholar? * * * What means this yearning of the soul for him?—He has bidden me come again.—I must come to-morrow or at the latest, the day after.

CHAPTER II

MASTER AND DISCIPLE

A couple of days after, at about eight in the morning, M. called again.

The Master is going to be shaved by the barber. The winter cold is still lingering and he has on a moleskin shawl hemmed with red muslin. On seeing M. the Master says, Well, you are come. Very good. Take your seat here.

It was on the southern verandah leading to his room that the meeting took place. Seated before the barber, he had a pair of slippers on and the shawl described above.

He talks to M. while the barber is attending to him. His face is, as usual, smiling. Only he stammers a little, while talking.

Master (to M.): Where is your home?

M.: In Calcutta, Sir.

Master: With whom have you been staying here at Barahanagar?

M.: With my sister, Sir, at Ishan Kaviraja's house.

Master: At Ishan's? O, I see.

Do you know how Keshab is doing at present? I heard he was seriously ill.

Keshab Chandra Sen.

M.: Yes, Sir, I too heard the same. I trust by this time he is doing well.

Master.: I made a vow to offer gifts—green cocoanuts and sugar—to the Divine Mother for Keshab's recovery. I would sometimes wake up in the middle of my sleep at night and cry out: O Mother, grant that Keshab may get well. If Keshab does not live, whom shall I talk with, Mother, when I go to Calcutta?

Do you know that one Mr. Cook has recently been in Calcutta. He has, I think, been delivering lectures. Keshab took me on board a steamer the other day and he was there.

M.: Yes, Sir, I have heard a good deal about him. I have never had any occasion to hear him giving lectures. Nor do I know much about him.

Duty of a father.

Master: Pratap's brother came and stayed here for a few days. He said he had come here to stay. He had no work to do, and he had left his wife and children in the care of his father-in-law. But here we took him to task for his want of self-respect. Do you not think it very wrong of him to go about in such a way when he has so many children to bring up? Must strangers come to feed and look after them? I wonder he is not ashamed that somebody else has to take care of his family,—that his father-in-law should be asked to bear his burden ! I rated him rather severely and told him to look about for work. It was when his folly was thus pointed out to him that he went away.

The Master reproves M. for having married.

Master (to M.):—Are you married?

M.: Yes, Sir.

Sri Ramakrishna, startled at these words, said: Ah Me! He has already taken a wife! May the Lord help him.

At these words M. was covered with confusion. He sat speechless, hanging down his head like one guilty of a serious offence. He then says to himself: Is marrying then so wicked?

Master: Have you any children?

M. can hear the beating of his own heart! Yes, Sir, he answers in a feeble voice.

The Master is shocked. He rebukes M., saying: Alas! and there are children too to bring up!

M. feels that a terrible blow has been dealt to his egotism.

After a while the Master looks up kindly and says in an affectionate tone: You see, my boy, there are some good signs about you. I know them by looking at the eyes and the brow. The eyes of Yogis have a peculiar look—those that in previous incarnations passed their days in communion with God. In the case of some it seems as if they have just left the seat[1] of divine contemplation!

Well, now, your wife,—what do you think of her? Is she of a divine nature[2] leading Godward and to light? Or the reverse, leading only to darkness[3] and away from God?

M.: She is good enough, but ignorant.

Master (sharply): *She* is ignorant and *you* are wise! You think you have attained wisdom! Do you?

M. knows not what wisdom and ignorance truly consist in. His idea is that a wise man is he who reads books. [This false notion was of course afterwards taken away and he was then taught that to know God is alone true wisdom and not to know Him ignorance.]

When the Master said, "Do you think you have attained wisdom?" M.'s egotism received a second blow.

Image worship: Is God with form or without form?

Master: Do you like to meditate upon God as 'with form' or 'without form'?

This question makes M. again look confused and sets him thinking: Is it then possible that one could have faith in the Formless God, and at the same time believe that He *has* a form? Or if one believed Him to be 'with form', how could one also think that He is 'formless'? Could two contradictory attributes co-exist in the same substance? Could white things like milk be black also at the same time?

After thinking for a while M. said: I should like Sir,

[1]Asana. [2]Vidya Sakti. [3]Avidya Sakti

to meditate upon God as the Formless rather than as a Being 'with form.'

Master: That is good. There is no harm in looking at Him from this or that point of view. Yes, yes, to think of Him as the Formless Being is quite right. But take care you do not run away with the idea that that view alone is true and all others false. Meditating upon Him as a Being 'with form' is equally right. But you must hold to your particular point of view until you realise—until you *see* God, when everything will become clear.

At this M. becomes once more speechless. He hears again and again from the lips of the Master that *contradictories are true of God*! Never has he come across so strange a thing in all his books and to these his learning is confined. His egotism has received another blow, but it is not yet completely knocked down and crushed. So he goes on questioning and reasoning a little with the Master.

M.: Then, Sir, one may hold that God is 'with form.' But surely He is not the earthen images that are worshipped!

Master: But my dear Sir, why should you call it an earthen image? Surely the Image Divine is made of the Spirit!

M. cannot follow this. He goes on: But is it not one's duty Sir, to make it clear to those who worship images that God is not the same as the clay forms they worship, and that in worshipping they should keep God Himself in view and not the clay images?

Public lectures and Sri Ramakrishna.

Master (sharply): It has grown to be a fashion with you Calcutta people, to think and talk only of 'lecturing' and 'bringing others to light'! Pray, how are you going to bring light unto your own self? Eh? Who are *you* to teach others? The Lord of the Universe will teach mankind if need be—that Lord Who has made the sun and the moon, men and brutes, the Lord Who has made things for them to live upon, Who has made parents to tend and rear them, —that Lord Who has done so many things, will He not do something to bring them also to light? Surely, if need be, He will! He lives in the temple of the human body. He knows our inmost thoughts. If there is anything wrong in image worship, does He not know that all the worship is meant for Him? He will be pleased enough to accept it knowing that it was meant for Him alone. Why must you worry yourself about things above you and beyond your reach? Seek to know and revere God. Love God. That is the duty nearest you.

M.'s egotism is now completely crushed. He thinks to himself: What this God-man says is indeed perfectly true. What business have I to go about preaching to others? Have I myself known God? Do I love God? It is, as the proverb has it, like bidding my friend Sankara lie down on my bed when there is no bed even for myself to lie upon! About God I know nothing. It would indeed be the height of folly and vulgarity itself—of which I should be ashamed—to think of teaching others! This is not mathematics or history or literature, it is the science of God! Yes, I see the force of the words of this holy man.

This was M.'s first attempt to argue a point with the Master, and happily the last.

Master: You were talking of 'images made of clay.' Well, there often comes a necessity of worshipping even such images as these. God Himself has provided these various forms of worship. The Lord has done all this——to suit different men in different stages of knowledge.

The mother so arranges the food for her children that every one gets what agrees with him. Suppose she has five children. Having a fish to cook, she makes different dishes out of it. She can give each one of her children what suits him exactly. One gets rich *polow* with the fish, while she gives only a little soup to another who is of weak digestion; she makes a sauce of sour tamarind for the third, fries the fish for the fourth and so on; exactly as it happens to agree with the stomach. Don't you see?

M.: Yes, Sir, now I do. The Lord is to be worshipped

in the image of clay *as a spirit* by the beginner. The devotee, as he advances, may worship him independently of the Image.

Master : Yes. And again when he *sees* God, he realizes that everything—image and all—is a manifestation of the Spirit. To him the Image is made of Spirit—not of clay. God is Spirit.

M.: Sir, how may one fix one's mind on God?

Master: To that end one must chant without ceasing the Name of God and His great Attributes. One ought always to seek the company of holy men. One must always go among the Lord's devotees or those that have given up things of this world for the sake of the Lord. It is hard, no doubt, to fix one's mind on God in the midst of the world's cares and anxieties. Hence one must go into solitude now and then in order to meditate on Him. In the first stage of one's life in the Spirit, one cannot do without solitude.

The value of Solitude.

When plants are young, they have need of a hedge to be set about them for their protection; or else goats and cows will eat them up.

The Mind, the retired Corner, and the Forest are the three places for meditation[1]. One must also practise discrimination[2] between the Real (God) and the Unreal (the phenomenal world). Thus a man may be able to shake off his attachment to the things of this world, to wealth, fame, power and pleasures of the senses.

M.: Sir, how ought one to live in the world as a householder?

Master: Do all your duties with your mind always fixed on God. As for your parents and wife and children, serve them as if they were your own, but know in the inmost recesses of your heart that they are not really yours, unless they too love the Lord. The Lord alone is really your own, and also those who love the Lord.

Problem of Life: How solved for the House-holder.

[1]Dhyana. [2]Vichara.

A rich man's maid-servant will do all her duties, but her thoughts are always set upon her own home. Her master's house is not hers. She will, indeed, nurse her master's children as if they were her own, saying often; 'My own *Rama*,' 'My own *Hari*.' But all the while she knows full well the children are not hers.

The tortoise moves about in the water in quest of food; where do you think her mind abides? On the bank of the river to be sure—where her eggs are laid. In the same way you may go about doing your work in the world, but take good care that your mind always rests at the Hallowed Feet of the Lord.

Suppose you enter the world before you have acquired by means of spiritual exercises[1] a deep love[2] for the Lord, then, you may depend upon it, you shall get entangled. Grief, misfortune, and the various ills that flesh is heir to, will make you lose your balance of mind. The more you will throw yourself into the affairs of the world and trouble yourself with worldly matters, the more will become your attachment to the world.

First rub the hand with oil if you wish to break open the jack-fruit. Otherwise the milky exudation will stick to your hands. First anoint your hands with the oil of devotion,[3] and then deal with the affairs of the world.

Divine Contemplation in Solitude

But to this end solutude is the one thing needful: Suppose you want to make butter, then let the curds be set in some place out of reach. They will not set if they are distrubed. The next step for you is to begin churning, seated in a quiet place.

If you give your mind to God in solitude, you will receive the spirit of renunciation[4] and devotion. If you give the same mind to the world, it will become vulgar and think only about the world which is another name for 'Woman and Gold.'[5]

[1]Sadhana. [2]Bhakti. [3]Bhakti. [4]Tyaga.

[5]Sri Ramakrishna's own position was that woman should be renounced until the realisation of God—after which she should be worshipped as a manifested form of the Deity.

The world may be likened to water and the mind to milk. Milk once mixed with water cannot be brought back to the pure state again. Its purity is kept only in another state, that is, if it is first turned into butter and then placed in water. Let the milk of your mind then be turned into the butter of Divine Love[1] by means of religious practices[2] done in solitude. The butter will then never mix with the water but will come up to the surface. In like fashion your mind will remain unattached to the world. Though in the world it will not be *of* the world. True knowledge[3] or devotion being once attained, it now stands apart unattached to the world.

Along with this, practise discrimination. 'Woman and Gold' are both unreal; the one Reality is God. What use has money? Why, it gives us food and clothes and a place to live in. Thus far it serves, and no further. Surely you cannot see God with the help of money. Money is certainly not the end of life. This is the process of discrimination. Do you see?

M.: Yes, Sir, I do. I recently had occasion to go through a Sanskrit play, called *Prabodh Chandrodaya*, Therein I read of discrimination.

Master: Yes, yes, discrimination. Tell me, what is there in money or in the beauty of woman? Using your discrimination you shall find that the body of the most beautiful woman is made up only of flesh and blood, skin and bones, fat and marrow,—nay, of the entrails, as in the case of other animals, of urine and excreta, and the rest. The wonder is that a man can lose sight of God and give his mind entirely to things of such a kind!

M.: Sir, is it possible to see God?

Master: Certainly; there is no doubt about it. These are some of the means by which one can see God:—One may go from time to time into solitude and chant His Names and His Attributes;

How to see God.

[1]Bhakti. [2]Sadhana. [3]Jnana.

one may strive for discrimination; and then one may offer earnest prayer with a yearning for the Lord.

M.: Sir, what state of the mind leads to God-vision?

Master: *Cry unto the Lord with a yearning heart and you shall see Him.* People would shed a jugful of tears for the sake of *wife and children*! They would suffer themselves to be carried away on the stream of their own tears, weeping for the sake of *money*! But who ever cries out for the Lord? Cry to him not to make a show—but with a longing and yearning heart.

The rosy light of the dawn comes before the rising sun. Likewise is a longing and yearning heart the sign of the God-vision that is to come.

You may *see* God if your love for Him is as strong as the three attachments put together, namely, the attachment of a worldly man to the things of the world, the attachment of a mother to her child, and the attachment of a chaste and devoted wife to her husband.

The thing is that in order to see God one must love Him, heart and soul. One must offer one's prayers so that they may reach the Divine Mother.

The kitten knows only to cry to its mother, crying 'mew' 'mew'. All the rest the mother-cat knows. She hides her young wherever she pleases—now in the kitchen, and again in the soft downy bed of the householder. Yes, the kitten knows only to cry to its mother.

CHAPTER III

M. MEETS VIVEKANANDA

M. is putting up at his sister's house in Barahanagar, which is about a mile distant from the Temple. Since he saw Sri Ramakrishna, M. has never ceased to think of him. It seems as if he has always before his eyes the smiling face of the Master—that he is always listening to his words, sweet as nectar. How could this poor Brahmin, M. thinks within himself, have gone into these deep problems of life and soul! And his teachings, how clear they are! M.'s feelings are worked up to a high pitch of excitement; and he thinks day and night of taking the earliest opportunity to see him a second time. The following Sunday between three and four in the afternoon he comes again to the Temple in the company of Nepal Babu of Barahanagar.

The Master is in the same room as before, seated on the lounge. The room is filled with devotees. It is Sunday and they are free. M. does not as yet know any of them. After saluting him with folded hands, M. takes his seat on one side. The Master smilingly talks on with the devotees who are present.

Vivekananda: How to deal with bad men.

M. observes that the Master's words are specially addressed to a young man called Narendra (Vivekananda) who is now only nineteen years old. He is a college student and a member of the *Sadharan Brahmo Samaj*. His words are full of spirit. His eyes are large and dark. They beam with intelligence and tell of the great soul within. He has the looks of one who loves the Lord.

M. sees that the subject of talk is the conduct of worldly men—of such persons as throw ridicule upon those who seek after God. The question is, how to deal with such people?

Master (smiling, to Narendra): What do you say, Narendra? Worldly men say all manner of things against the godly. When the elephant wends its way along the public road, there are, indeed, a lot of curs and other animals running after, barking and clamouring. But it turns a deaf ear to all their noise and goes its way. Suppose, my boy, people do speak ill of you behind your back. What will you think of them?

Narendra: I shall look upon them as street dogs barking behind me.

Master (laughing): No, my child, you must never go quite so far as that (*laughter*). Know that God makes His abode in all things,—animate and inanimate. Hence everything should be the object of our worship, be it man or beast, bird, plant or mineral.

In our dealings with men all that we can do is to take heed that we mix with the good and avoid the company of bad people. True that God is even in the tiger; but surely it does not follow that one should fall on its neck and hug the brute to one's bosom. (*Laughter.*)

Some one may say, but why should I run away from the tiger seeing that after all it is God in one form? To this the answer is, that those who wish you to run away from the tiger are also God manifested in other forms. Why should we not pay regard to *their* words.

In a certain forest there lived a holy man who had a number of disciples. One day he taught them saying, 'God is in all things; knowing this we should bend our heads in adoration before every object in the world'. It chanced that a disciple of his went out to gather firewood for the sacrificial fire. Suddenly he heard a shout, 'Get out of the way! Get out of the way! Here comes an elephant rushing madly about!' At this everyone ran away except this disciple. He reasoned within himself, 'The elephant is God in one form; why then should I fly away?' So he stood where he was, saluted the elephant as the Lord, and began to chant His praises. The driver of the elephant continued to shout 'Run away! Run away!' but this disciple would not stir a single step. At last the elephant seized him with his trunk and cast him to one side. The poor boy, stunned, scratched and torn, lay bleeding on the ground.

His master heard of this and came with his other disciples to the spot. They carried him home and applied restoratives. When he came to himself they asked him, 'Well, why did you not quit the spot when you heard the man shouting that the mad elephant was coming?' The boy answered, 'Our master once told us that it is God who reveals Himself in man and in every other living creature. I looked on the Elephant-God and thus did not care to quit the spot.' His Guru said, 'My son, it is indeed true that it was the Elephant-God that was coming,—but the Driver-God, did he not warn you to get out of the way? It is true that God manifests Himself forth in everything. But did He not warn you to get out of the way as the Driver-god? It is true that God manifests Himself forth in everything. But if He is manifest in the elephant, is He not equally, or more, manifest in the driver? Tell me, then, why you paid no heed to His warning voice.'

In the Sacred Books it is written that Water is the same as God Himself. But some water is fit to be used for divine service, some only for washing plates or soiled linen, or for washing the face and the hands after meals. The latter may not be used for drinking or for the service of the altar. In the same way there are good men and bad men, lovers of God and those who do not love Him. In the hearts of them all, indeed, God abides. But one cannot have dealings with bad men and those who love not God. Our relations with such cannot be very close. With some, indeed, a nodding acquaintance is all that is possible. With many others even that is out of the question. It is meet to live apart from such people.

Vivekananda: Doctrine of Non-Resistance.

Narendra: Should we hold our peace, if evil men come to offend us or actually do so?

Master: A man living in society, especially as a citizen and a house-holder, should *make a show* of resisting evil for the sake of self-defence. At the same time care should be taken to avoid paying back evil for evil.

In a field certain cow-boys kept watch over their cattle. In that same field was a terrible and venomous serpent. One day there came a holy man that way. The boys ran up to him and said, 'Your Holiness, please go not that way. A tremendous snake is over there.' 'My children,' said the holy man, 'I thank you, but I am not afraid of your snake. I know holy texts[1] that will keep me from harm of all kinds.'

[1]Mantras.

So saying he wended his way in that direction. The boys did not go with him,—they were so much afraid of the snake. At the sight of the holy man the snake came swiftly towards him with its hood raised. He muttered a spell, and it fell at his feet as helpless as an earthworm.

'Well,' said the holy man, 'Why do you go about doing evil to others? Let me give you a Holy Name (of God). Repeat this always and you will learn to love God; you will *see* Him in the end; the desire to do evil to others will at the same time leave you. The snake had the Holy Name whispered into its ear. It bowed down before its preceptor and said 'O Lord, what more must I do in order to get salvation'?, 'Repeat the Holy Name,' said the teacher, 'and do no harm to any living thing. I shall come again and see how you fare.' So saying he went away.

Some days passed. The cow-boys noticed that the snake would not bite. They pelted it with stones. But it only looked as meek and inoffensive as an earthworm. One of the boys took it one day by the tail, and whirling it round, dashed it several times against the ground. The snake vomited blood, was stunned and left for dead.

Late at night it came to life again. Softly and slowly it moved and dragged itself into its hole. Its body was broken. In the course of a few days, it was reduced to a skeleton, and it was many many days before it could even come out of its hole to look for food. For fear of the boys it would come out only by night. Ever since its initiation by the holy man it had ceased to do harm to any creature of God. It tried to live as well as it could on leaves of plants and things of that kind.

The holy man[1] soon came back. He looked about, seeking the snake; but in vain. At last the boys said that it was no more. It was hard for the holy man to believe this, for he knew that the Name of the Lord which it repeated carried such spiritual power that death was out of the question

[1]Mahatma.

before the problem of life had been solved, that is to say, before it had *seen* God. So he made a search and called it repeatedly by its name. The snake came out of its hole and bowed down before its preceptor. They talked to each other thus:—

Holy man: Hallo, how are you doing?

Snake: O Lord, I thank you: by the grace of God I am quite well.

Holy man : How is it then that you are brought down to mere skin and bone? What is the matter?

Snake: Lord, in obedience to your bidding I strive to do no harm to any living creature. I feed upon leaves and things of that kind. Thus it may be that I am thinner than before.

Holy man : Well, I am afraid it is not the food alone that has brought you to this pass! There must be something else to do with it. Just think it over.

Snake: Ah, now I see it all! The cow-herds dealt with me rather severely one day. They held me by the tail and dashed me against the ground with great force—several times. They, poor fellows, had no idea what a great change had come over me! How could they know that I was not going to bite anyone or do them the least harm?

Holy man: What nonsense! You must be an idiot not to know how to save yourself from being handled in such a fashion by your enemies. What I forbade you was to *bite* any of God's creatures. Why did you not *hiss* at those who wanted to kill you so as to put them in fear of you?

Sri Ramakrishna then went on saying: So raise the hood and hiss, but don't *bite*. There is no harm in hissing at bad men, your enemies. Keep them off by showing that you are ready to give tit for tat—that you know how to resist evil. Only one must take care not to pour one's venom into the blood of one's enemy. Resist not evil by doing evil in return. All that you may do is to make a show of resistance with a view to self-defence.

The Problem of Evil: Are all men equal?

A Disciple: Sir, why are there bad men in God's world? Why is there Evil in this world?

Master: In God's Creation diversity is the universal rule. There must be evil as well as good. Again, there are various kinds of objects—animals, plants, minerals. Amongst animals again, there are some which are gentle and inoffensive, and others which, like the tiger, are ferocious and live upon other animals. Some trees bring forth good fruits, sweet as nectar: while others bring forth poisonous fruits which cause death. Likewise there are good men and bad men, holy men and those who are sinful. Some, again, are just and devout and others are attached to the world.

Men may be divided into four classes:—(1) Worldly men[1] (those who are bound in the fetters of the world); (2) The Seekers[2] after Liberation; (3) The Liberated[3] and (4) The Ever Free.[4]

The EVER-FREE, like Narada, the Holy Sage, are those who abide in the world for the sake of others,—in order to teach the Truth to others.

The WORLDLY are they who are attached to the little things of this world—money, honours, titles, sense pleasures and power. They forget God and never give a thought to Him.

The SEEKERS AFTER LIBERATION do their best to avoid the world, made up as it is of 'Woman and Gold.' But it is given to only a few amongst them to find what they seek, namely, Liberation.

The LIBERATED are those who are not attached to either 'Woman' or to 'Gold.' Holy men are examples of these. In their minds there is not a trace of attachment to the things of this world. They meditate always on the Hallowed Feet of the Lord.

Suppose a net is cast into a tank. Some of the fish are much too clever for the fisherman and take care never to be caught. But these may be counted on one's fingers,

[1]Baddha. [2]Mumukshu. [3]Mukta. [4]Nitya Mukta.

and to them may be likened the Ever-Free.

But most of the fish are caught in the net. Of these some try their best to make their escape. Such are the Seekers after Liberation, and of these a couple or so only are able to leap out of the net into the water. We often see such; they leap out with a splash, the fisherman as well as others shouting 'Look ! Look! There is a big fish getting away!'

But most of the fish are not able to get out at all. And what is more, they do not want to get out! They would rather rush into the mud at the bottom of the tank, head foremost, entangled in the net as they are, and there lie still; thinking all the while, 'We are quite safe and secure, and we need fear no more.' The poor things know not that in a short while the fisher-man will draw them in the net to the land. To these last may be compared the 'Worldly.' They feel secure in their muddy homes; but alas, they are entangled in the meshes of the world, soon to be deprived of the Water of Life and hauled up to the land to be killed!

The bondage of the world is bondage made up of the fetters of 'Woman and Gold.' Worldly men are bound hand and foot. They think they will find peace and rest and security in the mud at the bottom of the tank, that is to say, in 'Woman and Gold' They know not that these cause the death of the soul. When one of these 'Worldly' men is on his deathbed, his wife says to him, 'You are departing from this world, but what property do you leave to me?' The wife speaks not one word about the Lord. The dying man himself is so much attached to the world that the light of a lamp burning in the sick-room troubles him and he cries out, 'Who is there? See that not more than one wick is burnt and that no more oil is wasted than is absolutely needed.'

The worldly man does not think of God. If he has time and nothing to do, he will either talk empty twaddle or do things that are of no use to anybody. Upon being asked, he says 'To sit still I am not able. Hence am I planting a hedge.' Time hangs heavy on his hands. So he must play at cards or at dice! (*Deep Silence in the room.*)

A Disciple: But a man of the world, Sir,—how may he be saved? Is there no help for him?

The Power of Faith.

Sri Ramakrishna: Certainly. Let him seek the company of holy men. Let him from time to time go away from his family into retirement, in order to meditate upon the Lord. Let him practise discrimination. Let him pray earnestly to the Divine Mother, saying, 'O Mother, grant unto me love and faith.' Once you get faith, your work is done. *Verily, verily, there is nothing higher than faith.*

(*To Kedar*): You must have heard of the power of Faith. Ramachandra was God Incarnate; you know how he had to build a bridge across the sea (between India and Ceylon[1]). But Hanuman, the great lover of the Lord, had infinite faith in the power of His Name. He repeated that Name and behold, he found himself at once on the other side! Here, you see, to show the power of faith, the Lord Himself had to build a bridge while the devotee who had faith in His Name needed no bridge to carry him across. (*The Master and his disciples all laugh.*)

Another devotee wrote the name of Rama on a leaf and handed it to a man who wanted to cross the sea, saying, 'Fear not, my friend; have faith and walk across the deep. But mind you do not show any want of faith: for then you will be drowned.' The man had tied up the leaf within the folds of his cloth. He went his way, walking on the sea. As he went, he was seized with a desire to look at the writing. He brought out the leaf and read the name of Rama (God) written large upon it. At this, he thought to himself, 'Only the name of Rama! Is that all?' And on the instant with loss of faith, down he went under the water!

The Sinner and the power of God's Name

Let one only have faith in the Lord, and, depend upon it, he will reach salvation—no matter if he has committed

[1]Lanka.

the vilest of sins—the murder of Brahmins, of woman and the rest! Let him only say 'Lord, I shall not do this again', and take His Hallowed Name.

And the Master sang:

> Let me but die, O Mother, with Thy Holy Name on my lips.
> Then shall I see whether or not Thou givest me Liberation at the end.
> With Thy Name on my lips I care not if I have killed holy men[1] or woman or the child in its mother's womb!
> I care not if I have been guilty of drinking wine! My sins do not trouble me, even for one moment!
> Taking Thy Name indeed I may aspire to the very throne of Him[2] whom Thou hast appointed to be the Creator of the Universe.

Narendra and the signs of the Ever-perfect.

The Master now turned to Narendra who was seated before him and said: You all see this boy, so gentle and unassuming. Of course even a naughty boy is gentle in the presence of his father. But he is quite another when he runs about and plays at the *Chandni*. A boy like this belongs to the class of the EVER-PERFECT. (By the *Chandni* the Master meant the long porch of the Temple next to the landing-ghat.)

These are never bound by the fetters of this world. When they get a little older in years, they feel an awakening within the heart and walk Godward at once. They come down into the world as teachers of mankind. They love not the things of this world,—their minds never go after 'Woman and Gold.'

There is mention made in the *Vedas* of a bird called '*Homa*.' It lives high above the clouds away from the din and bustle of this world. There it brings forth an egg which begins to drop as soon as it is brought forth. For days together it goes on falling and is hatched during the fall. Such is the height that the young bird which comes out of the egg goes on falling while it is getting its eyes and wings!

Then it comes to know that it is being carried down with a tremendous force, and that the mere touch of the

[1]Brahmins. [2]Brahma.

earth will bring on death. Afraid of being thus dashed against the ground, it suddenly shoots upwards in quest of its Mother who lives so high up above the clouds.

The parent-bird is the Divine Mother who abides above with the Infinite—high up above and beyond the world of the senses. Those of her children who are nearest to Her are these pure young souls to whom life continues to be a mystery until their eyes are opened and they can fly upon their wings. When their eyes are opened, they see clearly the death that is before them—if they only touch the world and the things that are of the world—money, honours, sense pleasures and the rest! The moment their eyes open, they change the course of their life and turn Godward, knowing that the Divine Mother is the one *Reality* in Whom they live and move and have their being, and to Whom they must always look up for light and life.

At this point Narendra left the room.

Kedar, Prankrishna, M. and many others were still in the chamber with the Master. The Master still talks of Narendra and smiles as he talks.

Master (to the disciples): You see, Narendra excels in everything, be it singing, playing on instruments, or reading and writing. The other day he had a discussion with Kedar. But Kedar's words were chopped off by him as it were as soon as they were spoken. (*The Master and the others present laugh.*)

(To *M.*): Is there any book in English on the art of reasoning?

M.: Yes Sir, it is called logic.

Master: Well, give me some idea of this book.

It is a sore trial for M. But he plucks up courage and says:

'One part of logic deals with reasoning from general propositions to particulars. Thus:

All men are mortal,
Pandits are men,
Pandits are mortal.

Another division deals with reasoning from particulars to general propositions. Thus:

This crow is black,
That crow is black,
That other crow is black; and so on.
Hence all crows are black.

The reasoning by simple enumeration like this is open to fallacy however, for it may be that in some unknown land there may be found *white* crows.'

Sri Ramakrishna did not appear to pay much attention to these words. It seemed as if they fell flat upon his ear. Thus the conversation on the subject came to an end.

The meeting broke up. The disciples were walking about the garden. M. walked by himself at the 'Cluster of five trees.[1]'

The Master in Samadhi

It is about five in the afternoon. Coming back to the verandah, north of the Master's chamber, M. comes upon a strange sight. The Master is standing still. Narendra is singing a hymn. He and three or four other disciples are standing with the Master in their midst.

M. is charmed with song. Never in his life has he heard a sweeter voice. Looking at the Master M. marvels and becomes speechless. The Master stands motionless. His eyes are fixed. It is hard to say whether he is breathing or not.

This state of divine ecstasy, says a disciple in low tones, is called *Samadhi*. M. has never seen or heard of anything like this. He thinks to himself, 'Is it possible that the thought of God can make a man forget the world? How great must be his faith and love for God who is thrown into such a state!'

The song that was being sung ran as follows:

1. Meditate thou upon the Lord, O my mind! He is the essence of spirit. He is free from all impurity! Without equal is His glory, beautiful is His shape; how much is He beloved in the hearts of His devotees!

[1]Panchavati.

2. Behold. His Beauty is enhanced by fresh manifestations of Love! It throws into the shade a million moons! Verily, the lightning flashes out of His Glorious Beauty! The Blessed Vision causes the hair to stand on end.

The Master is deeply touched when this line of the hymn is chanted. The hair of his body does actually stand on end. His eyes are bedewed with tears of joy. The smile on his lips shows the ecstatic delight that he feels at the sight of the Blessed Vision. Yes, he must be enjoying a vision of unequalled beauty which puts into the shade the refulgence of a million moons! Is this God-vision? If so, what must be the intensity of faith and devotion, of discipline and austerity which has brought such a vision within reach of mortal man?

The song went on:

3. Worship His Holy Feet on the lotus of thine heart!
Gaze thou upon the matchless beauty of that Beloved Form, now that the mind enjoys peace and the eyes are filled with Divine Love.

That bewitching smile once more! Behold, his body becomes motionless again! His eyes are half closed and fixed, as it were, on vacancy. It seems as though he beholds some strange vision—of things that are beyond the sense-world—and is thus filled with ecstasy!

The song draws to a close. Narendra sings the last lines:

Inspired with Love Divine be thou immersed, O my mind, in the sweetness of Him who is the Fountain of Absolute Intelligence and Bliss!

* * * *

M. wends his way back home with this unique picture in his mind of *Samadhi* and the ecstasy of Divine Love. The sweet music which he carried in his heart bubbles up, as it were, from time to time as he goes along:

'Be incessantly merged, O my mind, in the sweetness of His Love and Bliss! Yes, be thou drunken with the joy of the Lord!'

CHAPTER IV

THE DISCIPLE AGAIN

The next day is a holiday and M. calls again at about three in the afternoon.

The Master is seated in his chamber. The mat is spread on the floor. Narendra, Bhavanath and one or two other disciples are seated before him, all young men, nineteen or twenty years old. Smiles as before play about his lips. He sits on the lounge and laughing and talking converses with the boys.

M. enters. Looking at him the Master laughs and laughs. He cries out, 'Why look! There he is again!'

The boys all join in the merriment.

M. falls at his feet. On previous occasions he had saluted the Master with folded hands,—after the manner of those persons who had received an English education. But to-day he has learnt to fall down at his feet. He takes his seat and the Master tells Narendra and the other disciples what has made him laugh. He says:

'Once upon a time a small quantity of opium was given to a certain peacock at four o'clock in the afternoon. Well, punctually at four the next afternoon, who should come in but the selfsame peacock longing for a repetition of the favour—another dose of the opium!' (*laughter.*)

'Yes,' thinks M. to himself. 'He has indeed said well. I go back home, but I leave my heart behind me with this God-Man, the like of whom I have never seen before. Night and day one thought presses me,—when shall I see him again? It seems as if a hand draws me to this place. It is impossible for me to go anywhere else or give up the idea of coming here.'

Thinking this M. sat watching the Master as he amused himself with the boys. He kept up a running fire of chaff, and it seemed as if these boys were of his own age and he was playing with them. Peals of laughter and brilliant flashes of humour follow one upon another, calling to mind the image of a fair, where the Joy of the Lord is to be had for sale.

M. marvels at the sight of a personality so unique. He thinks to himself, 'Is this the man who was in a state of *samadhi* yesterday and who gave us an example of Divine Love never seen before? Is this the man who took me to task the first time I saw him because I had entered into the married state?' It was he again who rebuked me, saying 'Do you indeed look upon yourself as one who has attained Knowledge?' Was it he who declared that God is *with form* and that likewise God is *without form*? Was it he again who declared that God is the one Reality, all else is unreal, transitory,—now is, and the next moment has vanished out of our sight? Was it indeed he who taught the other day, saying, 'Do your work in this world unattached—with your mind turned always to your Home—the Abode of the Everlasting, the Abode of our Divine Mother; even as the maid servant does her work—with her mind dwelling always in her country home, where her own people, her dear ones, reside?'

In the midst of his merriment the Master from time to time looks on M.—who is seated speechless, motionless, gazing up into his sweet face!

He says to Ram Lall, 'This young man here (M.)is a little older than these boys; that is why he is a little grave. He holds his peace, as you see while they laugh and make merry.' M. is about twenty-seven years old at the time.

Renunciation

The Master talks of *Hanuman*, one of the devout characters of the *Ramayana*. How ready is *Hanuman*, says he, to give up everything for the sake of the Lord—money, honours, pleasures of the body and the rest!

The Master sings:

What need have I of sweet fruits? I have the Fruit that makes Life fruitful,
—the fruit of Liberation borne by the Divine Tree[1] which is planted in my heart!

[1]Kalpa.

I sit down at the foot of this Celestial Tree called the Lord[1] of the Universe—whatever fruits I gather I get from that tree.

Talking of fruits let me assure thee once for all, I am not one to accept fruits that the world can give.

Thus he is singing of Hanuman's renunciation of the world and its pleasures, and as he sings he loses sense-consciousness.

He is now in a state of *Samadhi*—the superconscious or God-conscious state. The body is again motionless! The eyes are again fixed! He is seated just as we see him in the photograph.

The boys only a moment ago were laughing and making merry! Now they all look grave. Their eyes are steadfastly fixed on the Master's face. They marvel at the wonderful change that has come over him. M. sees the Master in *Samadhi* for the second time.

It takes him long to come back to the sense world. His limbs now begin to lose their stiffness. His face beams with smiles, the organs of sense begin to come back each to its own work. Tears of joy stand at the corners of his eyes. He chants the sacred name of *Rama* (God-Incarnate). M. thinks to himself, 'Was it the self-same God-man who was only a few moments back sporting with the boys like a five-year-old child?'

He has returned to his former state and says to M. and to Narendra, 'I should like to hear you both talk in English and question and reason between yourselves.' At these words, both Narendra and M. laugh. They talk, however, but not in English. For M. to take part in any discussion in the presence of the Master is now quite out of the question; the chamber of his mind which formerly furnished materials for such things has been closed now, so to speak, once for all. The Master presses them once more but the talk in English does not come about.

[1] Rama.

It is five in the afternoon. The disciples must go back to their homes and all leave the Temple except Narendra and M. Narendra is going to spend the night with the Master.

With some of his members nearest to his heart

He will wash his face, hands and feet; he takes his brass pitcher and goes towards the *jhau* trees and the Goose-tank,—in the northern part of the Temple garden. M. paces up and down the garden path thinking of the extraordinary Man whom it has been his good fortune to meet. Walking round the *Kuthi* and coming up to the Goose-tank, he is surprised to find Sri Ramakrishna talking with Narendra, alone, by the tank-side. They stand at the head of the steps leading to the water. Narendra has washed and stands talking, pitcher in hand.

'You see,' says the Master smiling, 'you are a new comer; let not your visits be few and far between. During the first love, the meetings between lovers come oftener than at other times. Is that not so?' (*Narendra and M.both laugh.*)

The Master smiles and goes on, 'Well then, you should come here oftener. What do you say?'

Narendra smiles and says, 'Yes Sir, I shall try to come.'

The Master turns back and goes in a southern direction towards his chamber.

Narendra and M. walk with him on either side. Coming near the *Kuthi* he says to M., 'Do you know how peasants buy their bullocks for the plough? O they are very expert in these matters and know very well how to choose good bullocks from bad. They know quite well whether the beasts have mettle or not. They touch the tail, and the effect is miraculous. Those that have no spirit, will offer no resistance, but lie down on the ground, as if they were perfectly satisfied. Those that have mettle, on the other hand, will jump about as if to protest against the liberty taken with them. The peasant will choose these. Now Narendra is a bullook of this latter class; he has true mettle within.'

The Master smiles and goes on saying, 'But there are

many who have no grit at all in them—who are like popped rice put in milk; soft and loose! no strength within! no capacity for sustained effort! no power of will!'

It is evening. The Master is meditating on God in his own chamber.

Looking up he says to M., 'Will you go and find Narendra who is walking about in the Temple garden, and have a talk with him? You shall tell me what sort of boy he is.'

It is evening and the temple priests are worshipping, waving lights and flowers and other sacred offerings before the Holy Images. M. meets Narendra once more on the river-ghat west of the *Chandni.* They were, as they both said, very glad to meet each other. Narendra said, 'I belong to the *Sadharan Brahmo Samaj*; I am a college student;' and so on.

What do you think of me?

It is getting late and M has to take his leave. Something, however, seems to hold him back. Leaving Narendra he looks about for Sri Ramakrishna. The charm of his songs has gone to his heart and he is longing to hear more from his lips. Not finding him in his chamber he directs his steps towards the choir[1] in front of the Sanctuary of the Divine Mother.

The Master is pacing up and down the hall alone, in the dim light. Within the Temple stands the Image of the Mother of the Universe with a brilliant light burning on either side. But the dim light burning in the choir gives just that soft blending of light and darkness which is so very good for religious contemplation.

M. was beside himself with joy when he heard Sri Ramakrishna chanting the name of the Divine Mother. He was spell-bound!—like one helpless under the spell of the exorcist!

He draws near the Master and says with great diffidence

[1]Nata-Mandir, the music hall or choir placed in Hindu Temples in front of the sanctuary.

and humility, 'Are any more hymns going to be sung to-night Sir?'

The Master thinks for a moment and then says, 'No, there will be no more songs to-night. But look, I am coming to Balaram's house in Calcutta one of these days. Come there and you shall hear me sing.'

M.: As the Master pleases.

Master Don't you know the house? Do you know Balaram Bose?

M.: No, Sir; I do not.

Master: Balaram Bose? At Bosepara?

M.: Very well, Sir, I shall make enquiries.

Sri Ramakrishna walks up and down the choir with M.

Master: Well now, let me ask you a question *What do you think of me*?

M. holds his peace—deep in thought.

Master: What do you think of me? I mean, how much, how many *annas*, of True Knowledge have I got?

M.: The meaning of *annas* of Knowledge is not clear to me. All I can say is *Never till now has it been given to me to see such marvellous Wisdom, and Love of the Lord, and Faith and Renunciation, and Communion with God, and Catholicity all in one and the same person*. Never—and nowhere else!

The Master laughs.

M. takes his leave and bows down before the Master bending his head and falling at his feet. He comes as far as the northern gate, but turns back as if put in mind of something.

He comes back to the Master, who is still pacing the hall alone.

Yes; walking up and down the hall in that dim light, half-light, half-darkness. Alone. By himself. Companionless! So walks alone in the depths of the forest the king of animals—the Lion—with his Self, the only Companionship[1]!

[1]Atmarama

So does the King of Men rejoice to go about companionless in the wilderness of the world!

Awe-struck, speechless, does M. look on the Master! He thinks to himself, 'Here is Man's Ideal realised indeed! Man scorning the ground and communing with the Infinite!'

Master (to M.): Oh! Why have you come back?

M.: Sir, I am afraid it is some rich man's house to which you ask me to go. There may be porters and other people standing in the way. I think I had better not go. It is here that I should always like to meet with you.

Master: Why, my dear Sir, you have only to mention my name! Say that you desire to *see me*; and do not doubt but someone will lead you to me.

M.: As the Master pleases.

Saying this, M. bows down and departs.

SECTION II

1882

VISIT TO PANDIT ISWARA CHANDRA VIDYASAGAR

CHAPTER I

THE MASTER IN SAMADHI

Present:—Vidyasagar, Bhavanath, M., Hazra and many others.

The Master had a great desire to see Pandit Iswara Chandra Vidyasagar. One afternoon, he was seen taking a carriage and coming with his disciples all the way from Dakshineswar, a distance of about six miles, to see the Pandit in his house at Badurbagan, a district in Calcutta.

It was Saturday, 5th August 1882, about 5 p.m.; the seventh lunar day in the dark fortnight of the month of *Sravana*.

The carriage drew up in front of the door of the Pandit's house. The Master alighted, supported by M. Before reaching the staircase that led up to the Pandit's library, which was also his drawing-room, he said to M. with some concern: 'Well, do you think I ought to button my coat?'

M. answered, 'Oh don't trouble yourself, Lord, on that account. Things of this kind are not at all binding upon you.'

The Master, childlike, seemed to be convinced, for he paid no further attention to the matter. He looked as teachable as a five-year-old child!

The party was then led upstairs into a room next the landing with a door looking towards the south. In this room the Pandit was seated on a chair, facing the south. A table, after the European fashion, with his usual books and papers lying about, was before him.

M. then announced the Master's arrival and at once

introduced him to the Pandit, who stood up to receive him. The Master stood with his face to the west, and with one hand resting on the table. He looked on the Pandit in silence. But his sweet, radiant, childlike face was wreathed in smiles.

There was some company present, including the Pandit's friends and pupils. One of these was a boy who had come to ask for a free studentship in connection with one of the schools of which the Pandit was founder and proprietor.

The Master in Samadhi

Standing thus and looking on the Pandit, the Master again lost all sense-consciousness. He had passed into the state of Samadhi. After a while, taking his seat he said, as was his wont, 'I want some water to drink.' Thereupon, Vidyasagar inquired of M. whether the Master would like to take some sweetmeats also, which he had just received from Burdwan. Finding no objection, the Pandit went into his inner apartments and soon came back with the water and the sweetmeats. He placed them before the Master. The disciples also partook of them.

When they were offered to one of the disciples, Vidyasagar said, 'Oh, he is a child of this house. Never mind him.' Thereupon the Master said, 'Yes, this young man is good. He is like the River *Falgu* with an apparently dried-up bed, but with an active, invisible current underneath. Internally he is full[1] of pith and marrow.'

Knowledge which leads Godward[2]

Master (to Vidyasagar): This day I am at last fortunate enough to come down to the ocean[3]. Up till now I have come across canals, marshes, or at most, rivers. (*Laughter*). (Here the Master referred to the literal meaning of the word Vidyasagar, which is 'Ocean of knowledge.')

Vidyasagar: Then you are welcome Sir, to take home some salt water from your ocean. (*Laughter*.)

Master: No, my dear Sir, you are surely not the salt

[1]Antassita. [2]Vidya. [3]Sagar.

ocean. You are not the ocean of *Avidya* (ignorance which leads one away from God). You are the ocean of milk, the ocean of *Vidya* (true knowledge leading Godward). (*Laughter.*)

Vidyasagar: Well Sir, I am afraid you may say *that.* (*Laughter.*)

Master: Your nature is made of the *sattva* element of man's nature which leads to Illumination or True Knowledge. Only your *sattva* is in that phase which makes you active and devoted to the doing of good works. Charity[1], compassion[2], kindness towards others are good if practised without attachment. So practised and with devotion[3] they will lead to God.

Work without attachment

Master: Further, I should say that you deserve to be called a Perfect Man: for has not your kindness to others, made you soft and tender of heart? Bear in mind potatoes and other vegetables do not get tender until they are *Siddha* (well-boiled). (*Laughter.*)

The Perfect Man

(The word Siddha may mean either 'a perfect man' or 'well-boiled.' Hence the pun on the word by the Master.)

Vidyasagar: But *Kalai* pulse pounded to pulp, when *Siddha* (well-boiled), gets hard and is by no means tender. Is it not so? (*Laughter.*)

Master (laughing) :Well, my dear Sir, you are no such thing: I mean, you are not a mere Pandit,—dry and hard and good for nothing.

In the Hindu almanac, it is mentioned that on a particular day there will be twenty *Adas*[4] of water. But you shall not be able to squeeze out of the almanac a single drop!

The Master on the value of mere book learning

Our learned men, so-called, will talk big. They will talk of Brahman, God the Absolute, of Jnana Yoga, Philosophy, Ontology and the rest. But there are very few who realise the things they talk about.

[1]Dana [2]Daya. [3]Bhakti [4]Adas are measures of Capacity

The highest learning[1] is that by which we know God. All else—the Sacred Books,[2] Philosophy, Logic, Grammar, etc. etc., as such, only load and puzzle the mind. They are good only when they lead to the highest learning.

The Substance of Bhagavadgita

In one sense there is no use of going through the whole of the Lord's Song[3]. Say 'Gita,' 'Gita' ten times. That is sufficient. For said ten times, it comes to be '*tyagi*,' '*tyagi*.' Now *tyagi* means a person who has given up the world for the sake of God—riches, honours, work with attachment, sensual pleasures, etc.

In one word, the Gita says 'Give up.' The ideal *sannyasin* (ascetic) will give up the world both outwardly and inwardly. He will give up secular work and the fruit of all work.

The ideal householder[4] will give up the world from the mind, that is, he will give up the fruit of all work for the sake of the love of God.

Thus the substance of the Gita is, 'O man, love the Lord alone—give up everything for the sake of the Lord.'

A holy man had a manuscript book. Somebody asked him what it was about. The saint opened the book before the man, who was surprised to find that on every page was written only the Name of God—the words 'Om Rama!'

Chaitanya Deva in the course of his pilgrimage through the Deccan came across a certain devotee who was in tears all the while that a Pandit was reading from the Gita. Now this devotee knew not letters. He could not follow a single text of the Gita. Upon being asked why he shed tears, he replied, 'It is indeed true that I do not know a word of the Gita; but all the while that it was being read I could see with my inner eye the beautiful form of my Lord Sri Krishna seated before Arjuna at Kurukshetra and saying all those things that are said in the Gita. It was this which filled my eyes with tears of joy and love.'

This man who knew not letters had the highest learning, for he had a pure love[5] for God and could realise Him.

[1]Paravidya. [2]Shastras. [3]Gita. [4]Grihastha. [5]Bhakti.

CHAPTER II

THE MASTER ON JNANA YOGA
THE VEDANTA OR ADWAITA PHILOSOPHY OR PHILOSOPHY OF THE UNCONDITIONED

Brahman of the Vedanta. The Absolute and the Unconditioned

Master: Well, I was talking of *Vidya*. But Brahman is above and beyond *Vidya* (the relative knowledge which leads Godward) as well as *Avidya* (the world which keeps all beings away from the knowledge of God).

Knowledge leading Godward is the last and topmost step of the stairs leading to the roof. The Absolute is the Roof.

The phenomenal world[1] is made up of that[2] which leads Godward and that[3] which does not. Thus God the Absolute[4] is above and beyond the phenomenal world.

The Absolute is perfectly unattached: The problem of Good and Evil solved

The Absolute is unattached to Good or Evil. It is like the light of lamp. You may read the Holy Scriptures[5] with its help. It is equally open to you to forge another man's signature in the same light

Again, the Absolute is like a snake. The snake has poison in its fangs. But it is none the worse for this. The poison does not affect the snake or cause its death. It is poison to others only, those whom it may chance to bite.

Whatever misery, sin or evil we find in this world is misery, sin, or evil only relatively to ourselves. God the Absolute is not affected thereby. He is above and beyond all these things.

Evil in the created is not evil to the Absolute and the Unconditioned any more than the venom in the fang of the snake is venom to the snake. God the Absolute is above and beyond God and Evil.

Yes, that Being is perfectly unattached. He is not to

[1]Maya. [2]Vidya. [3]Avidya. [4]Brahman. [5]Bhagavat.

be judged by any human standard of Good and Evil. His sun sheds light equally on the Evil and the Good.

Brahman is unspeakable[1]

Everything—even the revealed Scriptures, the *Vedas*, the *Puranas*, the *Tantras* and all other Sacred Books—has become with one sole exception, defiled[2] as it were like the leavings of food, having been uttered by the mouth of human beings. That One Exception is *Brahman*. For when one reads the Vedas and other Sacred Books one must use the vocal organs and thus bring these texts in touch with the mouth, so to speak. Thus they may be said to have all been defiled like the leavings of food. But no creature in this world has yet been able to give proper and adequate expression to God the Absolute. He is unspeakable, unthinkable, inconceivable!

Vidyasagar: I must say, here is, indeed, some thing that I have learnt to-day. The Absolute is the One Substance that has never been defiled by the mouth!

Master: Yes, that is so. It is Being not conditioned by anything—Time,[3] Space,[4] or Causation.[5] How can one give expression to it by any word of mouth?

The Absolute again is like the unfathomable ocean. Nothing can be predicated of It—the Being beyond the bounds of Relativity—of all existence! The last feeble attempt to describe this Being—the attempt made in the *Vedas*—is to call Him by the name of Bliss[6] Everlasting!

If you are asked to describe the ocean, you stand with your mouth wide open and can only stammer out, 'Oh, how vast an expanse! What a never-ending succession of gigantic waves! What thunderous sound, incessant and eternal'! That is all!

The utmost that Sukadeva and Holy Sages like him could ever do was to see and to touch the water of this Immortal Sea, and just taste a bit! Had he once gone down

[1]Avyapadesyam. [2]Ucchista. [3]Kala. [4]Desa.
[5]Nimitta [6]Anandam.

into that Sea, he would have been merged in It, never to come back into this world any more!

The Great Mystery is unfathomable by conditioned Knowledge
Parable of the Ants and the Mountain of Sugar

Once upon a time, there came some ants to a mountain of sugar. They, of course, had no idea that it was such a big thing. They ate up a few grains of the sugar and were filled. Then each took away a particle. As they went their way, they thought the next time they would be able to carry away the whole mountain to their place of habitation!

Such, alas, is the condition of man! It is given to some few, indeed, to realise the Supreme Being[1]. But many unfortunately, run away with the idea that they have fully known, fully enjoyed communion with, fully realised, the Infinite Being!

The mountain of sugar seems all but carried home by the ant; for is he not filled and satisfied with his meal? Thus, too, the self-deluded rationalist! He is satisfied with his ounce of reason. *Ergo*, he comprehends Brahman!—he knows what the Absolute is and what It is not!

People talk glibly of the Infinite, the Absolute, the Unconditioned, as if they had any conception of It at all!

Sukadeva and other holy sages were at best ants of the larger sort. If we say that they could eat up eight or ten particles of this sugar, we have said enough in their favour.

It is just as absurd to say that God the Absolute has been known and comprehended by any one, as it is to say that a mountain of sugar has been carried home by some ants to be eaten up.

The Goal of the Vedantin

The union between the Undifferentiated (the Universal Soul) and the Differentiated (the individualised soul[2]) is the goal of the Vedantin.

The parable of the Salt Doll

Once upon a time a doll made of salt went to the sea with a view to measure its depth. This salt doll had in its hand a sounding line and plummet. It came to the edge of the

[1]Brahman. [2]Jiva

water and looked on the mighty Ocean that was before it. Up to this point it had continued to be the doll of salt that it actually was, keeping in its own individuality. But no sooner did it take one step forward, and put its foot to the water, than it became one with the Ocean, lost, entirely lost to view! Every particle of the salt doll now dissolved in the sea-water. The salt of which it was made had come from the Ocean, and behold, it came back once more to be reunited to the original salt of the Ocean!

The 'Differentiated' had again become one with the 'Undifferentiated.'

The human soul is this salt doll—the Differentiated Individualised *ego*. The Absolute, the Unconditioned is the Infinite salt Ocean—the Undifferentiated Ego.

The salt doll could not come back and tell of the depth of the Mighty Ocean. Such is he who is fortunate enough to realise God the Absolute in the unfathomable depth of *Samadhi*[1] which wipes out all individuality. Undifferentiated as he is, he comes not back out of the deep to tell the world the nature of God, the Absolute and Unconditioned. For if it were ever possible, by my Mother's will for the salt doll to come back to the differentiated again, it must speak in terms of the finite—in the language of the differentiated. It must behave like an inhabitant of the relative phenomenal world.

This is why the *Great Mystery* defies all attempts at explanation. The Absolute and Unconditioned cannot be stated in terms of the Relative, the Conditioned. The Infinite cannot be expressed in terms of the Finite.

God the Absolute-beyond all predication: Parable of the Vedic Father and His Two Sons

A certain father had two sons. When they were of age he wished to start them on the first stage of life—that of the student.[2] To this end they were given into the care of a preceptor and with him made to go through the *Vedas* and other Sacred Books.

[1]Nirvikalpa. [2]Brahmacharin

In this way there passed some days. The father now wished to see how the young men were getting on with their studies. He sent for them and asked whether they had read the Vedanta, which purports to teach the Highest Knowledge to the aspirant. The sons replied that they had.

Father: So, my boys, you have read the Vedanta. Well, tell me what sort of Being is God[1] the Absolute.

Elder son (quoting the *Vedas* and other Scriptures): It, O Father, is not capable[2] of being expressed by words, or of being known by the mind. O, He is thus and thus and so and so; I know it all. (Here he quotes texts from the Vedanta.)

Father: Very well, that will do. So you have known *Brahman*; you may go about your business. Now, my boy, let me hear what *you* have got to say. What sort of Being is the Absolute?

The second son, to whom this question was put, hung down his head and sat quite mute. Not a word proceeded out of his mouth. Nor did he make any attempt to speak. He continued in this state for a long time.

The father thereupon said, 'Yes, my boy, you are right after all. Nothing can be predicated of the Absolute and the Unconditioned! No sooner do you talk of him one way or the other, than you state the Infinite in terms of the Finite, the Absolute in terms of the Relative, the Unconditioned in terms of the Conditioned. Your silence is more eloquent than the recitation of a hundred texts[3] and the quoting of a hundred authorities.'

Realisation

Yes, He who has True Knowledge ceases to have anything to do with talk or controversy. God the Absolute, is the one Substance to be realised—not described or known. The sign of True Knowledge or Realisation is cessation of doubt and therefore of all philosophical discussion.

How long does the clarified butter set in a pan over a

[1] Brahman. [2] Avangamanasagocharam. [3] Slokas.

cooking-stove go on making noise? Why, so long as it does not get to the right degree of heat at which no trace of water is left. The clarified butter not sufficiently hot bubbles up and gives out those well-known sounds *kawl, kawl.*

The butter melted to the right temperature and not giving any sound is he who has got True Knowledge—that is, who has realised God the Absolute.

The butter not heated is the aspirnat for knowledge. The water with which it is mixed must be taken out by setting it over the fire. This is the ego or self which gets very clamorous in the process of being got rid of. As soon as this egoism is shaken off it is *pucka.* No noise, no clamour. (*Laughter.*)

At the same time the impurities all settle down on the bottom of the pan. Worldliness and attachment to women —'carnality and gold' and their attendant evils are the impurities.

The Perfect Man again, is like a pitcher of water filled to the brim. While the pitcher is being filled, it gives a gurgling sound (*bhawk*, *bhawk*). As soon as it is filled, the sound ceases altogether. The sound is reasoning or discrimination leading up by my Mother's will, to True Knowledge. The sound tells us that the pitcher is not yet full. Discriminating[1], too, proves that the Goal has not yet been reached.

The bee buzzes so long as it does not settle down on the flower and begin to drink of the honey. As soon as it tastes the honey all buzzing is at an end.

Is discriminating possible after True Knowledge?

The question now arises how we explain the relation between a 'perfect' preceptor and his disciples? The preceptor must talk with a view to drive away the ignorance of the disciple. This is *discriminating*—which, however, does no harm.

The butter set over the fire in a pan when melted to the right degree of heat ceases no doubt to give any sound.

[1]Vichara.

But throw an unbaked cake[1] into this hot melted butter. The result is that the heated butter in contact with the water in the cake will once more begin to give off sounds. This noise will go on as long as the cake is not sufficiently fried and made ready for eating.

The cake is the disciple. The sound which the heated butter (the preceptor) gives the second time is the process of discrimination which he is called upon to go through in order that the disciple may be brought to light. The cessation of the sound tells us that the Master has stopped talking as soon as the disciple has been illumined.

The Higher Self alone knows the Higher Self

The result of the foregoing position is that the Higher Self[2] alone knows the Higher Self. He, Knowledge Absolute[3], is capable of being realised by Himself, the *Knowledge Absolute* alone.

The Differentiated Soul, so long as it continues to be differentiated and walks on the lower plane cannot as such realise God the Absolute.

The Undifferentiated alone realises the Undifferentiated.

This is the true meaning of the expression 'God is unknown and unknowable.'

The World-system (Maya) is unreal: Vedanta Philosophy intepreted by the School of Sankara

All differentiation takes[4] lace in the domain of *Maya*. In other words, it is *Maya* that causes the differentiation. It ends with the cessation of *Maya*.

All the facts of the universe—every object, every phenomenon—that comes under creation, preservation and destruction—under body, mind and soul; under waking, dreaming, dreamless sleep, even meditations,[5] all come under *Maya* (the World-system). All these are looked upon as unreal by those[6] who interpret the Vedanta philosophy after Sankara and the like.

According to these the Absolute is the only Reality;

[1]Luchi(Poori). [2]Atman. [3]Bodhaswarupam [4]Dhyana.

[5]Vedantists or JnaniNs. [6]Vedantists or Jnanins.

the universe[1] is unreal[2] that is when looked at from the point of view of the Absolute. To the Absolute or the Undifferentiated the universe and man and other creatures[3] are unreal, for the only Reality is the Absolute.

When *Maya* is realised as unreal the differentiated *ego*[4] has been completely shaken off or effaced, so to speak. There is no trace of the *ego* left behind. It is perfect *Samadhi.*

It is absurd to say 'the world is unreal' so long as we remain convinced that we ourselves are real! A person who has not realised the Absolute cannot realise that the world is unreal.

On the other hand, a saint returning from *Samadhi* to a lower spiritual plane gets back by my Mother's will, has differentiated, attenuated, though purified, *ego.*

Getting back his *ego* the saint is thrown once more upon the world of relativity. So long as his *ego* is real to him (real relatively), the world is real too, and the Absolute is unreal (unreal relatively)!

With his differentiated *ego* restored to him he perceives, the World-system (Maya) as real. Only the *ego* being purified by God-vision, he sees the phenomena of the universe as manifestations of the Absolute to the senses.

He also sees the World-system (Maya) as either *Vidya* or *Avidya.*

Vidya leads Godward. To this belong discrimination,[5] non-attachment,[6] love of God,[7] etc. *Avidya* leads away from God. To this belong carnality,[8] riches,[9] honours, work with attachment, and the rest.

Realisation: The reconciliation between the Non-dualist and the Dualist

Vijnanis are they who have realised God in *Samadhi* both (1) as the Impersonal or the Undifferentiated, and (2) as God Personal. (Literally *Vijnani* means, he who possesses an intimate knowledge of God.')

Vijnanis have realised that it is the Absolute and un-

[1]Jagat. [2]Mithya. [3]Jiva. [4]Aham. [5]Viveka.
[6]Vairagya. [7]Bhakti. [8]Kamini. [9]Kanchan.

conditioned who as the Primal Divine Energy causes this differentiation[1] into God and the World-system, the soul and the universe. They have seen God both within and without and have received this Revelation from Him direct. God Personal has said to them, 'I am the Absolute (*Brahman Nirguna* of the Upanishads) realised in *Samadhi*. I have caused this differentiation. I am the Origin of the twenty-four categories—of the human soul and the world.'

The Personal God—creating, sustaining, destroying and causing the differentiation—has manifested Himself in various forms to those[2] who seek *the Personal God*[3] alone as well as to the *Vijnanis* as a Person with the three qualities.[4]

The *Sattva Guna* (material) of the Divine Person preserves, the *Rajas* creates, and the *Tamas* destroys. These three qualities dwell in the Divine Person. But He is not in them. He is quite unattached.

The only Proof of God Impersonal or Personal: Revelation

The *Vijnani* with his soul (his *ego*) purified has thus seen God, the Personal side of the Absolute as well as the Impersonal. He has heard His voice both within and without him. Not only so, He has talked to Him. He has ministered to Him as father, mother, son, wife, servant, brother, &c. According to the testimony, therefore, of these Perfect men—these *Vijnanis*—the World-system[5] is not an illusion, but the manifestation to the differentiated but purified *ego* of a Real Being as a Person who has created (or from whom have been evolved) the human soul and the soul of every created being as well as this universe.

This testimony is infallible, because it is based upon *Revelation*.

The Lord revealed Himself to the Rishis as both Personal and Impersonal. Such revelations are made from time to time for the salvation of mankind as well as for the joy of devotees.

[1]Bheda. [2]Bhaktas. [3]Sakti or Iswara. [4]Gunas. [5]Maya or Sakti

The Impersonal and the Personal God

When the Supreme Being is thought of as inactive[1]—neither creating, sustaining nor destroying, I call Him by the name *Brahman* or *Purusha* (the Male Principle) the Impersonal God. When I think of Him as active—creating, sustaining, destroying, I call Him by the name of *Sakti* or *Maya* or *Prakriti* (the Female Principle) or the Personal God.

The use of analogies

Analogies indeed do not go on all fours with the things to be made clear by them. They are at best one-sided[2] being intended to clear up some one particular phase of an unknown thing and bring it out from obscurity.

'So and so is a tiger' does not mean he is a tiger in every respect, even to the head, the teeth, the claws and the tail! It is not meant that he has claws or a tail like a tiger. The meaning is simply that he is *fearful-looking*.

No analogy can be perfectly satisfactory to explain the relation between the Impersonal and the Personal God. This is a thing to be realised alone.

Yet analogies enable us to catch a glimpse, however faint, of the truth regarding spiritual matters that go beyond the bounds of sense-consciousness.

One and the same Being

But in fact the distinction between Brahman, the Inactive or Impersonal God on the one hand, and Sakti, the Active or Personal God on the other, is a distinction without a difference.

The Impersonal and the Personal are one and the same Being, even as fire and its burning property are one. You cannot conceive of fire apart from its power of burning, nor the power of burning apart from the fire!

They are one, even as milk and its whiteness are one. One cannot conceive of milk without the whiteness.

They are one, just as a gem and its brightness are one. You cannot conceive of a gem without its brightness, nor of gem-like brightness apart from a gem.

[1]Nishkariya. [2]Ekadesi.

They are one, even as a serpent and its movement in a crooked line are one. You cannot conceive of the serpent apart from its serpentine tortuous motion nor of serpentine motion apart from the serpent.

CHAPTER III

THE OMNIPOTENT MOTHER

Is God Partial? Are all men equal?

Master: As I have already said the Personal God creates, preserves and destroys. She has made Herself manifest on the one hand as powers or phenomena leading Godward[1] and on the other hand as powers or phenomena leading away from God.[2] The manifestation of this omnipotent Power[3] varies in vaying centres of activity. In men as well as in other creatures, it varies. For variety is the law—not sameness.

Vidyasagar: Am I then, sir, to believe that we come into the world with unequal endowments? Is the Lord partial to a select few?

Master: Well, I am afraid you will have to take the facts of the universe as they stand. It is not given to man to see clearly into the ways of the Lord.

As the Omnipresent,[4] He is present in and through all creatures,—in and through all things—even in the smallest of His creatures, the ant for instance. Yes, God is immanent in all His creatures. But the fact remains that these creatures do vary in their endowments and powers.

If it were not the case how could one man often be a match for ten and beat them single-handed? We all know how another will flee from the face of a single individual who is more than his match.

As in the physical, so in the moral world. So, too, in the spiritual. Morality varies. And there are different degrees of spirituality.

[1]Vidya Sakti. [2]Avidya Sakti. [3]Sakti. [4]Vibhu.

Allow me to put it to you, why is it that you enjoy the respect of all so much more than others? Surely you do not mean to say that you are a phenomenon, that you have a couple of horns standing out from the front of your head and that, therefore, people come to see you! (*Laughter.*)

No. Variety is the law and my Divine Mother is that One Being who is manifest as many. Herself of Infinite Power, She has differentiated Herself into living creatures,[1] and all other beings[2] of this universe with all their varying powers and endowments—physical, intellectual, moral and spiritual.

And this my Divine Mother is no other than the Absolute, the *Brahman* of the *Vedanta*.

And the Master sang:

PSALM

MY DIVINE MOTHER: OMNIPOTENT, UNKNOWN, UNKNOWABLE.

1. Lives there one who knows Kali, my Divine Mother. She who is the Consort of the Absolute,[3] the Spirit of Eternity. Even the six schools of philosophy cannot get a sight of Her.

The Yogi always meditates upon Her at the Muladhara[4] and at the Sahasrara.[5]

There go about a Goose and a Gander in this lotus wilderness and these are mated with each other. Verily they are the Spirit of Eternity[6] and His Consort.

2. My Divine Mother is the most beloved of the Absolute,[7] even as *Sita* is the most beloved of *Rama*.

It is the Spirit of Eternity[8] (the Absolute) only who knows the greatness of My Divine Mother—greatness which is hidden from ordinary beings. Who else can know so well as He.

3. My Divine Mother gives birth to the Universe—now think of Her greatness!

---

[1]Jiva. [2]Jagat. [3]Kala.

[4] The Muladhara is the first lotus with four petals in which the Yogi meditates upon Siva and Sakti (God Impersonal and Personal) as manifest in their glory. It is the root of the Sushumna in the spinal cord.

[5] *Sahasrara* is the lotus with a thousand petals which is the goal of Sakti waked up by the Yogi at the Muladhara. When the Sakti reaches the *Sahasrara* and gets united to Siva or Brahman, the Impersonal God, the result is *Samadhi* in *Brahma-jnana*.

[6]Siva or Brahma. [7]Siva. [8]Mahakala.

She appears in Her majesty in each finite being[1] as an individual just as She pleases. She has Her own way[2] in everything.

4. Says Prasad, the Psalmist: To think that a man can know Her is to think that one can swim across the great mighty ocean. People will only laugh at the idea!

I understand this well enough by the mind, but alas! my heart[3] will not see this. It is a dwarf that must aspire to reach the Moon.

The Master in Samadhi: Revelations in Samadhi

At the end of this hymn the Master is seen to be once more in the indescribable region of *Samadhi*. The sweet angelic voice is still. The outer eyes are fixed and steadfast. The inner eye looks within and beholds the Vision of Glory. This Blessed Vision, the Master enjoys for a while. His face shines with a heavenly lustre and at last breaks into smiles.

Half returning to the plane of consciousness, he says: Yes, my Holy Mother is none other than the Absolute[4] She it is to whom the six systems of philosophy with all their learned disquisitions furnish no clue.

The Omnipotent Mother

When the differentiated *ego* is taken away by my Mother, there comes the realisation of the Impersonal in *Samadhi*, and then it is the Impersonal God, not the individual soul, that realises the Impersonal. When the *ego* is purified and so retained, the seeing or realisation of the Personal God or any of Her manifestations is possible by Her Grace—manifestations such as Sri Krishna, Chaitanya Deva and other Divine Incarnations; or as men, women, children, all living creatures; nay, all the twenty-four categories.

It pleases my Mother, the Personal God, to efface the self in self-less[5] *Samadhi*. The result is the realisation of the Impersonal God in *Samadhi*.

Sometimes it pleases Her to keep that self on in Her devotees and then to appear before them as the Personal God, and talk with them.

[1] Ghata. [2] Ichhamai. [3] Prana.

[4] Brahman of the Vedanta: *Atmani Chaibam Vichitra chahi:—Brahma Sutras*, 28 i, ii. [5] Nirvikalpa,

Revelation *vs.* Reason: The Personal God how proved; The Impersonal God how proved

The key to the realisation of the Absolute is with the Divine Person alone, the *Saguna Brahman* of the *Upanishads*, the Personal God of devotees. That power of discrimination[1] which the philosopher relies on comes from Her, my Divine Mother, the Personal God.

Prayer, meditation, devotion, self-surrender, are all likewise derived from my Omnipotent Mother.

Again, the sage in *Samadhi* is sometimes kept on in that state and sometimes not. Who keeps him on in that blessed state? Who brings him down to the lower plane of sense-consciousness? Why, it is the Divine Person, my Holy Mother.

Such a Person cannot be unreal. She is the Personal side of the one Reality, the Absolute (Brahman of the Vedanta). Yes, my Mother Herself has declared to Her children, 'I am the Mother of the Universe,' 'I am the *Brahman* of the Vedanta,' 'I am the *Atman of the Upanishads.'*

Thus the Personal God reveals Herself. That Revelation is the proof of Her existence.

Again, the Impersonal, Undifferentiated God, the Absolute, is *revealed* by the Personal God, that is, the Personal side of God the Absolute.[2] The Saint in *Samadhi* cannot say anything about the Absolute. Like the salt-doll, getting in touch with the Mighty Ocean, he is lost! Nor can he, coming down from *Samadhi*, say anything about the Absolute. Once differentiated, he is mute as to the Undifferentiated. Once in the relative world his mouth is shut as to the Absolute and Unconditioned.

My Mother (the Personal side of the Absolute) says, 'I am the Absolute,' (the *Nirguna Brahman* of the *Upanishads)*.

Thus too Revelation is the only proof of the Impersonal God.

However one may describe the Absolute or the Impersonal, one must throw one's differentiated *ego* into the

[1] Vichara [2] Mahakala.

description. His Absolute is covered, so to speak, by this *ego*.

Surely with our feeble powers of ratiocination and discrimination[1] we cannot reach the Absolute. Hence, Revelation not ratiocination! Inspiration not reason!

Spiritual Forms of the Deity

The manifestation of the Personal God is often a spiritual form which is seen only by the purified human soul. In other words, these Forms are realised by the organs of spiritual vision, belonging to that spiritual body which is derived from the Lord.

Not every one, but only the perfect man can see these Divine Forms through the grace of my Mother.

The Path of Knowledge and the Path of Devotion equally lead to Realisation

Once Ramachandra (God incarnate) said to his great devotee,[2] 'My son, tell me in what relation thou regardest me, and how thou meditatest upon me.' The devotee replied, 'O Rama, at times when the conviction.[3] I am the body, clings to me, I worship Thee as the one Undivided[4] God; then I look upon myself as part[5] of Thee—a fragment, as it were, of Divinity! At other times, I meditate upon Thee as my Divine Master, and think myself as Thy servant. When, however, I am blessed, O Rama, with knowledge[6] of God the Absolute, I see, I realise, that *I am Thou* and *Thou art me*.'

The devotee meant that after *Samadhi* his 'I' was merged or lost in Rama; by which he meant the Undifferentiated Ego, God the Absolute and Unconditioned. This is *Brahma-jnana*.

Water to Ice and Ice to Water.

Again, suppose there is an infinite expanse of water—water above, water beneath water in all directions. Portions of this water, we may imagine, get changed into ice by contact with cold. Again, the same ice may be exposed to heat, and thus get liquefied. It has become water once more.

[1]Vichara. [2]Hanuman. [3]Dehatma-buddhi. [4]Purna. [5]Amsa. [6]Tatwa-jnana.

The Absolute is the infinite expanse of water. The portions of this water that are changed into ice are the spiritual personal forms of the Deity manifest to devotees. The cold is the Bhakti of the devotee, his love, his devotion, his self-surrender. The heat again is his discrimination between the real (that is, God the Absolute) and the unreal or phenomenal universe, leading up to self-less[1] *Samadhi* and the total effacement of that self which says 'I,' 'I.'

To a devotee (dualistic worshipper) the Lord may manifest Himself in various forms. To one who has reached by my Mother's will, to the height of Absolute Knowledge in *Samadhi*, He is the Absolute once more, Formless, Unconditioned.

Herein lies the reconciliation between realisation by philosophy[2] and that by love.[3]

What is the external world? Identity of God, the Soul and Nature

To him unto whom it has been given to realise the Impersonal-Personal God, it has been revealed that the twenty-four categories[4] (taking in the external world) have all been evolved from the Mother.

Be it known that the Holy Mother is both one and many and the Absolute beyond one and many. She has not only differentiated into the *ego* within man but also into the various other categories.

The New Philosophy

The Advaitist's position, that Brahman is God, the Absolute and Unconditioned, must be accepted in its entirety; because, first, Brahman has been realised in *Samadhi*; and secondly, because Brahman has been revealed by my Mother as the Unconditioned that may be realised in *Samadhi* alone, and as being the Impersonal side of Her own Self. Let not any one, however, say, 'My position is the only correct, rational,

[1] Nirvikalpa. [2] Jnana. [3] Bhakti.

[4] The five gross elements, the five subtle elements the five external instruments, *viz.*, the eyes, &c., the five organs of sense, the mind, the determinative faculty (buddhi) and the ego.

and tenable position; those that believe in a Personal God are wrong. The Personal God is a myth. The Personal God has no power to give liberation'[1] etc.

The Problem for the Philosophical Advaitist: How can the Perfect Soul be led to think that it is imperfect?

The philosophical Advaitist, so long as he relies on the unaided powers of his reason, answers this question by saying, 'I do not know how this delusion, namely, the fact of the Undifferentiated Ego[2] being differentiated into the individual soul has come about.'

The answer which realisation gives is conclusive. My Mother (the Personal side of God, the Absolute) says: "It is I, the Brahman of the Vedanta, who have caused this differentiation. So long as you say, 'I know' or 'I do not know,' you look upon yourself as a person. Being a person, you must take these differentiations as facts—not delusions."

My Divine Mother says again, 'It is only when I efface all personality that the Undifferentiated (my impersonal aspect) may be realised in *Samadhi.*' And then it is all silence about delusion or no delusion, fact or no fact, knowing or not knowing. This is knowledge[3] of the Absolute.

CHAPTER IV

THE GREAT REVELATIONS AND THE NEW PHILOSOPHY

Necessity of a Personal God

Till then there is the 'I' in me and before me my Mother, Almighty (the Personal God) revealing Herself to Her children through various Forms[4] of Glory and through the Divine Incarnations, Sri Krishna, Chaitanya Deva, etc., and manifesting Herself under the twenty-four categories—as living creatures[5] and the whole cosmos.[6] Yes, it is owing to Her power that no created being can get rid of this self which says, 'I', 'I' in all created beings and which makes him of the earth earthy.

[1]Mukti. [2]Atman. [3]Brahma-jnana. [4]Rupa. [5]Jiva. [6]Jagat.

In the second place, it is She my Divine Mother, who teaches Bhakti (love, devotion, prayer and self-surrender) to the devotee and thus changes his *ego* of this world into the *ego* of knowledge,[1] making it thin like a line—a length without breadth. Lastly look at Her omnipotence!

If it pleases Her, She may take away the last trace of this *ego*[2] from any created being and bless him with the knowledge[3] of God, the Absolute and Unconditioned. This result comes about by the differentiated *ego* being merged or lost, *by* Her *Grace*, in the Undifferentiated Ego,—the Absolute—the Atman or the Brahman.

You cannot shake off the self. Even those[4] who have realised the Absolute in the ecstasy of *Samadhi* will yet come down by my Mother's will, to a lower plane and have just sufficient self[5] left to hold communion with the Personal God. Is it not difficult to raise the voice incessantly to *ni*, the highest note of the gamut?

So long as you are a person, an *individuality* of your own, God will, if it so pleases Him, manifest Himself to you as a person.

Nor can you conceive of, think or perceive God otherwise than as a person, so long as you are a person. Such is the constitution of your self.

The Advaitist and ordinary men

The goal of the Advaitist is the merging of the conditioned *ego* in the Unconditioned Brahman. This is not meant by my Divine Mother for everybody. For, with the majority of mankind the *ego* is a thing which cannot be shaken off in this life, or any other life in the near future.

Thus they (ordinary men) must, so long as they cannot attain to *Samadhi*, meditate upon, and commune with, the Personal God. For sages and the Scriptures and Revelation all agree in assuring us that the Unconditioned does manifest itself to man, both within him and without him, as a condi-

[1] Ego of Vidya. [2] Ahamkara. [3] Brahma-jnana. [4] Atmaram. [5] Aham.

[6] Corresponding to the *si* of the European musical scale.

tioned being;—the Impersonal as a Personal God. These Personal Manifestations are by no means less real, but infinitely more real than the body or the mind, or the external world. 'Hence,' says the knowing one, 'the necessity of a Personal God.'

Identity of the Mother with the Soul and Cosmos

It has pleased my Divine Mother to have become, in the course of creation (or evolution), not only my individualised self, but also the *external world.*

To him alone who comes down from *Samadhi* to the plane of sense-consciousness is left a thin self (like a line—length without breadth) just sufficient individuality to retain the spiritual vision.[1] This enables him to see the soul and the world, as well as himself, as my Holy Mother manifesting Herself in these different multifarious forms.[2]

This vision of glory of my Holy Mother manifesting Herself in the course of evolution as the twenty-four categories including the external world as well as the internal, is a vision not given to everyone to see and enjoy. The perception of this vision is granted unto him alone who has realised the Formless Impersonal God, Absolute and Unconditioned in Selfless-*Samadhi*, and the Personal God with forms in conscious-*Samadhi*.

The Omnipotent Mother and Karma: Can God Personal give Knowledge of the Absolute?

Yes, even the knowing one who loses his self in *Samadhi* and becomes one with the Absolute and thus realises It, is forced by the unseen power to come down to the lower plane of sense-consciousness. Who is this unseen power? This question brings us to my Omnipotent Mother (the Divine Person) who alone has it wholly within Her own power both to keep the self and to efface it in *Samadhi.*

The philosopher says it is Karma—works previously done either here or in previous incarnations—which causes the saint in *Samadhi* to come down to a lower plane.

Of course, so long as there is the self or *ego* there are

[1]Divya Chakshu. [2]Rupa.

both the actor[1] and the action.[2] There are both cause and the effect. Not only that. There are as facts, also, the millions of living creatures, and the cosmos with the twenty-four categories, time past, time present, time future, previous births, future births and all other differentiations.

But if there are these differentiations to be taken as stubborn facts, there is also the *Almighty Differentiator*, my Divine Mother, the Personal God.[3]

The position is made stronger by Revelation. For, my Divine Mother says, *'It is I who have caused this differentiation*. Good works and bad works all obey Me. There is, true enough, the law of Karma, but *I am the Lawgiver*. It lies with Me to make and unmake laws. I order all Karma, good or bad. Therefore, come unto Me through love,[4] devotion, prayer, self-surrender; or through philosophy[5] if you like; or with good works[6] leading Godward; and I will lead you across this world, this ocean of all work. I will give you knowledge of the Absolute[7] also, if you like. If there is still work after *Samadhi*, if there is still the *ego* and the body, be it known that such Karma, that *ego* and that body, I Myself order to be retained for purposes of My own.'

All this she has revealed to Her children, Her servants.

Can the lover of God (Bhakta) get Knowledge of the Absolute?

So if knowledge of the Absolute is the end in view, one may attain to it ultimately if one would earnestly pray for it to the Almighty Mother and throw oneself entirely upon Her mercy. The devotee[8] if thus anxious for such knowledge comes to my Mother (to any of Her Divine Manifestations) with *ego* of *Bhakti*, to find in the end the whole of his *ego* swept away in *Samadhi*, by my Mother's will.

It is the Personal God (the *Saguna Brahman*), my Divine Mother, who has caused this differentiation into subject and object. It is She who can and does efface the

[1] Karta. [2] Karma. [3] Saguna Brahman of the Vedanta.

[4] Bhakti. [5] Jnana. [6] Karma. [7] Brahmajnana. [8] Bhakta.

ego in *samadhi* and give a knowledge of the Absolute.

That it is She who does so, we learn from Revelation.

The philosopher, who does not rely upon Revelation so much as upon reason, says that the Personal God cannot give liberation[1] to the soul, or, in other words *the knowledge of the Absolute*.

It is from a lower plane (that of relativity or the phenomenal world), the plane of I and you, that the philosopher says: 'It is I that can give a knowledge of the Absolute[2] to myself.' But in this same plane we must, from the necessity of our nature, admit God Personal, my Omnipotent Mother.

It does seem strange that while it is supposed to be quite within the power of the individual with his limited faculties to give the knowledge of the Absolute to himself, my Omnipotent Mother has not that power! That although you can bring to yourself your own liberation, my Omnipotent Mother has not the power of giving you that liberation!

These philosophers forget that the same Being is both Personal and Impersonal. They do not see that the Supreme Being manifests Itself as a Person of Infinite Power so long as we are persons,—Infinite Power including the power of giving *Brahma-Jnana*.

But reason, alone and single-handed, is such an uncertain guide!

Moreover, the power of reason or discrimination upon which the philosopher relies also comes from God Personal.

Thus another thing is added to the position of the purely Advaitist philosopher, namely, that it is the Personal God who can and does give *Brahma-Jnana*.

Man's 'Absolute' must imply the 'Relative'

It is absolute knowledge so long as there is complete self-effacement and *Brahman* is realised in *Samadhi* and you are silent, postulating neither existence nor non-existence regarding it.

No sooner do you talk of *Advaitam* than you postulate *Dvaitam*. For if there is one, there are also two.

[1]Mukti. [2]Brahmajnana.

Talking of *Monism*, you take for granted *Dualism*.

Talking of the Absolute, you take for granted the Relative. For, your 'Absolute', until realised in *Samadhi*, is at best the correlative of the Relative, if not indeed a mere word put in certain letters of the alphabet!

Talking of the Unchangeable,[1] you take for granted the changeable[2] or this play-world.

Talking of the Impersonal,[3] you take for granted the Personal.[4]

Just as talking of light you postulate the existence of darkness, its correlative.

Just as where there is happiness there must also be misery, its correlative.

The same Being whose changeable play-world this is, is the Unchangeable. He who is the Unchangeable, the same Being, is the changeable.

It is through this changeable phenomenal world that you must feel your way up to the Unchangeable, Unconditioned. It is again from the latter that you must feel your way back to the former (now no longer *unreal*, but a manifestation to the senses of the Unchangeable).

When you talk of the Absolute you cannot possibly put it as it is. You must throw[5] over it a foreign element—*that of your own personality*.

After all we must fall back upon Revelation. It is the Divine Person (My Mother) who says, 'I am God the Personal,[6] I am the Absolute[7] realised in *Samadhi*.'

Yes, you cannot think or speak of the butter without postulating the *esse* of the *buttermilk*.

Reconciliation between Mayavada and Parinamavada: between Advaitam and Visishtadvaitam.

From the buttermilk comes the butter: so of the butter is the buttermilk. If the buttermilk is known by its relation to the butter, the butter is equally known by its relation to the buttermilk.

[1]Nitya. [2]Lila. [3]Avyakta. [4]Vyakta.

[5]*Adhyasa* superimposition, of the philosopher. [6]Saguna. [7]Nirguna.

In the plane of personality—the plane of sense and even of higher consciousness—you must admit both 'butter' and 'buttermilk.'

So long as you are a person, the *ego* being kept on by the Divine Mother, your Absolute must imply a 'Relative,' your Unchangeable must imply a changeable play-world, your Substance must imply qualities, your 'Impersonal' must imply a Personal Being, your 'One' must imply the 'many.'

When the Divine Mother wipes out your *ego* (personality) in *Samadhi*, *Brahman* is realised and it is all silence and whatever is, is there. For verily the salt-doll stepping down to measure the depth of the sea tells no tale when one with the Infinite Deep!

Were it ever possible to lay down the position by an analogy, you might say that the original milk was *Brahman* realised in *Samadhi*, the butter was the Impersonal-Personal God revealing Himself, and the buttermilk the universe made up of the twenty-four categories.

The path of Love as well as of Philosophy lead to Absolute Knowledge. The efficacy of Prayer and Faith

My Divine Mother (the Personal Phase of *Brahman*) has declared, 'I am the *Brahman* of the *Vedanta* (Impersonal-Personal God). It is within My power to give Absolute Knowledge. This I do when I cause the effacement of the lower self[1] and the realisation of the higher self in *Samadhi*.'

Thus, in the first place, you may come unto *Brahman* by my Mother's will through the path of philosophy.[2] But it is given only to a few, especially in this *Kaliyuga*, to come through this road; so very difficult[3] it is to shake off the conviction, 'I am the body,' which clings to us.

Again, you may come through prayer for light and for love. Self-surrender to Him and love of God are the

[1]Aham or the ego. [2]Jnana-yoga.

[3]*Klesodhikatarastesham Avyaktasaktachetasam Avyaktahi gatirduhkham dehavadbhiravapyate*:—Bhagavadgita.

various elements of *Bhakti*. First come to my Divine Mother, the Personal God, through these.

Take my word for it that if your prayer comes from the bottom of your heart, my Mother shall respond to it, if you will only wait. For, this She has revealed to Her children.

Pray to Her again, if you want to realise Her Impersonal Self. Should She deign to grant your prayer—for She is Omnipotent—you would be in a position to realise in *Samadhi* Her Impersonal Self also. This is precisely the same thing as absolute knowledge (*Brahma Jnana*).

The Bhakta's Wish

Only, I must add that the devotee as a rule will be quite content to realise the Divine Person alone—My Divine Mother, or any of Her Infinite forms of glory including the Divine Incarnations—Sri Krishna, Chaitanya Deva, etc., etc., the 'Visible Revelations of God.' As a rule, the *Bhakta* does not long for the realisation of the Impersonal. He is anxious that the whole of his ego should not be effaced in *Samadhi*. He would fain have sufficient individuality left to him to enjoy the Vision as a Person. He would fain taste the sugar in place of being one with the sugar itself.

To such, my Mother appears as a Person (the Personal God), for She is loving to Her worshippers—Her children.

Realisation: signs of God-Vision

He who has thoroughly realised the Deity must insist upon realisation as the only great fact in spiritual matters.

It won't do to say from the very beginning, 'I see God —Impersonal-Personal, manifest in and through all things. Why, everything that I see—man, woman, beast, bird, tree, flower—is God! Oh, I am full of joy and bliss! I am past all happiness and misery! *Soham* (I am He), *soham* (I am He), and so forth.'

What, as a rule, is absolutely necessary is the preliminary discipline. Without it, one cannot have *bhakti* (love of God.) Without this discipline it is indeed a far cry from absolute knowledge.

For the precious treasures are safe in the room under

lock and key. You have not yet unlocked those treasures. Surely it does not lie in your mouth to say, 'I have opened the lock and have got into the room. Behold, I have laid my hands on those longed-for treasures, those shining gems, diamonds, jewels! Behold, I have possessed them all!'

The Blessed One who has indeed beheld the Vision Divine, becomes like a child, simple, open (*Sarala*), turning his eye upon the fresh world as it is, stripped of its artificial name and formulas. Often he is intoxicated with the wine of Divine love at the sight of the revelation before him. He is one with the living fountain of holiness. With him, therefore, as a rule, there has ceased to be any distinction between *suchi* (purity) and *asuchi* (impurity).

Lastly, sense consciousness leaves him from time to time and in *Samadhi* he looks like a *Jada* (an insentient, motionless, inanimate thing).

CHAPTER V

Sri Ramakrishna and Bhaktiyoga

Sri Ramakrishna: But until realisation, one must be pure, one must renounce the world—*Kamini* and *Kanchana* —carnality and the worship of Mammon.

The necessity of God Personal: the Way to solve the Problem of Life

It is so difficult to get rid of this sense of 'I' which puts a barrier in the way of *Brahma-Jnana*. Even after Absolute Knowledge, the released soul is forced, as we have said, by an unseen power, my Divine Mother, to come down to the plane of sense-consciousness and have this sense of 'I', though in a thin form, attached to him.

You dream of a tiger. You tremble in every limb. Your heart throbs violently. You wake up to find that it was a mere dream. But all the same, in your waking state, your heart goes on throbbing.

The self as it should be

That being the case, the sense of 'I' refusing to leave, what should be done? Why, let it have one sole limiting adjunct[1]. Let it stay on as the 'servant of the Lord.'

But the 'I and mine' of worldly men is ignorance leading away from God.

Everything is ordered by the Lord. It is ridiculous for a man to say 'I am the Lord of creation,' 'I am the master,' 'All these things are mine.'

On two occasions, the Lord cannot help smiling: One is taken seriously ill. His end is very near at hand. The doctor steps in and says to the mother, Why, Mother, there is no cause for anxiety; I take it upon myself to save your son's life.'

The doctor does not see that it is the Lord who is bringing about the death of her son.

But the Lord smiles and says, 'It is I who am causing the death of this man, and the fool of a physician says that he is going to save his life.'

Again, when two brothers, busy making a partition of their lands, take a measuring tape, stretch it out across the earth and say, 'This side is mine, that side is yours.' The Lord smiles and says, 'These fools! They call the land their own! They see not that every bit of the ground belongs unto Me!'

Parable of the Rich man and his Steward

A rich man has a garden, which he has placed in charge of a steward. When visitors look in, the steward is all attentive. He takes them through the different parts of the garden and the house attached to it, saying, 'These, gentlemen, are our mango trees, these our *lichi, galop jam* (roseberries), *etc.* Here, you see, is our drawing-room. Over there are our oil-paintings and other pictures so beautiful.'

Now suppose the steward does something to merit

[1] Upadhi.

the displeasure of his master. Do you know how he is dealt with? Why, he is peremptorily ordered to leave the garden at once. He is not even allowed sufficient time to bring away his wooden chest!

And it was, bear in mind, the very same man who was so warmly talking away of 'our this' and 'our that'!

This 'mine' or 'our' of the steward comes of *ajnana* (ignorance leading away from God).

Reason is weak. Faith is omnipotent. Reason cannot go far enough and must stop at some point or other. But faith will work wonders.

The Omnipotence of Faith

Yes, by faith shall a man be able to cross the mighty ocean itself, without the slightest difficulty.

Ramachandra, God incarnate, worked hard to throw a bridge over that part of the sea which separates Ceylon from the mainland of India. But as if to prove to the world the majesty, the omnipotence of faith, He gave it to His devotee the great *Hanuman* to cross the ocean by the unaided power of faith!

Once a friend of *Vibhishana*, king of Ceylon, wanted to go across the sea. *Vibhishana*, to whom he appealed for help, had the name of Rama (God) written on a leaf without the knowledge of his friend. He then said to his friend, 'Take this and be sure you keep it tied to the end of your cloth. This will enable you to walk across the ocean in safety. But mind, never try to look into the leaf, for you will go under, the moment you open it.'

The friend put faith in his words. He walked over the ocean for sometime in perfect safety. But unfortunately, he took it into his head to try and see what precious thing was tied to the end of his cloth, which could take him unhurt over the mighty deep. He opened the leaf and down he went beneath the waves!

Yes, faith is omnipotent. Before it the powers of Nature all shrink and give way! You get over seas and mountains with perfect ease and the utmost indifference.

What is more, sin and iniquity, worldliness and ignorance, all go out of sight before faith.

...And the Master sang:

The name of God

1. O my Divine Mother,! let me but die with *Durga, Durga,* Thy (hallowed) name on my lips.

Then shall it be seen, O Giver[1] of all good, whether or not in the end Thou wilt take Thy poor child over to the other side of the sea of this world.

2. I may be the slayer of a cow or a *brahmin*! I may have made away with an unborn child yet in the mother's womb! I may be a drunkard! Nay more, I may have put a woman to death!

But I care not the least for the terrible sins. In spite of all these I have power enough to raise myself to the exalted position of the Creator[2] of the world.

Yes, faith is at the root of all spiritual progress. You can do without all other things; *only You must have faith.*

Have but faith in the Lord, and you shall become at once free from the vilest, the blackest, of all sins.

Faith at the Root

1 Many are the thoughts that arise in my mind when I think of my Divine Mother.

One's reward is just as much as the strength of one's love for God. At the root of all there must always be absolute faith.

2. The Holy Feet of my Divine Mother, the Consort of the God of Eternity, form the Lake of Nectar. If the mind be in that Lake of Immortality—if it goes on taking its dip into that Lake—then nothing more is needed—you may do without the rest—be it worship with flowers and incense, be it the pouring of oblations into the sacrificial fire, the silent recitation of the Name of God, or the sacrifice of animals.

3. The devotee of my Divine Mother, the Goddess of the Universe, has even in this life a soul released from the bondage of the world. O! he is made purely of joy everlasting.

Yes, the one thing needful is *faith* and *bhakti* (love, devotion, prayerfulness, self-surrender).

It is exceedingly difficult, especially in this *Kali* age, to come to my Mother through *Vichara*, the discrimination

[1]Sankari. [2]Brahma.

of the Real from the unreal phenomenal universe by the limited faculties of man, unaided by the Divine Person, *i.e.*, unaided by Revelation.

Verily has *Ramprasad*, the 'sweet psalmist' of Bengal, laid stress upon this difficulty in that well-known song, 'O my mind,' etc.

And the Master sang:

IDENTITY OF THE PERSONAL GOD AND THE IMPERSONAL GOD

DIFFICULTY OF JNANA YOGA

1. O my mind! what line art thou taking to realise that Being? Thou art groping about like a mad man in a dark room!

2. Do thou try thy best to bring under thy control the Moon[1] who is a door-keeper at the gate of the House (the Microcosm). In the House are various apartments and amongst them a Thief-chamber where the (Divine) Treasure is kept hidden:

Once the Moon is under thy control, thou mayest secretly like a thief work thy way to the Treasure in the Thief-chamber and make It thine own.

But when the Moon is beyond thy control and it is day-break, the Treasure in the Thief-chamber shall hide itself from thee.

3. With that Love as the Ideal, the great *yogi* practises, one decade after another, meditation for re-union with the Universal Soul.

Once this Love springs up in his (*yogi's*) heart, he draws the Supreme Being near unto him, much as the loadstone draws the iron.

4. Go into the six schools of philosophy. There that Being thou shalt not find! Neither in the *Tantras* nor in the *Vedas*! That Being is fond of the sweet syrup of *Bhakti*. A Being of Joy Everlasting, She resides in all Her Majesty in this city (*i.e.*, the Microcosm).

Says *Prasad*:

5. The Being whom I call my Mother and try thus to realise, shall I give out Her real name?,

Would not that be breaking my (sacred) cooking pot in the court-yard of the house (or in the market-place) before the eyes of the unfeeling multitude? Guess, O my mind! who that Being is, by the hints I have thrown out.

There is deep silence at the end of this song, which was listened to with rapt attention. Every one is moved. The Master remains for a long while with his mind fixed upon the hallowed feet of the Divine Mother, the great burden of this soul-stirring psalm.

[1]Desire.

CHAPTER VI

THE PARTING

A friend asks Vidyasagar the meaning of *chatar*.

Vidyasagar (smiling) : *Chatar*, *i.e.*, *chattara* or *uthan* the quadrangle of a house; or the market-place.

Master (to Vidyasagar): Oh! You must know, Pandit as you are. (*Laughter*).

Master (to Vidyasagar): Well, what is your idea of the Deity?

Vidyasagar (looking round on the company present): Excuse me, sir, I am afraid I must look for another occasion to talk with you by myself. (*Laughter.*)

Master (smiling): Oh, you must know all. Only, I suppose you do not care to say. The 'Lord of the Ocean' is the master of untold treasures,—gold, diamond, jewels. But it is hardly to be expected that the presiding God of the sea should take note of each of the valuable things that could be found in his vast domain. (*Laughter.*)

Again, very often, you will find a big *Babu*, the owner of vast wealth, quite ignorant of even the names of his servants! (*Laughter.*)

The *Babu* is too big to be on terms of familiarity with such commonplace people! (*Laughter.*)

* * * *

Master (to Vidyasagar): Will you not once come to the garden? It is a charming place, so grand, so beautiful!

Vidyasagar: Certainly. You have been so kind as to come here. Is it not my duty too to pay you a visit?

Master (smiling): Visit to me! Oh! For shame, for shame!

Vidyasagar: My dear Sir, this from you! I have a right to ask for an explanation.

Master (facetiously): Well, my good Sir, I tell you why. We are but fishing boats, small and light enough to row about to all sorts of places. (*Laughter*) You are a big merchant-man! Who knows but you may run against a sand-bank if you venture too far up stream? (*Laughter*) But the season—the present occasion—makes some difference. Does it not? (*Laughter*)

Vidyasagar (smiling): Oh, I see, the rains have recently set in. (*Laughter*)

It is about 8 P.M. The carriage is ready to take the Master back home to the *Thakurbari* at *Dakshineswar*. The Master becomes absent-minded for a while. He is evidently meditating upon the Divine Mother. Is he asking for Her blessing upon his good host?

It is the dark fortnight of the month of *Sravana*. The Master rising to depart, Vidyasagar with a lighted candle in his hand, leads the way downstairs, on through the compound to the gate. Near it is the carriage waiting to receive the Master and his companions from the *Thakurbari*.

An unexpected sight greets the eyes of the party as they come up before the gate. It is of a man who many be a little under forty, standing before the gate with folded hands. He is dressed in white and has a white *Sikh* turban on the head. He has a smiling face, has a fair complexion and expressive eyes. No sooner does he see the Master, than he falls at his feet with the head mounted with the big turban touching the ground.

The Master says:

'Is it you, Balaram? How is it that I find you here?' Balaram replies smiling:

'Oh, Sir, I have been waiting for some time here at the gate to see you.'

Master: Well, why did you not come in?

Balaram (smiling): I came rather late; so I would rather not interrupt you; and thought it better to stay here.

* * * * *

The Master then steps into the carriage with his companions.

Vidyasagar (to M.): Shall I see the *gharry* hire paid?

M.: No sir, you need not trouble yourself. It has already been paid by a friend.

The Pandit then folds his hands, and bends his head and body to make his *pranama* (salutations) to the Master.

All assembled about the carriage do the same. The coachman lets go the horses. Away rattles the carriage in a northerly direction.

The little crowd at the gate with the venerable Vidyasagar at their head still holding the lighted candle in his hand, stands for a while looking on in the same direction, wondering who this God-intoxicated man may be, so wise, yet so childlike, so full of joy, so sweet, so godly!

Verily a lightning sent down to set ablaze into life the dead bones of a dry work-a-day world! Embodied love like the dew of heaven falling on the thirsty heart of man! A voice crying unto sunken, self-weary man, *Thou must be born again and love*! A healer, from another clime, of this 'strange disease of modern life!' A man among men eager to solve for them the enigma of the universe!

SECTION III

1882

SRI RAMAKRISHNA AT THE TEMPLE OF DAKSHINESWAR WITH NARENDRA (VIVEKANANDA), RAKHAL, M. AND OTHER DISCIPLES

CHAPTER I

Story of The Master's Life as Told by Himself

Sri Ramakrishna is filled with joy to-day; for Narendra has come to the Temple to see him. Narendra has bathed here and has taken his morning meal[1] of the offerings accepted by the Gods.

It is Monday, the 16th of October, 1882, the fourth lunar day of the light fortnight of *Aswin*. The Durga Pujah will be celebrated on Thursday next.

Rakhal has been staying with the Master for some time. Ramlal and Hazra are also here. Two Brahmo boys are with Narendra. M. is also here.

After the morning meal, which has been taken between eleven and twelve o'clock, Sri Ramakrishna asks Narendra and the other disciples, specially Narendra, to rest a while. A bed is prepared for the purpose on the floor of the room. A quilt with a mat underneath and a white sheet spread out over it and some pillows and bolsters make up the simple bed. The Master squats on the bed by the side of Narendra and talks with him and the other disciples like a child. His eyes are fixed on Narendra and his face was radiant with smiles. He will place some ideals of life and

[1] Prasad.

character before the disciples—specially before Narendra —and teach them how to live.

Master (to Narendra and others): When this change (caused by God-vision) came over me, I longed to hear the word of God. I always looked about for places where the Sacred Books[1] were being read or recited—the books specially containing an account of the life and teachings of the various Incarnations of God—Sri Krishna, Rama, etc. I used to go to Krishna Kishore to hear him read the life of Rama.[2]

Krishna Kishore and his Faith

What a stupendous faith had Krishna Kishore! Once he had been to Brindaban on pilgrimage. There in the course of his walk one day, he chanced to feel thirsty. Seeing a person standing near a well, he asked him to draw a little water for him. The man said that he came of a very low caste so that he was not a fit person to draw the water for a Brahmin. Krishna Kishore said, 'Will you pronounce the name of God[3] and thus make yourself pure?' The man did so and then drew up the water for him; and he, a Brahmin, drank of the water! How great was the power of his faith!

A holy man once came to the river side and lived for some time at the *Ariada Ghat*. We thought of paying him a visit. I said to Haladhari at the Temple one day, 'Krishna Kishore and myself are going to see the holy man. Are you going too?' Haladhari replied, 'What is the use of one's going to see a being with a material body which is no better than a cage made of clay?'

Now Haladhari was a Pandit and used always to read the 'Song of the Lord'[4] and the Vedanta philosophy which says, 'God alone is real and everything else is unreal.' All these words were reported by me to Krishna Kishore. He was highly offended and said, 'What! And all this has been said by Haladhari! Is it possible that he looks upon the body of a holy man as a cage made of clay—a holy man whose only thought is God and who has given up the world

[1]Bhagavata, Mahabharata, etc. [2]Adhyatma Ramayana. [3]Siva. [4]Gita.

and its pleasures and excitements for the sake of the Lord? Does he not know that the body of one who loves the Lord is made up of spirit—not of matter as in the case of ordinary men?' When he came next time to the Temple in the morning to gather flowers for divine worship, he turned away his face to avoid Haladhari, so much had he been offended at his words.

State of Sri Ramakrishna after God-vision

Once he asked me, 'Why have you cast off the holy thread?' When this change came over me for the first time, everything was blown away as if by the great cyclone of *Aswin*.[1] The old land-marks were swept away. There was no outward consciousness; who was to take care of either the holy thread or even the piece of cloth that I used to put on?

Lost in intense God-consciousness, I was nude the greater part of the day. When, therefore, Krishna Kishore took me to task for having parted with the holy thread, I only observed, 'You shall see it all clearly if you are once seized with madness for the Lord!'

It all came about as I had feared. He, too, turned out mad after the Lord. He used to shut himself up in a room in which he sat still and only repeated, 'Om ! Om!'[2]

His people thought that he had actually gone mad. They called in a physician.[3] Dr. Ram of Natagore came to see him.

The True Self

Krishna Kishore said to the physician, 'Let me, good sir, be healed of my disease—and not of the *Om* which by the grace of the Lord I have learnt to value in these days.' (*Laughter.*)

Looking in on another occasion I found him musing. I asked what the matter was. He replied, 'The tax-collector was here. He held out the threat that he would dispose of my brass bowls and water-pots in case I failed to meet his demands! This has made me so anxious.' Upon this I smiled and said, 'Never mind, let him do his worst and sell

[1]Cyclone of 1864. [2]The Vedic symbol for God the Absolute. [3]Kaviraj.

off your goods and chattels. Let him bind your body and take it to the judge if need be; what matters it to you? Surely, *you* are not the body; so he cannot bind you—*your True Self*; for are you not *Kha*[1], my dear sir, as you often say?' (*Narendra and others laugh.*)

Like Formless Space

Yes, he used to say that his True Self, that is, God the Absolute, was like the formless space round about us. Oh,! he was an ardent reader of the *Ramayana*[2] in which Rama is always addressed as an Incarnation of God, the Absolute. I often amused myself saying, 'You are *Kha*; your True Self is not the body but the *Universal Soul.*' That day I assured him saying, 'No tax-collector shall be able to draw you away. Let them seize your gross body which you are not—according to your own showing.' (*Laughter*)

No Respector of Persons

In my state of madness for the Lord I used always to speak my own mind as to men and things. I regarded not the position of men. I was not in the least afraid of rich people or men of position.

One day Jatindra came into the adjoining garden belonging to Jadu Mallik. I asked Jatindra, 'What is the whole duty of man?' I asked again, 'Is it not our first duty to fix our mind on God?' Jatindra said' 'We are men of the world. Is liberation ever within the reach of worldly men? Witness Raja Yudhishtira who, pure as he was, had to bear the sight of the infernal regions for having once spoken what was not the truth.' This gave great offence to me. And I cried out saying sharply, 'What a curious man you are! You remember well the fact that Yudhishtira had to bear the sight of those regions! But, pray, what do you think of his love of Truth, his love of God, his forgiving temper, his perception of the Real, his non-attachment to things of the world?' I was going to run on like this when Hriday stopped my mouth. Jatindra soon after left, saying that he had some pressing business to attend to.

[1]Akasa. [2]Adhyatma.

On another occasion I went in company with the Captain[1] to Raja Sourindra's house. Upon first meeting him I said, "Look here, sir, I shall be unable to call you 'Raja' or such-like thing, for that would be speaking what is not true." (Raja in *Sanskrit* means the ruler of a kingdom.) He conversed with me for some time; during which we were frequently interrupted by visitors, amongst whom were some Europeans. I noticed that he was like other worldly people troubled with many things. He sent word to Jatindra (his eldest brother), informing him of our visit. A message came from the latter, which said that he had a trouble in the throat and could not come.

One day I observed an elderly Brahmin repeating the name of the Lord at the Barahnagore Ghat on the bank of the holy river Ganges. I observed that he was thinking of something else and gave him two slaps on his back to draw his attention back to the Lord! (*Laughter.*)

Once Rasmani (the foundress of the Temple here) came to visit the Temple. She came inside the Temple of the Mother when I was worshipping as priest. She asked me to chant the Holy Name. I sang, but observed that she was thinking of something else and sorting the flowers for worship. I gave her a couple of slaps. This made her sit quiet with hands folded in adoration. (*Laughter.*)

I repeated my sad story to my cousin[2], saying, 'How queer and offensive are my ways getting to be! Is there no help for this?' Well, I prayed to my Divine Mother with a yearning heart and at last I was able through Her grace to shake off this habit.

The value of Pilgrimage

In that state of my soul, words not relating to God jarred upon my ears. I used to sit by myself and cry whenever I heard people talking about worldly matters. Once Mathur Babu took me with him to various places of pilgrimage in the North. While at Benares we put up for a few days at the

[1]Biswanath of Nepal. [2]Haladhari.

house of Rajah Babu. One day I was in the drawing-room with Mathur Babu who was conversing with Rajah Babu and his people. They were talking purely of worldly matters: 'So much money has been lost or gained by the transaction,' and words like these. I cried bitterly by myself, saying to the Divine Mother, 'Where hast Thou brought me, O Mother? Verily, I was by far better off at the Temple at Dakshineswar than in this place of pilgrimage! They have come indeed to visit the holy shrines, but behold, O Mother, they talk only of Woman and Gold! The Temple was a far better place for me, because there I had not to hear such talks!'

The Master presses Narendra to take a little rest. And he himself lies down on the smaller bedstead to rest a while.

CHAPTER II

WITH NARENDRA AND OTHER DISCIPLES. CHANTING FORTH THE NAME OF THE LORD

It is afternoon, and Narendra is singing the sacred hymns. Amongst those present are Rakhal, Latu, M., Preo, a Brahmo friend of Narendra, and Hazra.

Narendra sang to the accompaniment of the drum[1]:

SONG

Meditate, O my mind, upon the Lord, the Embodiment of Spirit and of Purity.

Vide song, page 48

SONG

In the Temple of the Heart shines the Blessed Vision of the Lord who is the One Reality, who seeks the good of all His creatures, and whose form is so beautiful. Let us behold this beauty over and over again and be thus immersed in that Sea of Beauty.

[1]Khole

O Lord, come into my heart as Infinite Wisdom Divine! Speechless, but with a mind that knows not peace, shall I then throw myself on Thy Hallowed Feet!

O! arise in the firmament of my Soul as the Embodiment of Immortal Bliss, that at the blessed Vision we shall rejoice, drunken with the joy of the Lord, much as the bird *Chakore* rejoices and sports about in the sky drunken with joy at the sight of the Moon!

* * * * * * * * * *

SONG

Be filled with Joy and Gladness and say on the sweet Name of the Lord!

At His Name shall arise a flood out of the Sea of Nectar: of this ye may drink without cessation (yes, drink and give away just as you please).

The thunder of His Name shall snap the fetters of sin by which you are bound.

Come, let us be intoxicated with the joy of the Lord and thus have all our heart's desires fulfilled.

* * * * *

Narendra and the other disciples sing and dance about the Master to the accompaniment of the drum. They sing in a chorus:

Be immersed for ever, O my mind, in the sweet nectar of Divine Love.

And again:

In the Temple of my Heart shines the glorious beauty of the Lord who is the Only Reality—the Being who seeks the good of all His creatures, the Embodiment of all that is beautiful.

At last, Narendra with the drum hanging from his neck, sings:

Speak the sweet Name of the Lord by thy mouth filled with joy.

At the end of the song the Master embraces Narendra saying, 'Peace be unto you, my boy, and the joy of the Lord! How shall I tell of the joy unspeakable that you have given me to-day!'

The fountain of Divine Love within the heart of the Master swells up to-day and overflows.

It is close upon 8 P.M. He paces up and down the northern verandah alone, drunken with the joy of the Lord!

He paces from one end of the verandah to the other with quick and excited steps. He holds converse with the Divine Mother.

Like one who has gone mad he cries out, 'What (evil) can you do to me?'

Does the Master say that the powers[1] of evil cannot do any harm to him who has the Divine Mother to protect him?

They are going to stay to-night. Narendra will stay; hence to his joy there is no end.

The supper is ready. Mother at the concert-house[2] has made everything ready for the supper—the thin cakes of bread, *dal*, &c. Surendra bears the greater part of the expenses. The disciples stay here off and on.

The supper is ready to be served on the south-eastern verandah into which the Master's chamber opens.

The supper is being served. Narendra and other disciples stand before the door of the chamber and talk.

Narendra on School and College Discipline

Narendra (to M.): How do you like, Sir, our boys and young men of the present day?

M.: Well, they are not bad; but they stand in need of religious instruction.

Narendra: So far as I have seen, they are going from bad to worse. *Bird's-eye*, the company of young men, foppishness, playing truant, these are things that may be seen almost every day.

M.: In our day, when we were students, I never came across such things!

Narendra: I suppose you never mixed with such boys. I myself have seen persons of questionable character talking with boys, whom I know, on terms of familiarity. The wonder is how and when they could know one another.

M.: Is it indeed so?

Narendra: O, I know it myself how some of my friends have in this way lost their character. School and college authorities and the guardians of boys ought to have an eye on these matters.

One Thing is Needful

They were thus talking on, when the Master stepped out of the chamber and with a smile asked, 'Well, what were you talking about?'

[1]Maya. [2]Nahabat.

Narendra said smiling, 'We have been talking on matters connected with schools and colleges. The character of boys is not all that could be desired.' Upon this the Master turning to M., looked grave and said, 'Talking on these matters is not good: talk of the Lord and nothing else! You are older than these boys. You ought to have known better. It was your duty to put them on their guard and to warn them not to talk on anything but the Lord.'

M. feels a little abashed. Narendra and other disciples hold their peace for a time.

Narendra is about 19 or 20 years old; while M. is about 27 or 28.

They sit down for supper. The Master is happy; He smiles as he sees Narendra and other disciples going on with their repast.

Chanting the Name of the Lord

The Master rejoices very much to-day. After supper the disciples have come together inside the chamber and are resting on a mat spread on the floor. They talk with the Master and rejoice. It seems as if a fair is being held here, where the joy of the Lord may be had for sale.

The Master says to Narendra: Will you sing the hymn beginning with—'The full moon of Divine Love rises on the firmament of Divine Wisdom?'

Narendra began to sing to the accompaniment of the drum[1]:

SONG

The full moon of Divine Love rises on the firmament of Divine Wisdom.
The Ocean of Love overflows: O, how full of joy is the Lord!

VICTORY UNTO THEE, MERCIFUL LORD!
VICTORY! VICTORY!

Behold the gate of Heaven is flung open and the vernal breeze of the New Dispensation arises.

It breaks into waves of joy: it carries the fragrance of Divine Love, which makes the Yogis drunken with the joy of communion.

[1]Khole.

VICTORY UNTO THEE, MERCIFUL MOTHER!
VICTORY! VICTORY!

On the sea of this Universe is the Lotus of the New Dispensation.

Upon it is seated in Her Majesty the Divine Mother, The Embodiment of all Joy!

See, the Bees (the devotees) drink of the nectar therein!

They are filled with God-consciousness. Ah! behold the gracious countenance of the Mother!

It delights the heart: it fascinates the Universe!

Falling at Her Feet are bands of holy men, singing and dancing drunken with joy.

What beauty unparallelled! O! What peace does the Blessed Vision bring unto the heart!

Prem Dass (the psalmist) falls at the feet of all men and cries 'Sing, Oh My brethren!'

VICTORY UNTO THEE, MOTHER! VICTORY! VICTORY!

The Master sings and dances. With him in their midst the disciples also are singing and dancing.

The song is over. The Master walks up and down the north-eastern verandah that leads into his chamber.

Here is Hazra seated. He repeats the name of the Lord, as he tells the beads of his rosary. The Master takes his seat by his side and holds converse with Hazra and M.

He says to a disciple: Do you see visions of God in dreams during sleep?

God-vision in Dreams

Disciple: Yes, sir, the other day I dreamt a most interesting dream. It seemed as if the whole Universe were a vast expanse of water. Water, water everywhere before me and nothing but water! Water without beginning or end! Suddenly there arose a storm. Some of the boats that were visible at a distance went down under the water. A few only escaped. Amongst these was one belonging to my Mother. Well, I was on board a ship which carried a chosen number of passengers. What was our astonishment to see a Brahmin walking over the water unconcerned—as if he were taking steps on firm ground! I cried out saying, 'How is it that you walk over the Deep?' The Brahmin replied smiling, 'Here is nothing to be afraid of; my feet rest upon a bridge which is under the water.' I asked, 'Whither are you going, Lord?' He replied, 'I am going to the *City of the Mother*.'[1] I felt eager to join the holy man and cried out, 'Tarry a little, O Lord, and I shall join you; for that is precisely the place whither I also long to go.' He only smiled and said, 'O, I am in a hurry to reach that place. It will take you some time to come down. Mark the path which will lead you safe to the City and then come and follow me.'

Master: A thrill passes through my body as I hear the dream thus related by you! The hairs of my body stand on end. The hour is come when you should be initiated.

CHAPTER III

Which to Seek First?—The Kingdom of Heaven or Social Reforms?

It is 11 P.M. Narendra and other disciples go to sleep. They lie down on a bed spread on the floor of the Master's chamber.

Sri Ramakrishna chanting his Matins

It is daybreak. Some of the disciples are already up. They are seated on the bed meditating on the Lord. What is the Master doing all the time? He is repeating the Names of the Lord in a voice sweet as nectar. He goes about the chamber perfectly nude like a five-year old child. He steps to the various pictures hung on the walls and salutes, touching the wall with the forehead. He opens the door and looks on the Holy River with reverential feelings. He chants the Holy Name of the Lord and says, 'O, my Divine Mother, Thou manifestest Thyself in everything.[2] Thou art one with Thy Word that has taken the form of the Sacred Scriptures—the Vedas, the Puranas and the Tantras—the Bhagavat Gita and the Gayatri. And, Mother, Thy devotees are but manifestations of Thyself! Thou art the same as God the Absolute[3] beyond time and space; on the other

[1]Bhavanipore. [2]Bhagavata—Bhakta—Bhagavan. [3]Brahman.

hand, Thou art the Divine Energy manifesting Thyself in this universe. Thou art the Being Inactive.[1] Thou art, again the Principle of Activity.[2] Thou art the *Formless* Being and Thou art *with Form*. Thou art the universe[3] before us. Thou art the twenty-four categories of the philosopher!'

It is daybreak and the priests are waving the lights before the Holy Images. The sweet and holy sounds of the conch-shell, of the bell, and of the cymbals come vibrating from the temples.

The disciples arise and see that the priests and the servants are already gathering flowers for the morning offerings. The concert[4] plays pieces of music proper for the morning hour.

Narendra and other disciples have washed themselves.

Narendra and the One Thing Needful

They now come smiling before the Master. He stands on the north eastern verandah close to his own chamber. His face is radiant with smiles.

Narendra : We noticed several *Sannyasins*—followers of Nanak—seated at the 'Cluster of five trees.'[5]

Master: I know; they arrived here only yesterday. (To Narendra): I should like to see you all seated together.

The disciples seated themselves on a mat. The Master looks on them with delight and converses with them.

Narendra raises the question, 'What are the means of attaining God?'

Master: The one thing needful is love or devotion[6] to God. As to renunciation[7] and discrimination[8] (between the real and the unreal), these will come of themselves if one loves the Lord.

Woman as Mother

Narendra: Sir, in the Sacred Books it is stated that one may practise communion in the company of women. Is that not so?

Master: To practise in the company of women! Why,

[1]Purusha. [2]Prakriti. [3]Virat.

[4]Nahabat. [5]Panchabati. [6]Bhakti. [7]Vairagya. [8]Viveka.

that is not good. There is, indeed, such a path spoken of in the Sacred Books,[1] but walking along such a path, it is exceedingly difficult to reach the Goal. The risk of a fall is almost sure.

As a point of discipline woman may be regarded first, as mistress (the aspirant regarding himself as lover); second, as lady-mistress (the aspirant regarding himself as her hand-maiden); third, as mother. I, for my part, regard woman as my *Mother*. The part of a *hand-maiden* or *maid-servant* is not open to objection. That of a lover almost invariably brings on a downfall. That of a child is the purest and best of all.

Is Anything Impossible with God?

The Sannyasins who were the followers of Guru Nanak have now come to pay their respect to the Master. They salute him saying, 'Thou art the Lord[2] of the universe taking a human form! Salutation unto Thee!' The Master returned their greetings and asked them to be seated.

He says to the disciples and the holy men: Nothing is impossible with God. The nature of the Lord—no one can be dogmatic about it. Everything can be predicated of Him.

Once there lived two holy men;[3] they practised austerities with a view to see God. One day Narada, the holy sage, was going his way by their hermitages. One of them said to Narada, 'Are you come down from Heaven? If so, tell me what the Lord of Heaven is doing.' Upon this, Narada replied, 'Yes, that is so, I am come down from Heaven; I saw the Lord of Heaven causing camels and elephants to enter into the eye of a needle and saw the animals passing in and out.' One of the holy men observed, 'There is nothing here to marvel at. *Nothing is impossible with God.*' The other man said, 'O! that is impossible! It only shows that you have never been to the Lord's place.'

The first man had the faith of a babe and he was a

[1] The Tantras. [2] Namo Narayan. [3] Yogis.

true believer. For, nothing is impossible with God who has created this wonderful universe!

It is about nine in the morning. The Master is seated in his chamber. Manomohan, a disciple, is come from Konnagar with his family. He salutes the Master saying, 'I am taking my family down to Calcutta.' The Master makes kind enquiries and says, 'This is the first day of the (Bengali) month—an inauspicious day; and you are taking your family down to Calcutta! I really don't know what to say.' Saying this he smiles and passes on to other matters.

Narendra and his Calcutta friends have bathed in the Ganges. They come into the Master's chamber to dress themselves. The Master says to Narendra with great eagerness, 'Go to the foot of the banyan tree and there meditate on the Lord for some time; shall I give you something to sit on?'

Narendra and his Brahmo friends seated themselves on the terraced seat of brick-work built round the tree for meditating upon the Lord.

It is past ten in the morning. The Master comes up a little while after. M. is also here. The Master talks with Narendra and his friends.

How To Meditate

Master (to Narendra, &c.) : In the course of meditation one must be merged in the Lord. If one floats on the surface one cannot hope to reach the precious stones lying at the bottom.

Saying this, the Master sings:

SONG

1. O, my Mind, take thou the Name of the Mother and dive deep—into the depth of the heart—the ocean which is the repository of all precious gems.

2. You may not get the treasures after a few immersions, but that proves not that the sea of thy heart has no treasures within.

3. In this sea there are the alligators, the six passions (lust, anger, etc.) They move about in quest of food. Hence rub your body with the turmeric of discrimination.[1]

[1] Viveka.

The scent of the turmeric will keep you from being touched by the alligators.
4. Many are the precious gems that lie scattered at the bottom of the sea. Take a plunge to the bottom, says Ramprasad, and you shall get them.

Seek First the Lord

Narendra and his friends come down from their seats at the foot of the 'Five Trees'[1] and stand round the Master.

The Master walks with the disciples to the south in the direction of his chamber. He talks as he walks. He says, 'Rub your body with turmeric and the alligators will be kept off. Love, anger, avarice, etc., are the six alligators.'

Master (continuing): Discrimination is the turmeric. It enables one to understand that God is the only Reality and all else is unreal.

Of what avail is book-learning or the delivery of lectures if there is no discrimination—the sense that God is the one Reality and all else is transitory?

Lectures and Social Reforms afterwards

First, set Him up in the temple of the heart; first realise God. Speeches, lectures and the rest, these may be taken up after you have *seen* God,—not *before*. People talk gliby of Brahman—God the Absolute—all the time that they are attached to things of this world. What does all this come to? Mere blowing of the conch-shell without any gods to worship in the temple. Let me tell you a parable.

God in the Temple of the Heart

There was once a young man named Podo in a certain village. In that village there was an old dilapidated temple. The holy image of God once worshipped had disappeared and it was now the home of small bats. One day at night-fall the villagers were surprised to hear the sound of bells, conch-shell and gong issuing from the deserted temple. Men, women and children, all flocked to the place. They thought some devotee must be worshipping an image of God recently set up within the temple and performing the evening ceremony[2], waving the lights and flowers, fruits, holy waters,

[1]Panchavati [2]Aratrika.

etc., before the image. With folded hands they all stood before the temple listening to the sacred sounds.

One of them, more curious than the rest had the courage to peep in. What was his surprise to see Podo ringing the bell and blowing the conch-shell! The floor was as dirty as before with impurities of all kinds and there was no image of God to worship! He then called out to him, 'O Podo, you have no image of God in your temple! How is it thou hast raised all this clamour by blowing the conch-shell? And behold you have not yet taken the trouble to cleanse the temple, to remove the dirt and impurities of years and to wash the floor with the holy waters of the Ganges! And the building continues to be soiled as before night and day by the small bats,[1] eleven in number!

First, realise God in the Temple of your heart. To that end you must cleanse it of all impurities—all sin and iniquity—all attachment to this world caused by the sense-organs. One must free oneself of one's sensuous nature in order to realise God. It is then that the time comes for blowing the shell, if need be. Do you talk of social reforms? Well, you may do so *after* realising God. Remember, the Rishis of old gave up the world in order to attain God. This is the one thing needful. All other things shall be added unto you, if indeed you care to have them.

If you seek the gems lying at the bottom of the sea you must first take a plunge to the bottom, giving up all other works. First set up the image of God; then talk of blowing the conch-shell. First see God and then talk of lectures and social reforms.

The Divine Teacher

It is a most difficult task—that of teaching others. He who sees God receives His commandment. He alone who receives the Lord's commandment is competent to teach others.

[1] Eleven sense-organs or *Indriyas*; five organs of perception; five of *Karma* or work (hands, feet & c.); and the head organ or, *mind*.

CHAPTER IV.

The Married Man's Problem

By this time, the Master has come up to the northern verandah which runs east and west. He stands on that verandah close to his chamber with Narendra, Mani and other disciples.

The Problem for The Householder

The Master says repeatedly that God cannot be seen by one who does not possess discrimination[1] and non-attachment.[2] Mani who is 27 or 28 years old has received an English education. He has married and thinks to himself, 'Do these (discrimination and non-attachment) mean renunciation of the world like a *Sannyasin*—outward renunciation of woman and gold?'

Mani (to the Master): Sir, what if the wife says to the husband, 'You are neglecting me; I shall commit suicide?'

Master (in a solemn, serious tone): A wife who stands in the way of her husband seeking God should be given up and left to her fate. It matters not even if she puts an end to her life. Let her do anything that she likes. A wife who stands in the way of the husband seeking God is an ungodly[3] wife who leads to ignorance and spiritual death.

Mani is absorbed in deep thought and leans back against the wall. Narendra and other disciples stand speechless for a moment.

The Master is talking with them for a while. Suddenly he turns to Mani who is still in the same posture leaning back against the wall. He speaks these words to him aside, 'But the case is different with a person who has a sincere and genuine love for the Lord; everybody then comes under his control—kings, bad men, wife. The wife may even come round and follow in his foot-steps and walk in the path which leads to the Lord. If the husband sincerely loves the Lord, the wife may come under his control, be

[1]Viveka. [2]Vairagya. [3]Avidya.

religious and help him in his struggle to attain eternal life.'

Mani feels that the fire blazing up in his breast has been put out. He enjoys peace of mind once more.

Mani (to the Master): What a fearful place is the world![1]

Master (to Mani, Narendra and others): The life of a worldly man is terrible, indeed! Chaitanya Deva once said to Nityananda:

> 'Listen, listen, O my brother,
> For a worldly man there is hardly any hope of salvation.'

(Aside to Mani): Hardly any hope of salvation for the worldly man who has lost sight of God! This does not apply to a person who sincerely loves the Lord. One who has realised the Lord can remain in the world and yet be fearless. Let such a person retire into solitude from time to time and thus attain sincere devotion and love to the Lord.

Well, such a person can remain in the world and yet be fearless. Chaitanya Deva had several house-holders amongst his disciples. They were in the world but not of the world. They lived unattached to it.

It is about noon. The morning service is over with the performance of the ceremony of waving the lights, holy water, flowers, &c. The Gods in the Temple will take their rest. The music which is being played by the concert[2] announces this. The Master sits at meal. Narendra and other disciples will also, like the Master, take their meals out of the sacred offerings presented to the Gods at the Temple and graciously accepted by Them.

[1]Samsara. [2]Nahabat.

SECTION IV

1882

STEAMER TRIP WITH KESHAB CHANDRA SEN LEADER OF THE BRAHMO SAMAJ

CHAPTER I

THE MASTER IN SAMADHI

This is the day when the Goddess[1] of wealth and prosperity is worshipped in India. It is the full moon after Durga Puja, Friday, 27th October 1882. Sri Ramakrishna was seated in his room in the Temple-garden with Bejoy Goswamy and Haralal. Some one came in and said, 'Keshab Sen has come; he is on board the steamer which has just come up and stands before the Ghat.'

A short while after, Kashab's disciples came in and bowed down before Sri Ramakrishna. They said, 'Sir, the steamer is here for you; Keshab Babu is on board, and has sent us to you with a request that you will kindly come on board and join him. You may be assured that you will enjoy the trip.'

It is just 4 o'clock. A boat takes the Master to the steamer. Bejoy is with him. Stepping into the boat Sri Ramakrishna loses all sense-consciousness! He is in *Samadhi*!

M. is on board the steamer. As the Master's boat is coming up, M. looks at the blessed sight—the picture of the Master with the senses stilled; motionless before the Blessed Vision that his soul is enjoying. M. came on board at about 3 o'clock. He is very eager to see the meeting between the Master and Keshab and witness the joy that is sure to come of such a meeting. He wishes very much to

[1] Lakshmi.

listen to their conversation. The mind of many a young man like M. has been captured, so to speak, by the saintly character of Keshab and by his unrivalled eloquence.

Indeed, many regarded Keshab as their own flesh and blood and had thus given him their hearts' love. Keshab has received an English education! He is well versed in English Philosophy and Literature; in the next place, he has on different occasions called the worship of images by the name of 'Idolatry.' It is certainly curious that such a man looks upon Sri Ramakrishna with reverence and admiration and visits him at the Temple off and on! It is a most interesting task for M. and others to find out the common ground on which they both meet.

The Master, indeed, holds that God is without form. He is thus at one with Keshab on this point, but he also holds that God is with form too! He meditates upon God, the Absolute.[1] At the same time He does not neglect to worship with flowers, incense and other offerings, the images with forms—manifest as gods and goddesses in the Hindu pantheon. What is more, he sings and dances before them with the madness of the joy of the Lord. The Master unlike an ascetic lies down on a bed supported by a bedstead; the cloth that he puts on is red bordered. He uses also coats and stockings and slippers. With all this he is not of the world. The signs of him are all like those that mark out an ascetic from a householder; hence people call him a Paramahamsa. On the other hand, Keshab holds that God is without form; he lives the life of a householder in the midst of his wife and children; he delivers lectures in English; he brings out a paper dealing with religious subjects; he does also attend in his own way to worldly affairs.

The boat has come alongside. Everybody is eager to see the Master. They crowd to the gangway. Keshab is anxious to see that he gets on board the steamer in safety.

It is with great difficulty that he is brought back to

[1]Brahman.

sense-consciousness once more in order to be taken inside the cabin on the upper deck. The state of divine ecstasy has not left him even now. He leans on a disciple as he is led into the room. He takes his steps mechanically, but his mind is fixed on God.

He enters the cabin on the upper deck. Keshab and others bow down to him. But what little sense-consciousness has returned, is now beginning to leave him altogether.

Inside the cabin are a bench, a table and a few chairs. The Master is seated on one of the chairs; Keshab on another; Bejoy has also taken his seat. Other devotees, most of them *Brahmos*, are also seated, many of them on the bare floor. The cabin is a small one. Many remain standing at the door and the windows, and they eagerly peep in.

The Master is now in *Samadhi* again; absolutely devoid of outer consciousness! Everybody is watching his face. Keshab sees that many people have come together within the cabin and that the Master is in need of more air. Bejoy, until lately a follower of Keshab, has, after the schism, become a member of another sect, the *Sadharan Brahmo Samaj*. He spoke against Keshab on different occasions with reference to his having given away his child-daughter in marriage in opposition to the well-known principles of his sect. Keshab is thus a little unprepared to meet Bejoy, whose visit to the steamer is most unexpected.

Keshab leaves his seat. He will open the windows.

The Prison house of the World

All look earnestly on the Master with fixed eyes. He comes down from his *Samadhi*; but the consciousness of the Divine Presence continues to be as intense as before. He talks to the Mother of the Universe in words that are hardly articulate.

He says, 'Oh Mother! Why hast Thou brought me here? They are hedged round and are not free! Is it indeed possible for me to save them out of their prison-house?'

Is it that the Master looks upon men of the world as beings who are shut up within a prison-house (*Samsar*); who cannot get out into the free air of God-consciousness who cannot so much as catch a glimpse of the light divine; who, in short, are bound hand and foot by affairs of the world? Men of the world can indeed see only the things within their prison-house—pleasures of the senses and worldly things. Is it thus that he says to the Divine Mother, 'Why hast Thou brought me here?'

Nilmadhab of Ghazipur is present at this unique meeting.

The Soul and The Body

Observing that the Master has come to himself, he and a Brahmo devotee begin to talk of Powhari Baba, the great saint of Ghazipur.

A Brahmo (to the Master): Sir, these gentlemen have been fortunate enough to see Powhari Baba at Ghazipur. The Baba is another holy man like your good self.

Not even yet has the Master got back the power of speech. His heart is full; he cannot speak. He only smiles on the good man who talks of the Baba.

Brahmo (to the Master): Sir, Powhari Baba has your photograph too, which he has put up in his own room.

The Master smiles again and points to his own body with his finger. At last in subdued tone he says, 'A pillow-case ! It is nothing but a pillow-case.'

The pillow and the pillow-case! The soul and the body! Does the Master say that the body alone dies and the soul dies not,—that the photograph is of the body which will not last for ever? Does he for this reason say, 'Let us not set very high value on a photograph which is of the body, but rather worship Him who is the ruler of the soul within?'

The Lord's Drawing-room

Master (continuing): But there is one thing to be borne in mind. The heart of the devotee[1] is the temple of the Lord. It is indeed a fact that the Lord is more or less manifest in all things. But He is manifest in a special sense within the heart of the devotee. Thus, a Zemindar can be met at any of the houses

[1]Bhakta.

of which he is owner. Still people would say, the Zemindar may be usually seen in a particular drawing-room. The heart of the devotee is the Lord's drawing-room. If one wants to meet the Lord, one had better seek an audience in the drawing-room. (*Laughter.*)

One God with Different Names

The same Being whom the *Vedantists* call *Brahman* (the Absolute), is called *Atman* (Universal Soul) by the *Yogis* and *Bhagavan* (or God Personal with Divine attributes) by *Bhaktas* (Devotees or God-lovers).

The high-caste Brahmin always remains one and the same person. When his duty is to worship the Lord he is called the priest, but when the same man is employed in the kitchen he is called a cook.

The Non-dualist

The Vedantist who seeks to realise God the Absolute, reasons, saying, 'not this, not this'; that is, the Absolute is 'not this, not that'; nor any finite object; nor the individual soul, nor the external world. When as the result of this kind of reasoning, the mind ceases to be moved by desires, when in fact, the conditioned mind vanishes, then is it that one can attain true knowledge,[1] then is it that one's soul goes into *Samadhi.* Such a man truly realises God the Absolute and finds the phenomenal universe to be consequently unreal. He realises that names and forms applied to finite objects are like dreams; that God the Absolute cannot be described by word; that one cannot, indeed, so much as say that God is a person.

The Dualist or The Bhakta

Such is the point of view of a Non-dualist. Devotees or lovers[2] of God, however, think and feel differently. Unlike the Non-dualists they look upon the waking state as a real state and upon the external world as real and not like a dream. They believe also in names and forms. They say that the objects of the universe before us are the works of God, who is a Personal God and is possessed of many attributes.

[1]Brahma-jnana. [2]Bhaktas.

The starry heavens, the sun, the moon, the mountains, the sea; men, birds, and beasts; all are His glorious works. He is the rich man and these are his riches. He is both within and without. The most advanced among devotees further says, 'It is He who has become manifest to us as the human soul and the external world, as the twenty-four categories[1] mentioned by the philosopher.'[2] The devotee wants not to be one with the sugar but would rather have a taste of it. (*Laughter.*)

Do you know how the devotee actually thinks and feels? He says, 'Oh Lord! Thou art the Master, I am Thy servant: Thou art my Mother and I Thy child;' or again, 'Thou art my child and I Thy father or Thy mother, or thus, 'Thou art the whole and I Thy part.' The devotee will not say 'I am God.'[3]

The Yogi (or the aspirant who seeks to commune with God) wishes also to realise the Universal Soul.[4] His object is to bring by self control the finite human soul[5] into communion with the infinite Soul.[6] He tries first to put together his mind which lies scattered in the act of running after the world of senses; he then seeks to fix it on the Universal Soul. Hence the necessity of meditating on Him in solitude and in a posture which causes no distraction.

But it is one and the same Substance,[7] the difference being only in the names. It is the same Being whom men call by the name of the Absolute,[8] the Soul of the Universe, the Personal God[9] with Divine Attributes. The first is the name applied by the Vedantist philosopher (monist), the second by the Yogi and the third by the devotees[10] (dualists).

[1] The twenty-four categories are the following: *viz*:—the five elements (Earth, Water, Fire, Air, Space): the five fine elements: the five organs of sense, the five organs of work: the mind: the determinative faculty (Buddhi): the ego: Prakriti.

[2] Sankhya.

[3] Brahman [4] Atman. [5] Jivatman. [6] Brahman. [7] "Substantia"—*Spinoza*. [8] Brahman. [9] Bhagavan. [10] Bhaktas.

CHAPTER II

GOD PERSONAL, THE OMNIPOTENT MOTHER[1] AND HER POWERS

The steamer has already left and is on its way back to Calcutta. Many are those who look on Sri Ramakrishna with eyes that do not move and who drink in the nectar of the words that drop from his hallowed lips. They cannot feel that the steamer is in motion. The Temple-garden is left behind and the eye can no longer see the picture of that beautiful Temple. Beneath are the sacred waters that reflect the blue firmament above. But the murmur of the waves with crests of foam into which they are broken as the steamer cleaves through the water is lost on the devotees. The magic of the Blessed Vision has thrown a charm over them. They have before them a wonderful being, a God-in-Man and a Man-in-God, with smiles playing about his sweet face radiant with the joy of the Lord, with eyes the beauty of which is enhanced by the collyrium of divine love. They look, as if charmed, on one who has given up the world and its pleasures, on one intoxicated with the love of the Lord, on one who looks not for anything except the Lord.

The conversation goes on:

God the Absolute and God the Creator

Sri Ramakrishna: According to the Nondualistic Vedanta Philosophy as explained by *Sankara*, God the Absolute (Brahman) is the only reality; and the phenomenal world before us is unreal. The Personal God, the Divine Mother Who manifests Hereself to us as the creator, preserver and destroyer, too is not a reality in the absolute sense, that is, in the sense in which the Absolute is understood to be Real. But it is impossible for an ordinary mortal to go beyond the jurisdiction of God Personal, however he may reason, saying, 'Not this,

[1] Sakti or Kali.

not this,'—unless, stripped of his relative sensuous nature, his soul becomes one with the Absolute[1] Unconditioned God, in that blessed, serene and ecstatic state called *Samadhi*. When one says, 'I am meditating upon God,' even then, one is going about within that jurisdiction. One cannot shake oneself free from the idea of a Personal God possessed of attributes.

One God

Thus God the Absolute and God Omnipotent and Personal are the same. A belief in the one implies a belief in the other. Thus fire cannot be thought of apart from its burning power. Nor can its burning power be thought of apart from the fire. Again, the sun's rays cannot be thought of apart from the sun nor can the sun be thought of apart from its rays.

What is milk like? Well, people say it is a whitish sort of thing. Now, you cannot think of the milky whiteness apart from the milk, nor can you think of the milk apart from its milky whiteness.

Thus God, the Absolute, cannot be thought of apart from the idea of God with Attributes, of God Personal, and *vice versa*. The Unconditioned, the Absolute, the Noumenon, the Substance on the one hand, and the Conditioned, the Relative, the Phenomenon, the Attributes, on the other hand, are correlatives—the one cannot be thought of apart from the other.

God Personal with Attributes, the Primal Divine Energy, as we conceive that Being to be, creates, preserves and destroys. The Sacred Books[2] call that Being by the name of Mother[3] of the universe.

Thus God Personal and God Impersonal are one and the same substance. I call that Being the Absolute or Unconditioned when I cannot think of It as active or as creating, preserving or destroying. I call that Being Personal and possessed of attributes when I think of It as active, creating, preserving, destroying,—and under all possible aspects.

[1]Brahman. [2]Tantras. [3]Kali or Sakti.

Reconciliation of all Religions

The Being is the same; only the names are different under different aspects like the same substance expressed in different languages as Jal, water, Pani, Vari, and Aqua. A tank may have four Ghats (landing-places with steps). The Hindus drink at one Ghat, they call it *jal.* The Mahomedans drink at another and they call it *pani.* The English who drink at a third call it *water.*

God is one, only the names are different. Some call Him by the name of *Allah*, some *God*, some *Brahman*, others *Kali*, others again *Rama, Hari, Jesus, Buddha.*

Keshab (smiling): Do say it once more, revered Sir, in what different ways Kali, the Mother of the universe, is making Herself manifest in this world of her sports.

The Divine Mother

Sri Ramakrishna (smiling): Oh! The Mother sports with the world, Her toy, under various aspects and various names. Now She is the Goddess[1] Unconditioned, Absolute, Formless; now the Everlasting[2] as distinguished from Her works. Under another aspect, She is the Goddess[3] of burning Ghats or crematories, the Dreaded Being that presides over Death; now again does She stand forth before us ready to bless, ready to preserve,[4] Her children. Under another aspect, She appears pleasing to the eyes of Her devotees as the Mother[5] with dark blue complexion—Consort of the God of Eternity and of Infinity. Those Sacred Books, the Tantras, speak of the Goddess[6] Unconditioned, the Absolute. When nothing was—no sun, no moon, no planets—nothing but darkness deep, there was my Divine Mother alone, Formless! As Mother with dark-blue complexion worshipped in Hindu homes, She is more accessible to man; She calls up human interest in a greater degree—coming to us with Her favours and saying to Her children, 'Fear not.' She is the Goddess that is worshipped in Hindu households.

[1]Mahakali. [2]Nitya-kali. [3]Smasan-kali. [4]Rakshya-kali. [5]Syama. [6]Dakini.

As Preserver She appears in times of plague, famine, earthquake, drought or excess of rain. At burning ghats of crematories, She appears in the form of Death. The dead body, the jackal, the spirits[1] of destruction are Her terrible companions. She lives in the midst of those horrible scenes, those fearful environments. Streams of blood, a garland of skulls thrown round Her neck, a girdle made of the hands of those that are dead, are the symbols that mark Her out as the Dreaded Mother, the All-Destroyer.

What is Creation?

Now look at Her mode of creation. At the end of a cycle—upon the destruction of the world—my Mother, careful Matron that She is, puts together the seeds of creation. The mistress of a house has a hodge-podge pot of her own in which she keeps sundry things for household use. (*Keshab and others laugh.*)

Sri Ramakrishna (smiling): Yes, my friends, that is indeed so. The mistress of the house has such a pot in her possession. In it are kept the sea-foam in a solid state, small parcels containing seeds of the cucumber, gourd, &c. She brings them out when wanted. In the same way my Mother keeps the seeds of creation after the destruction of the world at the end of a cycle. (*Laughter*)

The Spider and Her Web

My Mother, the Primal Divine Energy, is both within and without this phenomenal world. Giving birth to the world, She lives within it! She is the spider and the world is the spider's web that She has woven! The spider brings the web out of herself and then lives in it. My Mother is both the container and the contained, the efficient and the material cause of this world-system.

Is Kali, the Mother, of a dark-brown complexion? Oh, no! She is so far away from human ken that She only seems to be so.

Does not the sky look blue from a distance? The sky near us is colourless. Pretty much the same is the case with

[1]Jogini.

sea-water. It is of a dark-blue colour when looked at from a distance. Come near it. Take a little up in the hands and you shall find it colourless. Thus go near and realise Kali (the Divine Mother), and She will appear to be the same as God, the Absolute, about whom no attribute can be predicated.

And the Master sang, drunken with the wine of divine love:

SONG

Identity of the Mother and God the Absolute

Is my Divine Mother black?
O my mind! What do you say?
The Infinite is the garment that She puts on!
Though black, She illumines the lotus of the heart!

The Enigma of Life

Sri Ramakrishna (to Keshab and others). Bondage and freedom are both Her making. That man is bound with the chains of 'Woman and Gold' is due to the illusory power of *Maya* that my Divine Mother has created as part of Her plan of the universe. That man can make himself free from her fetters is again due to the mercy and grace of the same Being, my Divine Mother. She takes Her children across the sea of the world and removes the chains with which they are bound hand and foot.

And the Master sang divinely with that voice which in its sweetness rose superior to the voice of the gods[1] in heaven who sing there the glories of the Most High:

SONG

The Divine Mother and the Liberated Soul

1. O my Mother of the dark-blue complexion, you are flying the kite of the human being in the market-place of this world!
That kite flies on the wind of hope and is fastened to string made of illusion.[2]

[1]Gandharvas. [2]Maya.

2. The framework of the kite is the skeleton—ribs, veins and the internal organs of the human body.

The kite is made purely of Thine own attributes[1]; the rest of the workmanship is merely ornamental.

3. The string is made sharp with the powdered glass of worldliness;

Out of a hundred thousand kites, one or two only have their string cut through, and they are thus set free; O. how dost Thou then, laugh and clap Thy hands!

4. Prasad saith, 'The kite thus set free will be carried rapidly on favourable wind until it drops into the Infinite, beyond the sea of this world.'

My Divine Mother is always in Her sportive mood. The world, indeed, is Her toy. She will have Her own way. It is Her pleasure to take out of the prison-house and set free only one or two among a hundred thousand of Her children!

Why is the Human Soul Imperfect?

A Brahmo: Sir, She can if She pleases set every body free. Why is it, then, that She has bound us hand and foot with the chains of the world?

Sri Ramakrishna: Well, I suppose, it is Her pleasure. It is Her pleasure to go on with Her sport with all these beings that She has brought into existence. The player amongst the children that touches the person of the Grand-dame, the same need no longer run about. He cannot take any further part in the exciting play of 'hide and seek' that goes on.

The others who have not touched the goal must run about and play to the great delight of the Grand-dame. She would by no means be glad if every body should touch Her person at the same time and thus bring the sport to a close. Hence Her joy and Her clapping of hands when one out of a hundred-thousand snaps the string that binds the kite of the human soul to the world! (*The devotees rejoice.*)

It is my Divine Mother who has said to the human soul, as if in confidence, with a twinkle of Her eye, 'Go and live in the world until further orders.' Surely, the human

[1]Sattva, Rajas, Tamas.

soul is not to be blamed. It is entirely possible that She out of Her grace can turn away the mind from things of the world and thus give it freedom once more and pure devotion to the Lotus of Her Feet.

And the Master sang, placing himself in the position of men of the world and laying the trouble of his heart before the Divine Mother.

SONG

THE DIVINE MOTHER AND HER CHILDREN

1. This indeed is the thought that weighs heavily on my heart:

Thou, my own Mother, art here and I am wide awake, yet behold thieves (passions) do rob me of my all!

2. Sometimes I form the resolution of repeating Thy Holy Name, but I forget to do so at the proper hour!

O, now I know, I feel, that all this is Thy trick.

3. Thou hast not given, so Thou hast not received aught, to keep or to eat; am I to be blamed for this?

Hadst Thou given, Thou wouldst have surely received, and I would have offered Thee, out of Thine own gifts!

4. Fame or calumny, sweet or bitter, all is Thine!

O, Thou the Ruler of all tender feelings! Why dost Thou break them as they are called forth in me instead of giving them play?

5. Prasad says: 'Thou hast given me the mind but hast with a twinkle of Thine eye confided to it a secret at the same time.

Thus do I roam about seeking joy through a world, which is Thy creation, taking the bitter for sweet, the unreal for real.

* * * * *

It is my Divine Mother who has created this delusion, which has left man struggling in this sea of the world. Prasad says, 'O Mother! Thou hast in giving me the soul secretly bidden it, 'Live attached to the world.'

CHAPTER III

WORK WITHOUT ATTACHMENT OR THE PROBLEM FOR THE MAN OF THE WORLD SOLVED

A Brahmo: Sir, is it a fact that one cannot realise God unless one gives up the world?

Master (smiling): Assuredly not. It is certainly not

for you to give up everything. You are very well off as you are. There are both pure and alloyed gold; are they not both useful? The pure crystallised sugar and the molasses with all its impurities, are they not both sweet? *(Laughter.)*

O! I should think that you are very well off. Do you know *nox*[1]? Having taken more cards from the play and scored more points than were necessary, behold I have lost the play! You are far too clever for the player. You rest content, some with ten points, some with six, some others even with five! You have been clever enough not to ask for more from the player; so you have not lost the play. The play still goes on. That is alright, do you not think so? *(Laughter.)*

Verily I say to you it matters not whether you live the life of a householder or that you are a man of the world. Only you must fix your mind on God. Do your work with one hand and touch the feet of the Lord with the other. When you have no work in the world to do, hold His feet fast to your heart with both your hands.

The power of environments

The mind is everything. If the mind has lost its liberty, you lose yours. If the mind is free, you are free too. The mind may be dipped in colours, red, orange, yellow, violet or green. It is like the white cloth just returned to you by the washerman. This white cloth you may dip in any colour you like. Study English, and you must speak in English in spite of yourself (*laughter*)—you put on boots, whistle, in fact do your level best to behave like a native of England. The Pandit who studies Sanskrit must quote couplets[1]. If the mind be kept in bad company, it will colour one's thought and conversation. Placed in the midst of devotees, one's mind shall meditate upon God and talk on God and God alone.

The mind is everything. It changes its nature according to the object—according to the things amongst which it lives and acts. The attraction for the wife is of one kind

[1] A kind of play with cards. One need score only 17 points to win this game.
[2] Slokas.

and the affection for the child is of a quite different nature. On one side is one's wife, on another side is the child; one caresses both, but moved by quite different impulses!

THE SENSE OF SIN: MESSAGE TO CHRISTIANITY AND THE BRAHMO SAMAJ

Sri Ramakrishna (to the Brahmo devotees): The bondage is of the mind. Freedom is also of the mind. I am a free soul; be it in the world, or in the forest, I am not bound. I am the son of God, the son of the King of kings. Who is there to bind me in fetters? In case you are bitten by a snake, one way of getting rid of the venom is to make use of your will power and say, 'There is no venom, there is no venom.' In the same way you should say, 'I am not in fetters; I am free.' Call your will-power into action and free you shall be.

They once placed a book in my hands written by Christians. I wanted them to read and explain passages from it. Would you believe me, the one theme in that book was—sin and sin—from the beginning to the end!

(To Keshab): The members of the Brahmo Samaj also talk only of sin and sinners. The fool who says without ceasing, 'I am in bondage', does indeed bring bondage on himself in the end! The wretch who says eternally, 'I am a sinner', 'I am a sinner' turns out a sinner, indeed!

The name of God, when uttered with faith by a sinner, shall bring salvation unto him. 'What! Have I not chanted His holy name, and must I be a sinner still? Must I still be in bondage?' are words of faith in the Lord. Kristo Kishore was a pious Hindu, a Brahmin of Brahmins, who worshipped the Lord with a single-minded devotion. He went to Brindaban on pilgrimage. One day, while visiting the various shrines, he felt very thirsty. He went to a well where he found a man standing whom he asked, 'My good man! can you not draw some water for me? Of what caste are you?' The man replied, 'Oh, divine Sir, I belong to a low caste, that of a cobbler.' Kristo Kishore thereupon told him,

"It matters not; utter the name of the Lord; say, 'Siva,' 'Siva', and draw the water for me."

Chant the name of God and, depend upon it, your body, mind and soul shall become pure.

Why talk of sin and hell-fire all the days of your life? Do say but once, 'I have, O Lord, done things that I ought not to have done and I have left undone things that I ought to have done. O Lord, forgive me!'

Saying this, have faith in His hallowed name, and you shall be purged of all sins.

And the Master sang of the power of God's Sacred Name:

SONG

God's Sacred Name and Its Power

1. O Mother! Grant unto me but to die with Thy Sacred Name on my lips. Then, O good Mother! It shall be seen whether Thou savest or not this poor helpless child of Thine.

2. I care not if I kill the sacred cow, or a godly Brahmana, or even a child in its mother's womb. O I care not if I am sinful enough to drink or even to kill a woman.

3. With all the sins of the darkest type, I have, within my easy reach, and can lay claim to the high office of the God appointed by Thee to be the creator[1] of the world.

* * * * *

The Lord's Prayer

To my Divine Mother, I prayed for pure devotion[2] alone. With flowers in my folded hands, I prayed, saying, 'Do Thou, O Mother, grant that I may have pure and unalloyed devotion.' Here is sin, here again is merit, O, take them both; I lay them at

[1]Brahma. [2]Bhakti

Thy feet. Here is knowledge (of many things), here again is ignorance, O, take them both and grant that I may have devotion alone. Here again is purification on the one hand and defilement on the other; I desire neither of them. Here are good works, here bad; both I lay at Thy feet; O, grant that I may have devotion alone and love for Thee!'

(To the Brahmo devotees): Listen to a song by Ram Prasad:

SONG

My Divine Mother and the Discipline of the Mind

1. Come, O my Mind, let us go out for a walk.
Let us gather the four[1] fruits at the foot of the Kalpa Tree,[2] my Divine Mother.

2. You have, O My Mind, two wives; take Non-worldliness[3] with thee on thy way to the Tree.
Ask—about the Lord—Her Son *Viveka* who knows the Real (God) from the unreal phenomenal world.

3. O, when shalt thou lie down in the abode of the blessed with purification[4] and defilement[5] alike by thy side.
Thou shalt see my Divine Mother as soon as all difference between the two co-wives shall cease to exist.

4. Do thou turn out thy parents, Egotism[6] and Ignorance.[7]
Should Mine-ness[8] try to draw thee into its hole, do thou cling to the post of patience.

5. Tie to a worthless post the two goats, Virtue[9] (due to good works) and Vice[10] (due to bad works).
Should they prove refractory, let them be killed before the altar of God with the sword of knowledge.

6. Admonish, O my Mind, the children of thy first wife, Worldliness from a safe distance:
Should they not obey thee, see that they are drowned in the Sea of True Knowledge.[11]

7. Prasad saith, "If thou goest on like this, thou shalt be able to render a satisfactory account of thyself to the Lord of Death;"
"And I shall be glad to call thee 'my child,' 'my darling,' the 'idol of my father' and by other pet names; and then thou shalt be indeed a mind after my mind."

---

[1]Four fruits: *Dharma* (good works); *Artha* (wealth); *kama* (desire); *Moksha* (liberation of the soul).

[2] Kalpa Tree—a tree in Heaven which grants everything that the believer prays for.

[3]Nivritti. [4]Suchi. [5]Asuchi. [6]Ahamkara. [7]Avidya. [8]Moha. [9]Dharma. [10]Adharma. [11]Jnana.

The Problem of Life for the Man of The World

It may be given even to the householder to see God. It was the case with Raja Janak, the great royal sage. A great devotee once called the world 'a structure of dreams.' But, according to Prasad, another great lover of God, that is not the whole truth, and one may be in the world though not *of* the world.

And the Master sang:

SONG

The World to a Lover of God.

1. The world is indeed a thing of joy; let me eat and drink and be merry.
2. Raja Janak, the great royal sage,—was he inferior in any respect to the holy men who had given up the world?

Oh no, he it was who was loyal to both Matter and Spirit,[1] who realised God and at the same time drank his cup of milk. (*Laughter.*)

The Brahmo Samaj and Janak Raja

But one cannot rise to the height of Janak Raja all of a sudden by leaps and bounds. Janak spent many long years in devotional practices, in solitude away from the din and bustle of the world. Thus it behoves everybody to go into solitude for some time. It is a great thing, if one can cry out for the Lord for three days steadily, in solitude, away from the haunts of men. Indeed, one day passed in such a way would be a great gain. People are ready enough to shed, for wives and children, tears that will fill a water-pot; but who cries for the Lord? It would do men of the world infinite good if they would now and then retire into solitude to the end that God may be seen and realised.

There are a thousand-and-one difficulties in the way of the aspirant in the first stage of his spiritual life. These

[1]Loyal to Matter and Spirit.—Compare 'Sensibility' and 'Rationality' of the Hegelian philosophers.

difficulties are caused by the world and its attractions. The tree planted on the footpath stands in need of a fence lest it be eaten up by goats and cows. The fence is to last so long as the plant is young and tender; when the trunk and roots get thicker and stronger, no fence will be needed. An elephant tied to the trunk of such a tree will not injure it.

The disease of a worldly man is of a serious type. His organs with their functions are entirely out of order. He has lost sight of the Lord, his own Father, and is attached to 'Woman and Gold'. These have brought all this trouble on him and he needs rest and solitude.

Would you keep a large water-jar and savoury pickles in the same room in which a patient is laid up with typhoid fever? If you wish to cure such a patient, you must have him removed from that room, in case it is impossible to send away the jar and the pickles!

A man of the world, a householder, is such a patient; worldly things make the water-jar; desire to enjoy those things is the patient's thirst. The mouth waters at the mere thought of the pickles; they need not be placed before us. Women looked at with a carnal eye are such things. Hence solitude is the best remedy for it.

First, have a sense of what is real and what is unreal; and secondly, know what it is to live unattached to the world. Having these two *viz.*, discrimination and non-attachment, we may live a family life. In the sea of the world are the crocodiles—passions and desires. Rub your body with turmeric pounded to a pulp, if you wish to bathe in that sea; for then, crocodiles will do no harm to you. The turmeric is discrimination, that is, knowing the Real from the unreal, and non-attachment. God is the only Reality; the phenomenal universe is unreal.

Yearning for The Lord

Along with this another thing is wanted—that is, intense devotion to God. The Gopis of Brindaban had such a devotion. They had an intense love for Sri Krishna—God-

Incarnate. Here is a song about their intense love for the God-Man.

SONG

Yearning for the Lord

1. O, the sweet flute is again being played in yonder wood! I for my part must go there!
My Beloved of the dark-brown colour stands waiting for me there!
O tell me, my dear ones, if you are coming too or not.
2. My Beloved—O, I am afraid He is a mere word—an empty sound to you, my friends!
But to me He is the vital part. O, He is my very life, my heart, my soul!

Sri Ramakrishna is in tears as he sings. He says to Keshab and other devotees with great feeling; you are Brahmos; you believe that God is formless and do not believe in God-Incarnate. Well, it matters not. You need not accept Radha and Sri Krishna or any persons as Incarnations of the Supreme Being. But the attachment, the intense love, the yearning which the Gopis felt for Sri Krishna is a thing which you may well make your own.

Yearning is the next step leading to realisation—God-vision.

CHAPTER IV

Master and Disciple: God the Only Master

It is the ebb-tide. The steamer is going fast down stream towards Calcutta. It gets to the other side of the Howrah Bridge within sight of the Botanical Gardens just below Calcutta. The Captain has orders to go a little farther down. How far the steamer has actually gone down the river is not known to those who are listening to Sri Ramakrishna and watching his movements. They listen with rapt attention! They have no idea either of time or of distance!

Keshab now offers the Master popped rice with the kernel of the cocoanut. All present are invited to partake of these. They take them within the folds of their cloth, eat and are very happy. It seems as if a festival was being held on board the steamer.

The Master notices that Bejoy and Keshab are not quite at home in each other's presence. He would see that they make up their differences. Is it not his mission to see peace on earth and good-will among men?

Master (to Keshab): Look here, my dear Sir, here is Bejoy. As to your quarrels and fights—well don't worry yourselves on that account. There was fighting enough even between Siva and Rama. (*Laughter.*)

Siva was Rama's spiritual guide! After a little fighting they made it up and became once more as good friends as ever. But the fighting went on among their followers. The gibberish of the ghosts and the chatter of the monkeys could not easily be quieted down. You too will be very good friends once again. But your followers — well, I dare say, they will take after you. (*Laughter.*)

One's own flesh and blood! That is how he (Bejoy) stands in relation to you. These differences, you know, are things that cannot be avoided. There may be tug-of-war even between the father and the son. Take the case of Rama and his sons—Lava and Kusha. Take another case. The welfare of the mother and of the daughter is the same; still they observe the Tuesday each on her own account as the day of fast and prayer. It is as if the welfare of the one went against that of the other.

In the same way, you, Keshab, have a religious society (Samaj) of your own; and Bejoy must have a separate society of his own, too! (*Laughter.*)

Well, there is room enough for all kinds of things under Providence — even for quarrels and differences. When it was God-Incornate Himself Who appeared at Brindaban, the question may very well be asked, 'Why did Jatilla and Kutilla stand in the way of His mission of Love?' I suppose, His sport as the Divine Lover would have died a natural death from want of nourishment, but for those obstructives, the Jatillas and Kutillas. (*Laughter.*) Opposition adds zest to a thing. Ramanuja held the doctrine of qualified Non-dualism. His spiritual guide, however, was a Nondualist without any compromise; so they had their differences. Master and disciple criticised each other. This sort of thing comes about every day. Be it so: still to the Master the disciple is his own. (*They all rejoice.*)

Sṛi Ramakrishna: That your disciples break away from you is no wonder. Never do you study their nature before taking them in.

Men are the same in form and appearance. But they differ in the qualities of their nature. In some the qualities lead them God-ward. In others they make them inclined to multiply work and duty. In a third class, they cause ignorance which turns the mind away from God. The cake *Pooli* may all have the same look, but they differ as to their contents. In some the contents are the sweet condensed milk: in others, it is the kernel of the cocoanut sweetened by treacle or sugar. In others again, the contents may be *Kalai* pulse boiled without any admixture of sweets. (*Laughter.*)

Sri Ramakrishna's relation to the Divine Mother

The way of thinking and feeling into which I for my part have been put by my Divine Mother is somewhat different. I go about eating and playing, child as I am of my Divine Mother. It is She who must know all the rest.

Indeed, there are three words which prick me to the core: Spiritual Guide, Doer or Free Agent and Father. I am not the free agent; it is my Divine Mother, I am only an humble instrument in Her hands. I for my part do not wish to lead a family life and be a father of children. I would much rather give all my time to God and minister unto Him—as manifest in all His creatures and not merely in the members of one particular human family. Again, God is our only spiritual guide.

God the only Master

It is He alone who will teach as master. I for my part am like a child that feels its weakness as soon as it cannot see its mother.

Men as spiritual guides can be had by hundreds of thousands. Everybody is anxious to be master. How many are there who care to be disciples?

The Commissioned Teachers

The task of a master teaching a disciple is very hard indeed. If the master has seen the Lord, if by Him he has been commissioned to teach, it is quite a different matter. So commissioned were Narada, Sukadeva: also Sankaracharya.

When you are without such a commission, who will listen to you? You know Calcutta and her fondness for the latest sensation. The milk in the kettle will, of course, puff up as soon as it is put upon the fire. But the puffing will cease when the fire is withdrawn from under the kettle. The people of Calcutta are remarkably fond of sensations. They begin digging the well at one place; but they will give it up as soon as they find that the earth is hard and strong. They then set to work digging at another place. The soil, suppose, is sandy here; they will readily give up digging at that spot. They will then look about for another locality. That is indeed the way of the people. Their good opinion is by no means worth having.

What is God's direct Commandment?

Again there are people who think a particular thought and believe it to be God's commandment. Such an idea is quite a mistaken one. One may look for God's commandment after seeing Him and talking with Him and not until then. God's word! What wonderful weight must it carry! A mountain may be moved by it! A lecture taken by itself has no force whatever, apart from God's direct commandment. People may care for lectures, only for a short time; after which everything will escape from their memory. As to living up to the things taught—well, they will care even less for it!

Making disciples and teaching without divine authority condemned

In that part of the country there is a tank called Haldar-pukur. People used to throw dirt round about the tank. Others who came there for morning ablutions called the offenders names in a loud excited voice; but all in vain. The offence was repeated on the following morning. Upon this they sent word to the municipal authorities. A peon, wearing a badge round his waist, came to make enquiries. He put a notice to all concerned not to 'commit nuisance.' Would you believe it! the nuisance abated at once! (*Laughter.*)

For the teaching of divine truth a badge of authority is the one thing needful. Else, for a man to teach others—O, it would be ridiculous! To think that a person must teach who does not himself know—that the blind must lead the blind! You shall thus do more evil than good. It is only when you have seen God that you can hope to see through other people and tell them what disease (of the soul) they have been taken with.

You must have the direct commandment of God. Else it would be asserting yourself to say, 'I teach' or 'I am the master and you are my disciples'. Self-assertion is the offspring of ignorance. One enjoys real freedom in this very world if one can but realise that God is the sole actor in this world-system and that we are only instruments in His hands. All trouble, all want of peace, comes of the notion 'I am the Lord—I am the Free Agent.'

THE WESTERN IDEA OF WORK: IS WORK THE END OF LIFE OR A MEANS TO THE END?

Sri Ramakrishna (to Keshab and other devotees): You talk glibly of doing good to the world. The world to which you desire to do good—is it contained in a nutshell? In the next place, who are you, pray, to do good to the world? First go through devotional practices and see God. Then it is that inspiration and powers will come down to you, and you may talk of doing good. Not till then.

A Brahmo devotee: Sir, do you mean to say that we are to give up all work until we have seen God?

Sri Ramakrishna: No, my dear Sir, why shall you give up all work? Meditation, the chanting of hymns, the repeating of His holy name, and other devotional exercises you must have to go through.

Devotee: I mean work connected with the world. Are we then to give up all our wordly affairs?

Sri Ramakrishna: No; you may attend to them too just so much as you cannot do without, in order to live in this world. But you should at the same time pray to the Lord with tears in your eyes for His grace and for strength to do your duties without the expectation of any reward or fear of punishment in this world or the next. Say when you pray, 'Lord, grant that my work in the world and for the world may grow less and less day by day. For I see that my work growing manifold only makes me lose sight of Thee. Sometimes I think I do my duties remaining unattached to the world, but I know not how I deceive myself and do them through attachment instead! I do my alms, and behold! I seek for fame, O, I know not how!'

The End of Life

Sambu Mallik once talked of founding hospitals and dispensaries, schools and colleges; of laying roads, sinking wells, and digging tanks for the good of all. I said to him, 'Yes; but you must be unattached while doing good to others, and you must be careful to take up only such works as come in your way—such works, again, as appear to be of a pressing necessity. Do not seek them—do not seek more work than you can well manage. If you do, you will lose sight of the Lord. Go to the shrine of Kali, the Mother of the universe; before you see the Holy of Holies, and on your way to the shrine, you may do your alms. But if you continue your charitable work until late in the evening when the doors of the temple have been closed upon all pilgrims, you will not see the Mother. Clever people would first see the Holy Mother pushing their way through the multitude that assembles at the gates of the temple; and after seeing Her they may turn their attention to alms-giving and other good works.

First see God and then talk seriously of your duties.

What, do you think, ought to be the end in view of those who go on performing their duties? Work, or the performance of one's duty, is the means,—and God is the end. Do not take the means for the end. So said I once to Sambhu. "Suppose," I said, "you see God, or God manifests Himself to you; will you then say to Him, 'Lord, do Thou grant that I may have lots of dispensaries and hospitals, and schools and colleges?' (*Laughter.*) No; they are wanted so long as you are in the world—which is only transitory compared to eternal life." A true devotee shall rather pray in this wise: 'Grant, O good Lord, that I may have a place at the lotus of Thy feet, that it may be my privilege to live always in Thy holy presence, and that I may have deep, true, unalloyed devotion unto Thee.'

The Path of Work and the Path of Devotion

Hard indeed is work without attachment. It is hard in this materialistic age to get through all the works—all the duties—laid upon us by the sacred books. Verily life in this age comes out of food! Work and duties—O, there is hardly time enough for them! It will be all over with the patient suffering from the high fever of this world if he is allowed to go through the slow process of treatment practised by the old-fashioned Hindu physicians. People are shortlived and the fever carries one off in a few hours. The specific for the present day is Dr. Gupta's patent fever mixture. This produces effect at once.

Yes, in this age, the one means of realising God is sincere devotion to and love for Him—and earnest prayer, and the chanting of His holy names and of His divine attributes.

(To Keshab and other devotees): Your path too lies through devotion and self-surrender to the Lord. Blessed are they who like you, sing His name. Your path is clear and rational. You cannot shake yourself free from egoism; thus it is proper for you not to go far like a non-dualist and hold that 'God, the Absolute, is the only reality and that the world is unreal like a dream.' You are not philosophers but devotees. You believe in a Personal God. That is right. Go on in this way. But have a yearning for the Lord and, depend upon it, you shall see Him as a reality!

CHAPTER V

At the House of a Disciple

The steamer has come back to Koyla Ghat (Calcutta). All on board get ready to land. Coming out of the cabin they see that the full moon bathes the bosom of the holy Ganges and the banks adjoining with her mellow light.

The Master with two or three disciples including M. gets into a cab which is waiting for him on the shore. Nandalal, Keshab's nephew, also gets in. He wishes to go with the Master some distance.

When all have seated themselves in the cab Sri Ramakrishna says, 'Where is he?' meaning Keshab. In a few moments Keshab comes up smiling, and saying, 'Who are the persons that are going with him?' Being satisfied with the answer, he bows down to the ground before the Master who affectionately bids him adieu.

The cab has set out. It is that part of the town where the Europeans live; beautiful well-watered streets lined on both sides with beautiful mansions! It is the full moon. The splendid palatial buildings seem to repose under the soft, serene light. Near the gates are gas lights; within are brightly illuminated rooms; the sweet sound of music reaches the ear; evidently European ladies are singing to the accompaniment of the piano.

The Master is filled with the joy of the Lord as the carriage drives along. Suddenly he says, 'I am thirsty; what is to be done?' Nandalal stops the carriage before the gates of the India Club and goes upstairs to fetch water. Water is brought in a glass tumbler. The Master asks, smiling 'Is the glass well washed?' Nandalal says 'Yes.' The Master drinks from the glass.

He is child-like in his simplicity. He puts forward his face to look at the various objects on both sides. His joy knows no bounds as he looks on men, animals, carriages, houses, the moon-light, the lighted streets.

Nandalal alights at Colutola. The cab comes to a stop before the door of Suresh Mitra's house. Suresh is very much attached to the Master, but he is not at home. He has gone to visit a newly-purchased garden at Kankurgachi.

His people open a room on the ground-floor and invite the party to be seated there.

The cab fare is to be paid. Who is to pay it? Had Suresh been at home, he would have paid it. The Master says to a disciple, 'Ask the ladies of the house for the fare. I suppose they know well enough that their husbands and elders are in the habit of coming to our place.' (*Laughter.*)

Vivekananda with The Master

Narendra (Vivekananda) lives in the same neighbourhood, so the Master sends for him. Meanwhile the inmates of the house have led him upstairs into the drawing-room. The matting of the floor is covered with a carpet and a white sheet. Three or four bolsters are lying about. On the wall there hangs a beautiful oil-painting which Suresh has prepared, a picture of the harmony of all religions. In that painting Sri Ramakrishna is represented as pointing out to Keshab that all religions lead to one goal, God — be it Hinduism, Mahomedanism, Buddhism, Christianity or any of their various sects.

He talks with smiles on his lips when Narendra comes up. His joy is redoubled. He says smiling to Narendra as he talks, 'We enjoyed such a pleasant trip on board the steamer with Keshab Sen. Bejoy also was there and many of these present here.' Pointing to M., he says, 'You may ask M. how I told Keshab and Bejoy about the mother and daughter both observing the fast on Tuesday—each for her own welfare, and how God's sports in this world would suffer for want of nourishment in the absence of obstructives like Jatilla and Kutilla!'

(To M.): Was this not so, M?

M.: Quite so, revered Sir.

It is getting late. But Suresh has not yet come back. The Master will go back to the Temple-garden at Dakshineswar. It is about half-past ten and he must leave for the garden.

The streets are flooded with moonlight. The cab is at the door. The Master gets in. Narendra and M.—each bows down low to the Master and goes back to his own house.

SECTION V

1883

SRI RAMAKRISHNA WITH KESHAB CHANDRA SEN AT LILY COTTAGE

CHAPTER I

The Divine Mother and Her Manifestations

'He looks for you with a yearning heart as you come'—Song by Jaydeva.

It was past 2 p.m. on the 28th of November, 1883. A young man was there seen walking up and down the footpath of the Circular Road before Lily Cottage. The footpath runs close to the cottage north and south.

Lily Cottage is south of *Mangalbari*—a locality where the Brahmo devotees belonging to Keshab's Samaj have settled. Here Keshab lives with his family. But Keshab is very ill—his friends say that there is little chance of his recovery.

Sri Ramakrishna loves Keshab. He will come to-day to see him. He has by this time left the Temple at Dakshineswar for Calcutta. It is this that kept this young man, his disciple, pacing up and down the footpath, awaiting his beloved Master's arrival. Carriages come to view one after another and every time he looks up to see if he is coming.

He will wait. He watches the passers-by. He looks on the building opposite—the Victoria College, where Brahmo girls and ladies receive instruction. North of the college building is a garden house, the residence of an English gentleman. The young man has this house also in full view before him.

All is not right there. As he observes for a long time, there is hurrying to and fro amongst the inmates of the house; and their looks are sad. Presently come on the scene the ominous hearse and the drivers and servants reserved in black: they wear the livery of Death, for it is he who has visited the house: a spirit has passed away; the human soul has left this body of clay! It came into this world out of eternity. It has left the world!

'Whiter?' says the disciple to himself, as he walks up and down. 'Whither does the soul pass as it leaves this world?—verily it is raised out of eternity into eternity!'

Carriages rattle away before the disciple. He lifts his eyes; but the Master has not come.

It is five in the afternoon. The Master has come up. Latu and two or three other disciples are with him; Rakhal and M. are also there.

He is received by Keshab's people and is led uptairs. In the corridor that runs south of the drawing-room, the Master has taken his seat.

The Master in Samadhi

He has been waiting for a long time. He will see Keshab who is lying ill in the inner apartment. He gets impatient. But Keshab is just taking a little rest in the midst of his great sufferings; so his people say, with great humility, that he will come and see the Master soon.

Keshab has been taken seriously ill. Hence his disciples are so careful about him. Sri Ramakrishna however gets more and more impatient to see him. He appeals to Keshab's disciples—Prasanna, Amrita and others.

Sri Ramakrishna (to Keshab's disciples): Well, there is no need of his coming here. Let me go in and see him.

Prasanna (humbly) : Sir, kindly wait one moment; he will be here presently.

Sri Ramakrishna: O dear, it is you who are standing in the way : how I long to see him!

Prasanna talks about Keshab to turn his attention.

Prasanna : Sir, a great change has come over him.

Talking with the Mother

Like yourself he is often found talking to the Divine Mother! Like yourself he hears Her voice and sometimes sheds tears!

Does Keshab talk to the Divine Mother and smile and cry like a child? The good news is too much for the Master. He loses all sense-consciousness and passes into the state of *Samadhi*!

There is this God-intoxicated man seated motionless, like a statue. It being cold weather he has on a coat made of green Kashmere. He is seated with folded hands. His body is erect. His eyes move not. Deep in *Samadhi*. He continues in this state for a long time. No sign that this unique state of divine ecstasy is going to leave him!

It is evening. They have lighted the drawing-room. He is returning to the sense-world. They are trying to take him into that room.

He is seated on a couch—with cushion-chairs and couches and mirrors on all sides—in the lighted room. But the state of God-consciousness has not entirely left him. He smiles like one who has been intoxicated. He looks on the couches and cushioned-chairs, mirrors and the rest. He talks to himself and to his Divine Mother!

God-vision

Sri Ramakrishna (at the sight of couches, etc.): These were of use, indeed, some time back! But now?—They are of little use.

Did the Master see with his inner vision that Keshab's hour was come and that he would depart out of this world and go to his Divine Mother?

He looks at Rakhal, a young disciple, and says fondly, Rakhal, is it you?'

He talks to the Divine Mother, saying, 'Here Thou art, O Mother! How beautifully dressed Thou art! Do not trouble Thyself, O Mother! but take Thou Thy seat!'

The Brahmo devotees have filled the room by this time. His disciples Latu, Rakhal and M., are seated near him. He talks on the immortality of the soul. Does he see with a clear vision that Keshab's soul must pass away?

Sri Ramakrishna: The body and the soul! The body has a beginning, it must have an end. The body must die. The soul dies not!

Immortality of The Soul

The soul stands apart from the body. Until one sees God, one cannot help believing that the soul is the same as the body. The idea clings to the ignorant—to him who has not seen God. To the knowing one it is plain that the soul is not the same as the body.

The shell of the unripe betel-nut adheres to the nut. It is so hard to part the one from the other. Such is not the case with the ripe nut. The shell does not adhere to it; the nut is felt rolling inside, if shaken.

Who is it that now enters the room? A figure made of skin and bones—a veritable spectre coming on towards the Master! He holds on to the wall for support. He comes near the couch. He falls down at the hallowed feet of Sri Ramakrishna, who is now seated on the carpeted floor and is still in a state of divine consciousness. The figure before him is Keshab or rather the wreck of him who was once Keshab, the hero of a hundred platforms, the observed of all observers, the idol of young Bengal, the god-like figure whose very presence was so often inspiring as he sat conducting divine services in the Brahmo Samaj and poured out his soul like a child in prayer to the Divine Mother—in words never to be forgotten—so forceful, so earnest, so sweet, so charming!

God-in-Man

Still in a state of ecstasy! He looks on Keshab as on one he knows not. Keshab is seated and says aloud, 'Here am I, Sir! Here am I!' Keshab softly stroke his left hand.

But no return to the sense-world! Drinking deep at the fountain of immortal bliss! A little while later he talks to himself—like one gone mad! Is this the madness of divine love? He says:

So long as I do not have a knowledge of my true Self,

The Omnipotent Energy

so long as the Reality gets out of sight behind semblances, I have a perception of many things and persons—as Keshab, Amrita, Prasanna. Perfect knowledge is knowledge of One-ness—of only one Reality behind the many things—One God behind the phenomenal universe.

The knowing one sees again that this Reality—this Universal Soul—has differentiated Itself into living beings and the world—in short into the twenty-four categories of the philosopher.

It is only the Divine Energy which manifests Itself more or less everywhere. The One Soul has, indeed, differentiated Itself into many things; but in some the manifested energy is greater—in some, less. Vidyasagar asked me, 'Is it a fact that the powers given us by God are greater in the case of some and less in the case of others. Is God partial?' I answered, 'If that were not the case how is it that one man is a match for ten, nay, sometimes for forty? If that were not the case again, how is it that we have come here all the way, from Dakshineswar to see you? Inequality is a fact in God's creation and must have a deep meaning. It certainly does not prove that God is partial.'

Different in Manifestations

Special Manifestation: The Divine Incarnation

He in whom the divinity of the Lord is manifested possesses powers far greater than those of anybody else.

The rich man may have many houses to live in. But he may be generally met in a certain drawing-room—of which he is especially fond. The soul of him who loves the Lord is a drawing-room of the Lord. Unto it there come down special powers from the Most High.

Do you ask, what are the signs of such a person? Well, great works wrought by him in the name of the Lord. Verily, they are the fruit of great powers!

God the Absolute same as God the Mother

This Primal Divine Energy of God the Creator is the same as God the Absolute. One cannot be thought of without the other being suggested. The refulgence of the gem cannot be thought of without the gem being suggested; nor can the gem be thought of without its lustre being suggested. Take again the snake and its tortuous motion: the one cannot be thought of without the other idea being called up.

The identity of God the Absolute and God the Creator cannot be made perfectly clear by means of words. Reasoning by analogy only throws some light on it.

Now, God the Creator, my Divine Mother, has manifested Herself as the twenty-four categories of the philosopher. It is a case of involution and evolution. In Her were involved the human soul[1] and the eternal world.[2] Why do I yearn to see Rakhal, Narendra (Vivekananda) and other young men? They have not as yet touched the world—they have not touched 'Woman and Gold.' Verily the Divine Mother is revelealed in the flesh—the Unmanifested Energy has manifested Herself in the form of this world and markedly in these human forms.

Hazra indeed often takes me to task saying, 'Why do you go about thinking of these young men? I wonder what you are going to do to give your mind to God?' (*Here Keshab and others laugh.*)

Special Manifestations of the Mother: Pure souls like Narendra untouched by the world

Well, Hazra's word did set me thinking seriously of the matter. I prayed to the Divine Mother saying, 'Mother, is all this true that Hazra says? Am I indeed losing sight of Thee?' Well, I also asked Bholanath and it was he who assured me that the *Mahabharat* made the matter quite clear. It is pointed out there that a person in *Samadhi* who sees God has nothing in this unreal phenomenal world for his mind to rest upon. He therefore cannot help seeking the company of pure souls who have a love for God and who do not love 'Woman and Gold.' This dictum of the *Mahabharat* at once relieved my mind. It was to me much as a precedent in a case at law is to a

[1] Jiva. [2] Jagat.

litigant before a court of justice. (*Laughter.*)

Hazra is not to blame. Until God is seen one must reason saying, 'not this,' 'not this,'—that is, God is a Being who abides quite apart from either man or Nature. It is quite otherwise with him who has seen God. He realises the fact of involution and of evolution—that the phenomenal world and the human soul were involved in God the Absolute and that they are the forms in which He manifests Himself—forms which have been evolved out of Himself. To get the butter as a distinct object one puts aside the butter milk: in the end one cannot help realising that for the butter-milk the butter is its own; the two are correlated. Yes, man and Nature are His manifestations—only in some created things He manifests Himself in a greater degree than in others.

The more the love of God is deepened in the human soul after realisation, the easier it becomes to feel His presence in all things. Until a flood causes the river to overflow, you must follow its round-about course in order to reach the sea. During the flood there is deep water on land itself, and you may row from any point to the sea, straight as the crow flies.

After the harvest has been reaped, one need not any longer go round along the balk—one may walk straight to any point over the fields.

Perception of those that have seen God

He who has once realised Him, sees that the Lord manifests Himself in all things. Above all, He reveals Himself in man—more specially in those pure souls who are of themselves fixed upon God and are turned away from the little things of this world—turned away from 'Woman and Gold.' (*Perfect silence.*)

It is indeed hard for a man who comes down from *Samadhi* and has seen God, to give his mind to the little things of this world. Hence he seeks the company of such pure souls, for they have not touched the world and the things that the world can give—money, honours, titles, power, sensual pleasures.

Brahmo Samaj and the Motherhood of God

The Divine Mother is the same as God the Absolute. When thought of as inactive, He is called the Absolute.[1] When again, He is thought of as active—as creating, preserving and destroying—then the Being is called the Divine Energy or the Divine Mother.[2] The Absolute expressed in terms of the relative is the same as the Divine Mother—the same as God the Father. The father leaves the management of of the household to the mother. The Mother receives all Her power and authority from the Father.

You cannot think of God the Absolute *behind* the universe without thinking of the God of the universe, the Divine Mother. The thought of the one must call up to you the thought of the other.

The thought of the Male Principle in the universe must suggest to you the thought of the Female Principle; and the thought of the Female Principle must suggest to you the thought of the Male. One who understands what is 'Father,' also understands what is 'Mother'. (*Keshab laughs.*)

One who has a sense of darkness has also a sense of light, its correlative. One who knows the meaning of night knows also the meaning of day, its correlative. One who has feeling of joy has also a feeling of grief, its correlative. Do you see this?

Keshab (smiling) : Yes Sir, I do.

Sri Ramakrishna : What Mother do I mean? The Mother of the universe—She who does create and does preserve—She who protects Her children always from evil and teaches them how to live in the world and how again to obtain liberation and true knowledge. A true child cannot live apart from the mother. He knows not anything—but his mother knows everything. The child only gets his meat out of his mother's hands and romps about in play. He casts all his cares upon the mother.

Keshab : That is quite true, Sir.

[1]Brahman or Purusha. [2]Sakti or Prakriti.

CHAPTER II

The Last Words with Keshab Sen

By this time Sri Ramakrishna has come down to the sense-world. The company assembled in the drawing-room eagerly watches him as he talks smiling with Keshab. Strange, that neither Keshab nor the Master says, 'How do you do?' or 'How do you feel?' No words are spoken but those about God.

Sri Ramakrishna (to Keshab): The members of the Brahmo Samaj—why do they dwell so much upon the glory of God's works? 'O Lord, Thou hast made the sun, Thou hast made the moon, Thou hast made the stars.' Why do you dwell so much upon these things? Many are they that are charmed with the beauty of the garden—its glorious flowers and sweetest odours—few seek the Lord of the garden! Which is the greater of the two—the garden or its Lord? Verily the garden is unreal so long as death stalks in our midst; but the Lord of the garden is the one Reality!

After having taken a few glasses at the bar of a tavern, who cares to enquire how many tons of liquor there are in the barrels there for sale? A single bottle suffices for one.

At the sight of Narendra I am drunken with joy. Never have I asked him, 'Who is your father? or how many houses has he got of his own?'

Men do value their own goods, they value money, houses, furniture; hence they think that the Lord would view His own works—the sun, moon, stars—in the same light! Men think He would be glad if they spoke highly of his works.

Sambhu Mullick once said, 'Sir, do bless me that I may die leaving all my wealth at the hallowed feet of the Divine Mother.' I replied, 'What do you speak? It is all wealth to you! To the Divine Mother it is no better than the dust over which you walk!'

There was once a theft committed in the Temple of Vishnu—the thief had stolen the jewels that adorned the divine images.

Mathoor (manager of the Temple and son-in-law of Rani Rasmani) and myself went up there to see what the matter was. Mathoor cried out saying, 'Thou, God, hast no worth! They took away all Thy jewels, but Thou wert unable to do anything.' Upon this I said to him sharply, 'How foolish it is of you to talk in this strain! The jewels of which you speak are as good as lumps of clay to the Lord of the universe whom you worship in this Image! Remember it is from Him that the Goddess of Fortune derives all power!'

Does the Lord care for all the wealth that one may offer to Him? O, no. His grace lights on him alone who can offer love and devotion. What He values is pure love, non-attachment and renunciation for His sake.

Various Classes of Lovers of God

One's idea of God varies with the way in which one's nature is made up. One man is fond of meat, and offers animals in sacrifice to his God. Another has his mind turned to many things, and his offerings to his God are of many kinds. A third man does not like to make a show of his worship to the world. He offers flowers, leaves of the bael-trees and the holy Ganges water. He offers the plainest things,—sweet cakes, or a preparation of milk, rice and sugar.

There is yet another class of worshippers. They are like children. Their soul is unattached to the elements that go to form the body and mind. Their worship consists purely in believing in the name of the Lord and repeating it with devotion. Yes, the name of the Lord alone and nothing else!

Sri Ramakrishna (smiling to Keshab) : You are ill;

The Lord's Hospital and the Treatment of the Soul

well there is a deep meaning in that. There has passed through your body many a deep devotional feeling that searches the Lord: your illness bears witness to those feelings. Of the havoc done by them to the system one can form no idea at the time they arise.

A ship goes past over the Ganges but nobody attends to it. A little while after, big waves are seen beating upon the bank and sometimes washing away portions of it.

An elephant entering into a hut soon makes it totter and at last pulls it down. The love for the Lord is like the elephant in its greatness. It very often pulls down the frail house of clay called the human body.

When a house is set on fire, some of the things inside are first burnt up; then the house is taken up as a whole by the fire and burnt. Much the same thing comes to pass when God is seen. The fire of God-vision first burns up the various passions—lust, anger, etc.;—then the false ego which says, 'I am the doer (Lord)'; and lastly, the whole house, *viz.*, the body.

You may think let the Lord's will be done. But no, the physician does not leave the patient until he is perfectly cured. Your name has been entered as a patient in the hospital-books and you cannot get away till you are seen cured by the physician in charge (the doctor saheb). Why did you suffer your name to be so entered ? (*Laughter.*)

Keshab goes into a fit of laughter at the Master's reference to the Lord's hospital.

Sri Ramakrishna (to Keshab): Hriday used to say, 'Never have I witnessed such love of God and such illness too joined with it.' I was at the time taken very ill with diarrhoea of a rather severe type. It then seemed as if myriads of ants were eating into my brain.

But the words that I used to speak were all concerning the Lord. Ram of the village Natogore, a Hindu physician, finding me—when he called—in the midst of a homily, said, 'Has this man really gone out of his wits, that he goes on talking like that with a body made of mere skin and a couple of bones!'

Master (to Keshab) : Everything is ordered by Her will. Thou doest Thy will alone. O Mother Divine! Thou doest Thy own work—but foolish man takes all the credit to himself, saying, 'It is I who have done it!'

The Divine Gardener

The gardener knows well how to deal with the common rose; and also with the rose bussora which is of a superior type. As for the latter, he clears the soil round about its roots to give it the benefit of the night dew. The dew adds freshness and strength to the plant. It may be that the same is the case with you. The divine gardener knows how to deal with you. He digs round about you to the very roots, to the end that the dew of His inspiration shall fall on you and you shall be purer, stronger than before, and your work even greater and more abiding than ever.

The Lord's Prayer for Keshab

Whenever I hear that you are ill, my heart is sorely troubled. The last time that you were unwell, I used to wake up during the last part of the night and cry to my Divine Mother, saying, 'O Mother! If it be that anything evil comes upon Keshab, with whom shall I converse about Thee when I go to Calcutta?' Coming to Calcutta I presented offerings of fruit and sugar to the Divine Mother, praying to Her earnestly for your well-being. I had made a vow to make these offerings to Her.

All present look with wonder and amazement at the Master—thinking of the depth of his indescribable love for Keshab. He continues:

To speak the truth, my anxiety for you during your present illness has not been as intense as it was on a former occasion.

I have been a little anxious, however, for the last two or three days.

At the door leading from the east into the drawing room, stood Keshab's venerable mother.

Umanath said in a loud voice to the Master, 'Sir, here

is mother bowing down to you.'

The Master smiles, Umanath continues, 'Sir, mother asks you to bless him so that he may soon get well.' The Master replied, 'Let your prayers be offered up to the Divine Mother who is made of bliss everlasting. She it is who removes all troubles—all the ills that flesh is heir to.' Speaking to Keshab, again, the Master says:

All power comes from the Divine Mother

'It would be better for you not to stay in the inner apartment for long hours. With women and children about you, you run the risk of sinking in the sea of ignorance and of losing sight of the Lord. You shall feel better if words about the Lord are spoken to you by your friends.'

Solemn Warning to Keshab

Solemnly does the Master utter these words. Presently he passes into the state of a veritable child from that of a serious teacher. He smiles, and says, 'Keshab, let me look at your hand.' He takes it up on the palm of his own hand and gently tosses it up and down as if he were going to find its weight. At last he says, 'No, it is all right, your hand is light enough; it is only the hands of those that think evil that are not so.' (*Laughter.*)

Mother orders everything. But foolish man, who now is and the next moment goes out of sight into eternity, seeks to take all the credit to himself!

It is on two different occasions that the Lord smiles. Once when He finds two brothers dividing with a rope, the land left by their father, and saying, 'This is mine and that is thine!' He smiles, saying, 'The fools call the land their own, not knowing that the universe is Mine.'

And once again does the Lord smile. The child is dangerously ill and the physician says to the weeping mother, 'Fear not mother, I take it upon myself to see that your child gets well.' The fool of a physician knows not that it is the Lord that slays and no human power will be able to save! (*Absolute silence.*)

A fit of cough comes upon Keshab. It lasts for a long

time. The suffering of the venerable patient touches the heart of every one present. All look for the end of the fit with bated breath. The suffering has been great indeed. And Keshab must leave the room and go back to his sick bed. He falls down at the feet of the Master and bows down with his head touching the ground.

Keshab goes out of the room into his own chamber holding to the wall as before.

* * *

They have asked Sri Ramakrishna to take some sweetmeats before he leaves for the Temple at Dakshineswar. He is talking with the company present. Keshab's eldest son is seated by his side.

The Divine Mother to bless

Amrita says, 'This is his eldest son. Will you be so kind as to give him your blessings?' Amrita watches the Master gently stroking the young man. Amrita says again, 'Sir, will you not put your hand upon his head and bless.' The Master replied, 'It is not given to me to bless, it is for the Divine Mother to do so. All blessings come from Her.'

He smiles, and continues fondling the boy as before. Speaking of Keshab, the Master goes on saying to Amrita and other Brahmo devotees, all disciples of Keshab:

The Lord's prayer

It is not given to me to say of a person, 'Let him be healed.' Of my Divine Mother I never asked such power. My constant prayer is 'O ! Mother, do Thou grant that I may have Bhakti pure, sincere love for Thee, unmixed with worldly desires of any kind, like the weal of the body, pleasure, money, fame, &c. Never have I asked of Her the power of doing such miracles as the healing of diseases.'

Estimate of Keshab before the disciples

How great is Keshab—honoured alike by men of the world that seek for wealth and by holy men that seek for the love of God.

I once met Dayananda in a garden house. He expected Keshab on that day and was asking every body if Keshab had come up. In his yearning for Keshab he frequently left his room to make enquiries.

Dayananda called the Bengali language *Gouranga Bhasha* (the language of Gour).

Keshab, I suppose, did not believe in the Vedic gods and the efficacy of the Vedic sacrificial fire. So Dayananda had said, 'The Lord hath made so many things; could He not make the gods as well?'

The Master speaks highly of Keshab before his disciples.

Sri Ramakrishna (continuing): Keshab is free from the vulgar pride of the preceptor who comes in his own name.

Fame for the Master

Very often has he said to many of his disciples, 'Go to the Temple at Dakshineswar where you will have your doubts solved.' It is my way also to say, 'Let Keshab increase a million-fold.' What shall I do with fame?

Yes, Keshab is great, honoured alike by men of the world and by holy men who seek God alone.

The refreshment over, he will now leave for the Temple. The Brahmo devotees have stepped downstairs with him to see him off.

The Presence of the Mother in our home

Coming downstairs the Master observes there is no light on the ground floor at the foot of the stairs. He says to Amrita and others, 'All these places should be lighted, for the Divine Mother abides in every house. Such an omission leads to poverty. See that such an omission does not take place again.'

With two or three disciples Sri Ramakrishna sets out in a cab on his way back to the Temple.

SECTION VI

1883

A DAY WITH SRI RAMAKRISHNA AT THE TEMPLE AT DAKSHINESWAR

CHAPTER I

VEDANTA

The 19th of August 1883 is a Sunday, and the first day after the full moon. So the devotees have leisure to come and see their beloved Master at Dakshineswar, at the Temple of the Mother of the universe, the Consort of the Spirit of eternity. Everyone has free access. He talks with everybody who comes. His visitors are from all classes of people —Sannyasins, Paramahamsas; Hindus, Christians and Brahmos; Saktas, Vaishnavas and Saivas; men as well as women. Glory be unto Rani Rashmani whose goodness has erected this noble Temple where people are coming to see and worship this God-Man.

It is noon. The Master is seated upon the smaller bedstead in his room. He has taken a little rest after breakfast. Here M. comes and salutes him, falling at his hallowed feet. He bids him sit down and kindly enquires about the welfare of himself and family. A short while and the Master begins to talk with him upon the *Vedanta*.

Sri Ramakrishna (to M.) : Well, the *Ashtavakra Samhita* deals with the knowledge of Self. The knowers of the Self declare, 'I am He,' that is, 'I am that highest Self.' This is the view of all the Sannyasins belonging to the Vedantic school. But it is not good that a man of the world should hold such a view. Such a man does everything, and how at the same time can he be that highest Self, God the Absolute, who is beyond all action?

The Vedantists hold that the Self has no attachment

to anything. Pleasure, pain, virtue, &c., can never affect the Self in any way, but they do affect men who think that their soul is the same as the body.

Smoke can blacken only the wall but not the space through which it curls up.

There was a certain devotee, named Krishna Kishore, who used to say that he was a mere 'void', or empty space. He meant to say that he was the same as the highest Self or God the Absolute, who is sometimes likened to empty space because nothing can be predicated of Him. A true devotee, he had some right to say so. As for others it does not lie in their mouth to give out such an idea.

But it is good for everyone to cherish the idea that he is free. 'I am free, I am free'; if a man constantly says this, he is sure to be free. On the other hand, he who always thinks that he is in bondage, brings bondage, indeed, on himself in the end.

The weak-minded man who always says, 'I am a sinner, I am a sinner,' is sure to have a fall. A man should rather say, 'I repeat the holy name of God, how can there be any sin in me or the bondage of the world?'

Then turning towards M. he says, 'To-day my mind is not at ease. I hear from Hriday that he has been ailing much. Is this anxiety due to attachment or to the feeling of compassion?

M. did not know what to say in reply. M. remained silent.

Love to one's own and love to all or Compassion

Sri Ramakrishna: Do you know what is *Maya*? Love towards one's own father, mother, brother, sister, wife, children, nephew, niece &c., is called *Maya*; and compassion means loving all beings. Now, what is this, my anxiety, due to? Attachment or compassion?

But Hriday did a great deal for me. He served me much. He never hesitated to do all sorts of menial services for me. But he proved a scourge in the end; so much so that unable to stand such treatment, once I went to the ramparts to die by throwing myself into the Ganges flowing below. But let that go; my mind will be set at rest if now he gets some money.

Now whom am I to ask for money? Who cares to make an appeal to the Babus for this purpose?

At two or three o'clock in the afternoon, two of his disciples, Adhar and Balaram, came in. They prostrated themselves before him and took their seats. They asked how he was doing. The Master replied, 'Well, my body is all right; but not the mind.' He did not mention anything about Hriday's illness.

CHAPTER II

Master and Disciple

In the course of conversation when the talk was about the Goddess Singhavahini (the Goddess seated upon a lion) worshipped by the Mallick family of Barabazar, he said, 'Once I went to see the Goddess. She was staying with a certain family at Chashadhopapara, a district in Calcutta. The house was almost a deserted one. The family had become very poor. In some places there were filth and dirt lying about. In others mosses could be found growing. The cement upon the wall was crumbling down, brickdust and sand dropped slowly from the walls. Other houses belonging to the Mallicks are very neat and clean, but this was not so.'

Then turning towards M. he said, 'Well, can you explain, why this was the case?'

Unable to explain, M. remained silent.

Sri Ramakrishna: The thing is, every one must reap the fruit of his past actions. We should believe in the law of inherited tendencies, etc.

The Divine Presence in Images

One thing I saw in that deserted house. The face of the Goddess was beaming with glory. We should believe in the divine presence infilling the images of the deity.

I went to Vishnupura. The Raja has several fine temples. In one of the temples there is the image named Mrinmayi. A big tank is before the temple.

(To M.): But how is it that I smelt in the tank-water the spices that women used to perfume their hair with? I did not know that they offered such spices to the Goddess when they went to worship Her. When near the tank—and I had not seen Her image—I saw Her divine form up to Her waist in the water, and in *Samadhi*. The Mother of the universe appeared to me in *Samadhi* in the form of Mrinmayi.

Misfortune and Devotees

By this time other devotees arrived. The talk turned on the Kabul War, and the civil war that came after. One of the devotees gave the news that Yakub Khan had been deposed from the throne; and that he is a great devotee.

Sri Ramakrishna : Well, pleasure and pain, happiness and misery, are things that one cannot separate from the body. We read in Kavi Kandan's 'Chandi' that Kaluvira, a great devotee, was shut up in jail. They placed a heavy stone upon his breast. But Kalu was a highly-favoured child of the Mother of the universe!

The fact is, pleasure and pain, happiness and misery, come with the body.

How great a devotee was Srimanta! How fondly did the Divine Mother love his mother Khullana! But what an amount of trouble he had to go through! They took him to the scaffold to be executed.

A woodman— a great devotee—was fortunate enough to see the Divine Mother; and She loved and showed Her kindness towards him very much, but he had to go on with the business of the wood-cutter all the same. He must sell the firewood to get his livelihood.

It does not follow that a devoted lover of God must be very well-off in the world. He is rich in spirit, though he may be poor in worldly things. Devaki in prison saw God in the form of a human being holding conch-shell, disc, mace and lotus in His four hands. But she with all her god-vision could not get out of the prison.

M. : Get out of the prison! It seems to me that she should have got out of her body, too, that being the source of all her troubles.

Master : The thing is, the body is the fruit of one's past actions; so a man must bear with it, as long as his actions are not cleared. A blind man, taking a bath in the holy water of the Ganges, gets all his sins washed off. But his blindness keeps on all the same. It is the fruit of his actions in his past life.

M. : The shaft that has gone out of the bow must run out its race. One has ceased to have any hold on such a shaft.

Master : The body may be happy or miserable. But the true devotee is all the time rich in spirit—rich in knowledge and in the love of the Lord.

Take for instance the Pandavas. How many dangers and difficulties had they to face! What privations and trials to go through! But amidst all these they never lost their love and devotion to God. Can you find others equally wise and devoted to God?

CHAPTER III

WITH VIVEKANANDA AND IN SAMADHI

At this time Narendra and Viswanath Upadhyaya came in. Viswanath was the Nepalese Resident at Calcutta. The Master used to call him Captain, and hence all his disciples too called him by that name. Narendra was about 22 at that time, reading in the senior B.A. class. He used to come off and on to see the Master, especially on Sundays. Bowing down to him Narendra took his seat.

The Master asked him to sing. There was hanging from the western wall of the room a stringed musical instrument. Narendra took it down and began to turn its keys to raise the note of the strings to the necessary pitch to the accompaniment of *bawa* and *tabla* (musical instruments).

Every one was intently looking upon his face, eager to listen to his songs.

Master (smiling to Vivekananda): This instrument no longer sounds as before.

Captain : It is filled; therefore there is no sound even as with a vessel filled to the brim with water.

Master : But how do you explain the life of Narada and other divine teachers? They had realised God but they spoke. They were filled but they gave forth sounds.

Captain : They spoke for the good of mankind.

Master : Yes, that is so. Narada and Suka Deva came down from highest state of *Samadhi*. Their heart went out to those that were weary and heavy-laden and knew not God. They spoke for the good of others.

Vivekananda sang the following song:

SONG

When shall we realise in the temple of the heart, the all-good and all-gracious form of God, the only Reality? Constantly looking on Him, when shall we dive deep in the sea of that divine beauty?

Thou wilt come into my soul as Knowledge Absolute, as God Infinite. The dumbfounded mind, made restless by its intense joy, will then take refuge at Thy feet. Bliss, like embodied nectar sweet and life-giving, shall rise in the firmament of the soul. Looking at Thee thus manifest unto us, I shall be mad with joy, even as the bird *Chakora* is mad with joy at the sight of the moon.

I shall kill myself at Thy feet. O Beloved! and then the aim of my life will be realised. Thou art king of kings, one without a second, all-peaceful, all-gracious.

Thus, even in this life shall I enjoy heavenly bliss; O, what glorious privilege! When shall I look at Thy holy and pure Self? O, all impurities shall fly away from me before that glory, even as darkness flys away before the light!

Do Thou light in my heart a burning faith, that like the polestar is ever a sure (and infallible) guide. O, Thou Friend of the weak, do Thou thus fulfil my only desire. Thus lost in the infinite bliss of Thy love, I shall forget myself entirely, having Thee as mine own night and day! Oh, when is that to come about?

Sri Ramakrishna lost himself in deep *Samadhi* as soon as he heard the words, 'Bliss, like embodied nectar sweet and life-giving!' There he sat, with clasped hands, erect, turning his face eastward; diving deep into the ocean of beauty—the all-blissful Mother. No external consciousness! Breath had almost stopped; no sign of motion in any one of his limbs; no twinkle in the eyes! Sitting like one drawn in a picture! He had gone, somewhere away from this kingdom,—from this world of the senses!

The *Samadhi* ended. In the meantime, Narendra, seeing him in *Samadhi*, had gone out of the room to the eastern verandah. There Hazra was seated upon a blanket, telling his beads. Narendra began to talk with him.

Sri Ramakrishna's room by this time was filled with devotees. After the *Samadhi* had left him, the Master looked for Narendra in the room. He was not there. The *Tampura* was left on the floor! The devotees all had their looks fastened on the Master.

Master (referring to Narendra): He has lighted the fire. It matters not now whether he remains in the room or leaves it! (Then turning towards the Captain and the devotees) Meditate upon God, the sole existence, knowledge and bliss eternal, and you also shall have joy everlasting.

That Being of knowledge and bliss is always here and everywhere; only it is hidden from view by ignorance. The less is your attachment to the senses the more shall be your love towards God.

Captain : The more we near our home at Calcutta, the farther are we away from Kasi (Benares), and the more we near Kasi, the farther are we away from our home.

Master : As *Srimati* (Radha) was nearing Sri Krishna, she was getting the charming odour of His sweet person. Yes, the more one approaches God, the more does one's love towards Him increase. The more does the river near the sea, the more is it subject to ebb and flow.

The Knower and the Lover

Master : The Ganges of knowledge flowing in the soul of a wise man (a Vedantist) runs only in one direction. To him the whole universe is a dream. He always lives in his own true self. But the Ganges of love in a devotee's heart runs not in one direction. It has its ebb and flow. A devotee laughs, weeps, dances, sings. He wants sometimes to merge into his Beloved. He swims in Him, dives and rises up in his joy as merrily as a lump of ice dances upon water.

God the Absolute and God the Creator

But in fact God the Absolute[1] and God the creator[2] are one and the same being. God the Absolute, Knowledge-Intelligence-Bliss, is the same as the All-Knowing, All-Intelligent, and All-Blissful Mother of the universe. The bright precious stone and its brightness cannot be separated in thought, for you cannot think of the stone without its brightness; nor can you think of the brightness apart from the stone.

The Absolute, Knowledge-Intelligence-Bliss, the Undifferentiated, is differentiated into the One and the Many. He has various names applied to Him according to the various powers manifested. That is the reason of His having many forms. Hence the devotee has sung, 'O my Divine Mother, Thou art even all that.' Wherever there is action, such as creation, preservation and destruction, there is Sakti or Intelligent Energy. But water is water whether it moves or not. That One Absolute, Knowledge-Intelligence-Bliss, is also the eternally Intelligent Energy, who creates and preserves and destroys the universe. Thus it is the same Captain whether he does not do anything or performs his worships or visits the Governor-General. In all cases it is the same Captain. Only those are his different *Upadhis* or adjuncts.

Captain : Yes, Sir, that is so.

Master : I said this to Keshab Sen.

Captain : Well, Sir, Mr. Keshab Sen does not respect our Hindu manners, customs and laws. How can he be a real saint? He is a Babu,—not a holy man.

Master (smiling and turning towards the devotees): Captain always wants me never to go to Keshab Sen.

Captain : But your holiness must go. What can I do?

Master (sharply): You go to the Governor-General

[1] Brahman. [2] Sakti.

who, according to your Sastras, is a *mlechha* (non-Aryan); and for money too! And may I not go to Keshab Sen? He meditates upon God, utters His name! It does not lie in your mouth to say so-you who often say, 'It is God who has in the process of differentiation become the human soul and the world itself!' What you say you must mean, what you mean you must say!

After this Sri Ramakrishna abruptly left the room and went to the north-eastern verandah. The Captain and other devotees remained waiting for him in the room. Only M. accompanied him to the verandah where Narendra was talking with Hazra. Sri Ramakrishna knew that Hazra posed as an out-and-out monist—all dry. He would say, 'All the universe is a mere dream. All kinds of worship and offerings are mental delusions. God is the one changeless entity. A man should meditate upon His Self and nothing else, and so on.'

Master (laughing): Hallo! What are you talking about?

Narendra (laughing): We are talking about themes too big for ordinary mortals.

Master (laughing): But however you may talk, know that pure selfless devotion and pure selfless knowledge are both one and the same thing. The goal is the same. Smooth and easy is the path of devotion leading to God.

Narendra : Yes, there is no use of reasoning after the philosopher. 'Make me mad with Thy love, O mother?'

(To M.) : Sir, I have been reading Hamilton, and he writes, 'A learned ignorance is the end of Philosophy and the beginning of Religion.'

Master (to M.) : What is the meaning of that?

Narendra explained it in Bengali. Sri Ramakrishna laughed and thanked him in English, saying, 'Thank you.' Everyone laughed at this, for the Master's knowledge of English was confined, at most to half-a-dozen such expressions.

CHAPTER IV

AN EVENING SCENE

Evening was drawing nigh. The devotees one after another took leave of the Master; and so did Narendra.

The day was drawing to a close. It was almost evening. The temple servants were arranging the lights. The two priests of Kali and Vishnu were busy making their prayers as they stood up to their waist in the sacred waters of the Ganges, purifying themselves, body and soul. They were shortly to go into their respective temples to perform the *aratrika* ceremony—the waving of lighted lamps &c., beofre the images of the deity, and other evening services. The young men of Dakshineswar had come with their friends to take a walk round the garden. They strolled about the rampart with their walking sticks, and enjoyed the sweet evening breeze made fragrant by the flowers. They watched the slightly-undulating breast of the swift-flowing Ganges of the month of August. Some of them, perhaps more thoughtful, might be found walking about by themselves in the solitude of the sacred trees called the Panchavati. Sri Ramakrishna also looked on the Ganges for some time from the western verandah.

It was evening, the lamp-lighter had lighted all the lamps of the big Temple. The old maid-servant came and lit the lamp in Sri Ramakrishna's room and burnt incense there. In the meantime the *aratrika* ceremony began in the twelve shrines dedicated to Siva. It began soon after, in the temples of the Mother of the universe, and of Sri Vishnu. The united and solemn sound of gongs, bells and cymbals, grew more solemn and sweet, re-echoed by the murmuring Ganges.

It was the first lunar day after the full-moon. A short while after night-fall the moon rose. Gradually the tops of the garden trees and the big temple compound were bathed in balmy light. At her magic touch the waters of the Ganges shone bright like silver, dancing along with great joy.

The Master, just after the evening, bowed down to the Mother of the universe. He repeated the holy names of God, keeping time by clapping his hands. In his room were pictures of various manifestations of God and of God-men. There were Sri Gouranga with His devotees singing the praises of God; the Baby Krishna with His mother Yasoda; the Goddess of Learning; the Mother Kali; Dhruva; Prahlada; Sri Rama crowned; Sri Radha Krishna, etc. He bowed down to every manifestation of God, as drawn in the pictures, repeating Their holy names. He repeated his favourite sayings, all having a grand unifying principle running through them:

Brahma — Atma — Bhagavan (*i.e.*), God the Absolute (God of the philosopher), God of the Yogi, and God of the devotee are three in one, one in three.

Bhagavata — Bhakta — Bhagavan : the Word, the devotee and the God of the devotee are three in one, one in three.

Brahma-Sakti, Sakti-Brahma, (God the Absolute is the same as God the Mother.)

Veda-Purana-Tantra. (The various Scriptures and their one theme *viz.*, God.)

Gita-Gayatri.

Saranagata. (I am thine, I am thine.)

Naham, naham—Tuhu-tuhu (not I, not I, but Thou; Thou art the true actor; I am only an instrument in Thy hands.)

Ami Yantra, Tumi Yantri (I am the instrument, Thou art the being who uses the instrument) &c., &c.

After all these repetitions were over, he meditated upon the Mother Divine with clasped hands.

Some of the devotees had been walking about in the garden during the evening. When the *aratrika* ceremonies were over in the temples, they came together one after another into Sri Ramakrishna's room. He was sitting upon the bedstead. M., Adhar, Kishori, &c., were sitting before him on the floor.

Master : Narendra (Vivekananda), Rakhal, and Bhavanath—these are *Nityasiddhas* (perfect even from their birth). They need no training. What training they go through is more than they need. You see, Narendra never cares for any one. He was going with me in the Captain's carriage the other day. When the Captain requested him to sit upon the seat of honour, he did not mind him at all. Moreover, he never shows to me that he knows anything lest I praise him before men. He has no *Maya*, no attachment. He looks as if he is free from all bondage. He is very polite in his manners. For a single individual, he has very many good and noble qualities, such as reading, writing, singing and playing upon musical instruments. At the same time he knows how to control his senses. He has said that he will not marry. Narendra and Bhavanath are affinities. Narendra does not come to me very often. That is good. For I always fall into *Samadhi* whenever I see him and do not know what to do.

SECTION VII

1884

VISIT TO SURENDRA'S GARDEN

CHAPTER I

THE MASTER SINGING AND DANCING WITH HIS DISCIPLES

On the 16th of June 1884, Sunday, the sixth lunar day (dark fortnight) of *Jaishtha*, Sri Ramakrishna was invited by one of his beloved disciples Surendra, a householder, to a feast at his garden-house at Kankurgachi near Calcutta. These invitations were invariably occasions for the gathering of his disciples, followers and admirers. They were really occasions of festivity and rejoicing, on which the name of God was chanted to the accompaniment of *mridangas* and other musical instruments. At these times the Master could be seen at his best,—singing and dancing with the joy of the Lord and frequently lost in that blessed state of the soul, in the enjoyment of God-consciousness, called *Samadhi*.

On this occasion, when the singing of devotional hymns and the spiritual excitement which came with it were over, the company present was treated by the Master to one of those divine talks so laden with sermons for the spiritual welfare of humanity—to a veritable 'feast of reason and flow of soul'—which shall linger in the memory of those that had the rare good fortune, the privilege, to listen to them.

The first part of the day was given to *Sankirtan* (the singing forth of the name of the Lord). They were singing the songs, telling of the separation of the Gopis from the Lord Sri Krishna who had gone to Mathura.

The Gopis were the milk-maids of Brindaban who loved the Lord Sri Krishna then living in their midst as a shepherd-boy. Sri Krishna is looked upon as an incarnation of God. He loved and was loved by everybody. He is the personification of divine love. When eleven years old he left Brindaban.

In the course of the songs the Master was frequently in a state of *Samadhi* (divine ecstasy).

They are singing. Suddenly he rises to his feet saying, 'O my friend, do thou bring my beloved Krishna to me, or take me over to the place where He is.'

The Master has lost his own personality in that of Radha, the first among the Gopis. He realises that he and Radha are one.

The Master in Samadhi

With these words he stands speechless and motionless, with fixed half-closed eyes, evidently losing all sense-consciousness. Coming to himself again, he in a voice that draws tears from the eyes of those that hear him, cries out, 'O my friend, do me this favour, and I shall be thy most devoted servant. Remember, it was thou who didst teach me my love for the Beloved.'

The chorus goes on singing. Radha is made in the song to say, 'O! I will not go to the bank of the Jamuna to draw water; for coming up to the Kadamba tree, I am put in mind of my own, my Beloved.'

The Master, heaving a sigh, says 'Ah me!' The chorus chanting aloud the name of the Lord, Sri Ramakrishna is again on his feet and in *Samadhi*.

Getting back his sense-consciousness, he can only say inarticulately 'Kistna, Kistna,' for 'Krishna, Krishna.' The proceedings are brought to a close by the Master himself leading the chorus in the well-known piece 'Victory to Radha, victory to Govinda.' He dances with his disciples who form a ring round him.

The Madness of Love for the Lord

The dancing and singing all take place in the reception hall. The Master then withdraws into one of the adjoining rooms to the west.

To M., one of the disciples, the Master talking of the Gopis says, 'How wonderful is their devotion! At the sight of the Tamal tree they were seized with the very madness of love.'

Disciple : This was also the case with Chaitanya Deva. Looking at the forest, he thought it was Brindaban that was before him!—the sacred city, the birth-place of Sri Krishna.

Master : Oh ! If any one is but favoured with a single particle of this ecstatic love (Prema)! What devotion! Of this devotion they had not only the full complement (sixteen annas) but a great deal more than the full complement—five *Sikas*, five annas.

The One Thing Needful

It is immaterial whether or not one believes in the incarnation of Radha and Krishna. One may believe (like the Hindu or the Christian) in God's incarnation; one may not. But let all have a yearning—this intensity of love for the Lord. That is the one thing needful.

If you must be mad, be not so for things of this world. But be mad with the love of the Lord.

He then comes back into the hall (the disciples coming after him) and seats himself.

Purity

A bolster is placed there for his use. Before touching it, he says, *Om Tat Sat*—The Lord is the only reality. The pillow is of course a thing which has been made impure by the unholy touch of worldly men and the Master is purity itself.

It is getting late, but no dinner is being served. The Master becomes a little impatient. He is like a child.

Surendra is the host. He is a beloved disciple of Sri Ramakrishna.

Serve only the Lord

The Master says, 'Surendra's disposition has grown admirable. He is very outspoken. He is always bold enough to speak the truth. Then he is generous. Those who go to him for help never come back disappointed.'

Master (to M.) : You went to Bhagavan Dass. What sort of man is he?

Here comes Niranjan, a young disciple of Sri Ramakrishna. The Master stands up saying, 'O ! You are come after all!' He is filled with joy.

Master (to M.) : This young man is remarkably free from guile. Openness as opposed to dissimulation is the fruit of the practice of a good many religious austerities in one's previous incarnations.

Freedom from Guile

In that well-known song by Tulsi Dass—'Oh my brother! Do thou cling to God,' occur the words 'give up dissimulation and cunning.' Do you not see that whenever God has taken a human form this great virtue of guilelessness has never failed to come to view? Look at Dasaratha, the father of Rama, and at Nanda Ghosh, the father of Sri Krishna. They were all free from guile.

Master (to Niranjan) : Like men of the world you have accepted service. But you are working for your mother. Otherwise, I should have said, 'For shame! For shame! The Lord alone you must serve.'

The Service of the Lord

Master (to Mani Mallick) : This young man is open and guileless to a degree; only, now-a-days he tells fibs a little, that is all. The other day he said that he would come to see me, but he did not!

Referring to the same disciple, the Master says 'A change for the worse has come over his face. It seems a dark shadowy film has spread over it. All this is due to office work. There are the accounts and a hundred other different matters to attend to!'

The Curse of Serving the World

Bhavanath is another disciple of his. He is talking to his fellow-disciple M.

Bhavanath (to M.): You have not been to the Lord's place for a long time. The Master was talking to me about your absence and was asking me whether it was a fact that he (the Master) had turned out to be an object of disrelish to you.

Anxiety for a Disciple

Sri Ramakrishna who has heard everything says kindly to M., 'Quite so. Why is it that you did not come?' Poor M. could only stammer out some lame excuses. Here comes in Mahima.

Master (to Mahima): This is indeed a visit quite unexpected! We expect a boat at most in this poor river of ours. But here comes a ship! But then it is the rainy season. (*Laughter.*)

The conversation next turns on the spiritual aspect of feasts.

Master (to Mahima): Why is it that people are fed in a feast? Do you not think it comes to offering a sacrifice to God who is the living fire in all creatures!

But bad men, not god-fearing, guilty of adultery, fornication, etc., should on no account be entertained at a feast. Their sins are so great that several cubits of the earth beneath the place where they eat become polluted.

On one occasion Hriday gave a feast. A considerable number of those that were invited were sinful men. I said to Hriday, 'Look here! If you feed these wicked people, I shall leave the house at once.'

Master (to Mahima): Somebody said that formerly you used very often to give feasts. I dare say your household and other expenses have since multiplied.

CHAPTER II

The European Idea of Work

Protap Chandra Majumdar, a member of the Brahmo Samaj, comes and salutes Sri Ramakrishna. He returned his salutation with his accustomed modesty, bowing down very low.

Protap: Sir, I had recently been to Darjeeling.

Sri Ramakrishna: But you do not appear to be much the better for the change. What's the matter with you?

Protap: The same complaint to which he (Keshab Chandra Sen) succumbed.

There is then a talk on Keshab's life. Protap takes part in the conversation and says, 'Keshab was in his youth marked by non-attachment to the world. He was seldom found merry or cheeful. While a student at the Hindu College, he formed a close friendship with S. Thus it was that he came across S's revered father Devendranath Tagore. Keshab assiduously practised communion both by meditation and devotion. He was subject even to fits of unconsciousness due to excessive devotion, but he always succeeded in keeping them in check. The great end of his life was to bring religion within the reach of the householder.'

Desire for Fame

The conversation next turns on a certain Mahratta lady. Protap says that she had been to England and that she had embraced Christianity. He asks the Master whether he has ever heard of the lady. The Master replies, 'No; but from what I hear from you I should think that she must be a woman who wants to make a name for herself!'

Egotism

Master (Turning to the company): Egotism of this kind is to be condemned. Those that seek fame are under a delusion. They forget that everything is ordered by the Great Disposer of all things— the Supreme Being—and that all the credit is due to the Lord and to nobody else. It is the wise that say always, 'It is Thou. It is Thou, O Lord!' but the ignorant and the self-deluded say, 'It is I, It is I.'

Parable of the Calf and its Fortunes

The calf says, 'Hamma or Aham (I),' Now look at the troubles caused by its self which says 'I, 'I.' In the first place, the calf, sometimes, is taken into the fields where it is yoked to the plough. It is there made to work on from morning to evening alike in the sun and in the rain. Its troubles are not yet over. It is very often killed by the butcher. Its flesh is eaten as meat. Its skin is tanned into hides. It is made into shoes. The sufferings of the calf in this state know no bounds. But that is not all. Drums are made with the skin, which is thus mercilessly beaten sometimes with the hand and sometimes with a stick. It is only when out of its entrails are made strings for the bow used for carding cotton that the troubles of the poor creature are over. And that is because it no longer says, '*hamma*' '*hamma*' but 'Tuhum! Tuhum!' (It is Thou, O Lord, It is Thou!).

The perfect liberation of the soul is within the reach of him alone who, being convinced that God is the disposer of all things, has learnt the lesson of complete self-abnegation and absolute forgetfulness of 'I,' 'Me,' 'Mine.'

The self after God-vision

The truly wise man is he who has seen the Lord. He becomes like a child. The child, no doubt, seems to have an individuality, a separateness, of its own. But that individuality is a mere appearance, not a reality. The self of the child is nothing like the self of the grown-up man.

He has seen the Lord and he is now a changed being.

The steel sword has no sooner come in contact with the touchstone than it is turned into gold. It continues no doubt to have the appearance of a sword, but it does no harm to anybody. Our ego of self, if purified by the realisation of God—if made pure by seeing God—cannot harm anybody.

The self of the child is again like the face reflected in the mirror. The face in the mirror looks exactly like the real face; only it does nobody any harm.

Signs of God-vision

The signs of one who has seen God are these: His conduct is like that of a child. He sometimes looks like an unclean spirit. He does not care for his body. He seems to make no distinction between purity and impurity; for he sees God in and through everything. Such a person looks like a mad man, now laughing, now weeping, and the next moment talking to himself; now dressed like a gentleman and again taking his only bit of cloth under his arm and thus going naked like a child. Next he looks probably like one who is brought to the state of, an insentient being—the condition of an inert, lifeless, material body.

England & America

Master (to Protap Majumdar): You went to England and America. Tell me of your experiences.

Protap : Sir, the national characteristics of the English people may be summed up by one word, namely, the worship of what you call *kanchan* (gold). I must say, however, there are a few honourable exceptions. As a general rule, *Rajas* or worldly activity is the one thing everywhere. Much the same thing is observable in America.

Sri Ramakrishna : The attachment to work which you say is the chief characteristic of the English and the American people marks all human communities. But remember, it is a mark of the earliest stage of life. Work for the sake of one's own worldly good—riches, honour, fame—is degrading. Worldly activity will only bring an increasing ignorance. It will make you forgetful of God and attached to 'Woman and Gold'. Therefore the attachment to work that is observable in England and America—an attachment leading to spiritual degradation—is to be condemned.

Work without Attachment

You cannot get rid of work, because Nature will lead you on to it. That being so, let all work be done as it ought to be. If work is done unattached, it will lead to God. Work so done is a means to the end, and God is the end.

To work without any attachment is to work without the expectation of any reward or fear of any punishment in this world or the next.

Difficulty of the Problem in this age

Work without attachment, however, is exceedingly difficult, especially in this age. The fact is, one must have true knowledge or love of God. It is possible for the ideal man alone to live a life of work without attachment. Others get easily attached more or less to things of the world and they know it not.

Hence it is our duty as imperfect men to find out, if possible, the shortest path that leads to God—the end of our life. Let us do the duty that is nearest us. Let us bring down our work to a minimum by earnest prayer and self-surrender.

Problem solved for this Age

Thus on account of the difficulty of work without attachment in this age, communion by prayer, devotion and love—by the practice of Narada's Bhakti Yoga—has been enjoined as better adapted to this age than the communion by work or communion by the path of knowledge or philosophy.

Communion by love (of God) will enable us to see God with much less difficulty than by any other kind of communion.

Effect of Devotion upon work

No one, however, can avoid work. Every mental operation is 'work.' The consciousness that 'I feel' or 'I think' involves 'work.' What is meant by the 'Path of Devotion' in its relation to work is that work is simplified by devotion, or love (of God).

In the first place, this love of God reduces the quantity of one's work by fixing one's mind upon one's highest ideal —namely, God. Secondly it helps one to work unattached. One cannot love the Lord and at the same time love riches or pleasure or fame or power. He who has once tasted the drink prepared with *ola* sugarcandy does not care for that made with molasses.

Work Is not the End of Life

No greater mistake can be committed than to look upon work as the be-all and the end-all of human life. Work is the first chapter of human life. God is the conclusion.

On one occasion, Sambhu, a householder, said to me, 'I should deem myself fortunate if I could build hospitals and dispensaries, lay roads where there are none, sink wells for the good of the people in seasons of drought, set up schools and colleges.' Thereupon I said to him, 'It is all very well that you should do all these works, but can you do them unattached? If you can, it will lead to God. Otherwise not. But to work unattached is exceedingly difficult. In any case, take care and do not confound the means with the end. Work is a means, if done unattached, but the *end* of life is to see God. Let me repeat that the means should not be confounded with the end—that the first stage on a road should not be taken for the goal.

'No, do not regard work as the be-all and the end-all—the ideal of human existence. Pray for Bhakti (devotion to God). Suppose you are fortunate enough to see God. Then what would you pray for? Would you pray for dispensaries and hospitals, tanks and wells, roads and serais? No, no, these are realities to us so long as we do not see God. But once placed face to face with the vision Divine, we see them as they are—transitory things no better than dreams; and then we would pray for more light—more knowledge in the highest sense—more divine love—the love which lifts us up from man to God, a love which makes us realise that we are really sons of the Supreme Being,—of whom all that can be said is that He exists, that He is knowledge itself in the highest sense, and that He is the eternal fountain of love and bliss.'

Therefore, never lose sight of this goal of life that I have pointed out to you. Never lose sight of the ideal.In this connection I will tell you a parable: A man was cutting wood in a forest, when he was accosted by a *Brahmacharin*.

The Wood-cutter and The Brahmacharin or Go on ahead

(A *Brahmacharin* is a holy man practising control over the flesh and preparing for the next stage of life—that of the householder or of the ascetic.) The holy man said, 'Go ahead!' The wood-cutter came back home with his load of wood, wondering why the sage had bade him go ahead. Thus passed away some days. One day he was put in mind of the holy man's words and he made up his mind that day to go farther deep into the forest to cut wood. What was his surprise to find that portion of the forest full of sandal trees! Of course, he brought cartloads of sandalwood to market and soon grew enormously rich. In this way again some days passed, when he was once more reminded of the injunction laid upon him by the holy man, 'Go ahead!' So again did he form the resolution of going into the forest and of making a further advance. What was his surprise to find a silver mine close to the bed of a river! This he had never looked for even in his dreams. He worked at the mines and brought away tons of silver with which he made a splendid bargain. It is needless to say that after this he turned out to be one of the millionaires of the day. But once more after the lapse of some years did the holy man's words come back to his mind. He thought within himself, 'The holy man did not bid me stop at the silver mine but he told me to go onward.' This time he went across the river and came upon a gold mine and finally on a diamond mine! Needless to add, that he grew as rich as the god of wealth, Kubera himself.

So go ahead, my children, and never lose sight of your ideal! Go onward and never stop until you have reached the goal. Reaching a particular stage, do not run away with the idea that you have come to your journey's end.

Work is only the first stage of the journey. Bear in mind that doing acts unattached is exceedingly difficult, that therefore the path of love is better suited to this age, and that work, even if unattached, is not the end of your life but only a means to the end.

So march on and never halt till you have come up to the great ideal of your life—that of seeing God.

CHAPTER III

Sri Ramakrishna, the Brahmo Samaj and the One thing Needful

The Schism in the Brahmo Samaj

The next subject of this conversation was the schism in the Brahmo Samaj following upon the passing away of Keshab.

Master (to Protap): I hear there is a difference between you and other members of your Samaj. Amongst your opponents, as far as I have seen them, there are many, Horay, Palla and Pancha (men of ordinary calibre).

With one of those bewitching smiles which made his face radiant with a sort of celestial glory, the Master pointing to Protap said to the company present, 'You see the conch-shells—Protap, Amrita, etc., give a loud powerful sound. But there are conch-shells and conch-shells! Others there are that are not at all sonorous. They do give no sound at all.

All the company present had a good laugh.

The conversation then turns on lectures given by members of religious bodies like Brahmo Samaj and Hari Sabha.

Sri Ramakrishna: One can form an estimate of the man from the lectures he delivers. S. was lecturing as the preceptor of a certain Hari Sabha. In the course of his speech he said, 'The Lord is totally devoid of sweetness. That being so, we must make Him sweet by lending to Him the sweetness of our own nature.' By sweetness he meant love and other divine attributes. When I came to hear this, I was put in mind of the boy who said that in his maternal uncle's house there were a good many horses. Of this the boy tried to convince his hearers by saying that a whole cow-house was full of horses. Of course the intelligent audience could at once see that cow-house was not exactly the place intended for horses, that the youngster must have told a lie, and that he had no experience or knowledge of horses.

God is Love

To say that God is devoid of sweetness, love, joy, bliss and other attributes, is an absurdity which proves that the speaker is totally ignorant of what he is saying and that he has never realised the Supreme Being, who is the fountain of eternal love, wisdom and bliss.

(Becoming serious and turning to Protap): You are an educated and intelligent man. You are not lighthearted but grave and serious. Keshab and you were like the brothers Gour (Chaitanya Deva) and Nitai. You have had enough of this world — enough of lectures, controversies, schisms and the rest. Is it not so? Your soul must be wearied by this

Love of God and Renunciation

time. It is high time now to have one aim—to give your attention to God alone—to plunge, to dive deep into the immortal sea of His love.'

Majumdar: Yes, Sir, I see that is the one thing needful. No doubt of it. All that I seek is to keep Keshab's work alive.

Egoism and Altruism

Master (smiling): You say indeed that you seek to keep Keshab's work going; well, wait a few days and you shall think otherwise. A person lived comfortably in a hut built upon a rock. He had to work hard to get the hut built. A few days after, there was a terrible storm. The hut seemed to reel on its foundation. In his anxiety to save it, he prayed to the god of winds saying, 'Lord be good enough not to pull down my hut.' The god turned a deaf ear to his words and the hut was about to come down with a crash. It now occurred to him that Hanuman was the son of the god of winds. So he cried out, 'Do not pull down the hut, O Father, its owner is no less a person than thine own son, Hanuman!' But the storm blew on with as much fury as ever and the hut was about to come down. In vain did he cry out over and over again, 'It is Hanuman's own house! It is Hanuman's own'! He then made a fresh appeal, saying, 'It is Lakshman's hut! O god, spare it!' Lakshman being the brother of Rama, the incarnation of God, and the hero of the epic Ramayana. But Lakshman's name carried as little weight as the name of Hanuman, and the hut was ready to come down with a crash; so the man cried out in the last resort, 'It is Rama's house, spare it, O it is Rama's house, spare it, O god of winds!'

The god of winds was inexorable and the hut began to come down with a crash. Seeing all his appeals had been made in vain, the man rushed out of the hut and cursed, saying, 'It is the devil's own hut! (*Laughter*) It is the devil's!'

You may be anxious to preserve Keshab's name. But console yourself with the thought that it was after all owing to God's will that the religious movement connected with his name was set on foot, and that if the movement has had its day, it is all owing to that same divine will.

Therefore dive deep into the sea.

And the Master sang:

SONG

DIVE DEEP, O MIND

1. Dive deep, dive deep, dive deep, O my mind! into the sea of beauty.
Make a search in the regions lower, lower down under the sea; you will come by the jewel, the wealth of *Prema* (intense love of God).

2. Within thy heart is the abode of the God of love. Go about searching, go about searching, go about searching; you will find it.
Then shall burn without ceasing the lamp of divine wisdom.

3. Who is that Being that doth steer a boat on land—on land on solid ground? Says *Kabir*, 'Listen, listen, meditate on the hallowed feet of the Lord, the Divine Preceptor.'

Fear not, it is the sea of immortality. I once said to Narendra (Vivekananda):

Majumdar (interrupting): Who is this Narendra?

Master : Oh, there is a young man of that name. Well, I said to Narendra, 'God is like a sea of liquid sweet, would you not dive deep into this sea? Suppose, my boy, there is a vessel with a wide mouth containing the syrup of sugar, and suppose you are a fly anxious to drink of the sweet liquid. Where would you sit and drink?' Narendra said to me in reply that he would like to drink from the edge of the vessel, adding that if he chanced to come to a point beyond his depth he was sure to be drowned and thus to lose his life. Thereupon I said to him, 'You forget, my boy, that if you dive deep into the divine sea, you need not be afraid of death or of any danger. Remember the divine sea is the sea of immortality. The syrup of this sea never causes death but gives everlasting life. *Be not afraid like some foolish persons that you may 'run to excess in your love of God.'*

What is the difference between charity and self-love?

Charity and Self-Love

Charity is love extending to all and not confined to one's own self, family, sect or country. Self-love is attachment to one's own self, family, sect or country. Cherish the first, which is elevating and will lead you Godward. Self-love is ruinous to the soul and will only take you down-hill.

What is the knowledge in the highest sense? The

True Knowledge

wise man says, 'Oh! Lord, Thou art the sole actor in this universe. I am only an humble instrument in Thy hands. Again, nothing is *mine*. Everything is *Thine*. Myself, my family, my riches, my virtues are all *Thine*.'

'Thou and Thine' is true knowledge;[1] 'I and mine' is ignorance.

Work without devotion to God has in this age no

Charitable and Other Works

legs to stand upon. It is a foundation of sand. First, cultivate devotion. All other things — schools, dispensaries, etc., shall, if you like, be added unto you. First devotion, then work. Work, apart from devotion or love of God, is helpless and cannot stand.

Protap made enquiries about the disciples. He asked whether those that came to the Master were getting better in the spirit day by day.

Master : I place before them the ideal life of a maid-servant—a nurse—as teaching them how to live in this world.

The maid-servant says with reference to her master's

The Problem for The Householder

house, 'This is our house'. All the while she knows that the house is not her own, and that her own house is far away in a distant village. Her thoughts are all sent forth to her village home. Again, referring to her master's child in her arms, she would say, 'My Hari (that being the name of the child)

[1] Jnana.

has grown very wicked' or 'My Hari likes to eat this or that thing,' and so on. But all the while she knows for certain that Hari is not her own. I tell those that come to me to lead a life unattached like this maid servant. I tell them to live unattached to this world—to be in the world, but not of the world—and at the same time to have their mind fixed on God—the heavenly home from whence all come. I tell them to pray for the love of God (*Bhakti*), which will help them to live so.

After a short interval the conversation turns on the

Agnoticism in The West

agnosticism of Europe and America. Majumdar said, 'Whatever people in the West may profess to be, none of them, as it seems to me, is an atheist at heart. The European savants do admit an unknown Power behind the universe.

Master : Well, it is sufficient if they believe in *Sakti*,—the Power ruling the universe.

Majumdar : They also admit the moral government of the universe.

Protap rising to take leave, the Master says to him, 'What shall I say? It is better that you cease to have anything to do with all those things (schisms, controversies &c.)'.

RENUNCIATION (A PARTING APPEAL)

'Woman (carnality) and attachment to gold, remember, keep men immersed in worldliness and away from God. It is remarkable that everybody has nothing but praise for his own wife, be she good, bad or indifferent.'

Here Majumdar left.

SECTION VIII

1884

VISIT TO A HINDU PANDIT AND PREACHER

Place—College Street, Calcutta.

Date—Rathayatra, 25th June 1884, 4 P. M. to 6-30 P.M., the second lunar day of Ashadha (bright fortnight).

THE MASTER IN SAMADHI

Sri Ramakrishna was about to get into a carriage which was to take him to the house of Pandit Sasadhar. He was then in *Samadhi*, that 'blessed and serene mood' in which the place of all sense-consciousness is taken by pure God-consciousness—a mood which he called His *avesh*. In this state the Yogi is carried away into the super-sensual world.

It was about 4 P.M. It was drizzling a little when he set out from Ishan's house. The roads were covered with mud. The disciples followed the carriage on foot. They were eager to assist at what promised to be an interesting meeting. It being the day of the Car-festival, they found on their way, children playing and blowing their pipes of palm leaves. The Master's carriage drew up at the entrance door, and he was warmly received by the host and his people.

Coming upstairs the Master met Sasadhar advancing towards him. He appeared to be a middle-aged man, was of fair complexion and had a rosary of *Rudraksha* beads thrown round his neck. He came forward with reverential air, saluted the Master and led him into the parlour which was intended for his reception. The disciples and others all went after him and seated themselves as near him as they could. . .

Among the many disciples present were Narendra M., Rakhal and Ram.

Master (smiling in his semi-conscious state and approvingly): Very well! Very well! Well, what kind of lectures are you in the habit of giving?

Sasadhar : Sir, I try to bring out the truths taught by the holy scriptures.

Master: For this age, it is communion with God by love, devotion and self-surrender as practised by the Rishi Narada that is enjoined. There is hardly time for doing the various works laid upon man by the scriptures.

Communion by Love and Not by Work

Do you not see that the well-known decoction of the ten medicinal roots is not the medicament for fevers of the present day? The patient runs the risk of being carried off, before the medicine has time to take effect. Fever mixture is, therefore, the order of the day.

Look here. Teach them work if you like. But do so, weighing the fish minus the head and the tail. I tell people not to trouble themselves with long rituals like *Sandhya* and the rest of it, but to say only the shorter form, *Gayatri.*

Workers like Ishan are exceptions. You are welcome to talk of work to such people if you must, and of conduct enjoined by the scriptures.

Worldly Men

Your lectures cannot possibly make any impression upon those who are immersed in worldliness.

Is it possible to drive nails into a stone? Should you make an atempt to do so, the chances are that the nails would sooner have their heads broken than make any impression on the stone.

The crocodile will in vain be struck with the sword or spear.

The mendicant's bowl made of gourd shell may have been to the four corners of India which a holy man is required to visit, but it still remains as bitter in taste as ever.

Therefore I say to such men, your lectures shall prove

useless. They are sure to remain as worldly as ever in spite of them.

Experience for a Religious Teacher

But I dare say you will become wiser with added experience. The calf is not able to stand upon its legs all at once. It drops down at first as it tries to do so. But it is precisely in this way that it at last learns to walk.

The Effect of First Love on the Power of Discrimination

It is not your fault that you cannot know the godly from the worldly-minded. When a strong wind blows, it raises the dust and makes it difficult for one to know one kind of tree from another; for instance, the mango from the tamarind. So in you is blowing, for the first time, the strong wind of first love. You cannot know the godly from the worldly-minded. They are the same to you.

Giving up of Work and Realisation

It is possible for him alone to give up all work who has seen, who has realised, God. The question arises, how long should rituals and other ceremonial works be practised? The answer is, the term of these is over as soon as there are tears visible in the eyes and horripilation at the sacred name of God.

When you say, 'Om Rama!' and when immediately tears stand in your eyes, then know it for certain that the term of your work is over. Then you are at liberty to give up all rituals and routine exercises. You have risen above work. When the fruit appears, the blossoms drop off. The love which realises God is the fruit. Work is the blossom.

When the daughter-in-law of the house is found to be with child, the mother-in-law takes care that her household duties become less and less every day. When it is the tenth month with her, she almost ceases to work.

Sandhya loses itself in *Gayatri*. *Gayatri* loses itself in *Om*, the sacred symbol in the Vedas for *Brahman*, the Absolute and Unconditioned. *Om* in the end loses itself in *Samadhi* (pure God-consciousness.)

The sound of the bell is symbolical of these states.

Dong (or the sound of the bell) gradually loses itself in Infinity. This symbolises the sound perceived by the Yogi as proceeding from the Absolute and being then lost in the Absolute.

In the same way, Karma (religious exercises like the *Sandhya*) in the end loses itself in *Samadhi*,—pure God-consciousness.

Thus the realisation of God cuts short work.

The Master is talking of *Samadhi*, and once more his mood goes through a remarkable change. A strange heavenly expression comes over his sweet, radiant face. He loses all sense-consciousness. Remaining speechless in this state for a time, he says, as is his wont, 'Give me a little water.'

The call for water is, as a general rule, a sure sign of the Master coming down to the plane of sense-consciousness.

He then goes on saying, "O Mother! It did please Thee to show me Iswar Vidyasagar. This time again I said to Thee, 'Mother! I desire to see a Pandit,' and Thou hast heard my prayer."

The Necessity of Practice

Master (Turning to Sasadhar): My son, do add to your strength a little. Go through the devotional exercises a little longer. You have hardly got upon the tree and you expect to lay hold on a cluster of its big fruits!

The redeeming feature of your conduct is that it comes of a laudable desire to do good to others.

Learning without Discrimination

(Bowing to Sasadhar): When I first heard your name I asked people whether the Pandit was a mere scholar or a person who had attained discrimination (between the Real, *i.e.*, God, and the unreal), in other words, a sense of the vanity of this world.

A man of learning without any sense of the vanity of this world is of no worth whatever.

The Commandment from God

Preaching does no harm if there has been a commandment, if one has received a commission from the Lord to preach the truths of religion. Made strong by such a commission, the preacher becomes one whom nobody can beat.

One ray of light coming from the Goddess of Wisdom, my Divine Mother, has the power to turn great Pandits (men of vast book-learning) into the meanest worms that crawl upon the earth.

The Commissioned Teacher and his Nature

When the lamp is lighted the insects that appear in numbers in cloudy weather wait not till they are called in. They are sure to rush upon the flame of the lamp without anybody bidding them come.

A man with a divine commission does not look out for an audience. It is the audience that looks out for him. Such a person cares not to get up lecture-meetings and such things. People all must come to him of their own accord. His magnetic influence none can resist.

Then princes and *Baboos* all flock to him and ask him, 'Lord, what would you take? Would you like to take these mangoes, these sweetmeats, gold, jewels, shawls?' and so on. He says to such people, 'Away with you; no, excuse me, I do not want anything.'

Surely it is not for the magnet to invite pieces of iron to be drawn to it. These latter run to the magnet because they must.

The Commissioned Teacher and the Wisdom of Life

Do you fear because such a teacher seems not to be learned,—seems not to be well-up in the truths taught by the Sacred Books? Do you fear because he is not a Pandit (book-learned)? No! No! He never falls short of the wisdom of life. He has a never-failing supply of divine wisdom—truths directly revealed—which rise superior to the wisdom taught by the books. In that part of the country (*i.e.*, where the Master was born and brought up) you may often find people measuring grain as it lies in a heap. One man goes on measuring with a standard measure; another man pushes the grain on to him as soon as he finishes measuring the portion of the heap that is within his reach. Much in the same way the divine teacher receives his supply of truths from the fountain of all wisdom, the Divine Mother. That supply is never used up.

Should it be the rare good fortune of a person to be favoured with one side-glance of love from the Lord, such a person becomes blessed at once with divine wisdom enough and to spare.

Therefore I ask whether you have received any commandment from the Lord.

Hazra (to the Pandit): Oh, I dare say there must have been something of that kind. Is it not so?

Pandit : No! I am afraid there hath been no such thing.

Host : No commandment. He is lecturing only from a sense of duty.

Lectures without Divine Commission

Master : What are lectures worth, if the lecturer hath not a good record—a sufficient force of character derived from a divine commission? Some one said in the course of a lecture, 'Brethren, I used formerly to drink,' and so forth. This revelation only made the position of the lecturer worse; for some of the people said to themselves, "Look at the fellow! What does he mean by saying 'I used to drink?' " A retired Sub-Judge from Barisal once said to me, "Sir, do you go about lecturing? In that event I shall be glad to follow suit and gird up my loins." I said, "My dear sir, listen to a story. There is a tank called Halder Pookur in the village of Kamarpukur. People used to throw dirt about the edge of the tank water. Every morning, abuses were showered upon the heads of those that offended. But it was all in vain. The act was repeated the following morning and went on as ever. At last there was a notice put up by a peon of the Municipality, forbidding people to commit such acts. The effect of this authoritative notice was miraculous. There was no more any repetition of such nuisance."

Therefore, I say, your lecturer must not be an ordinary man. He must be a person armed with credentials,—clothed with authority from the Most High. He must be one who has received his commission from Him.

A teacher of mankind must possess sufficient spiritual power. In Calcutta there are many veteran wrestlers like Hanuman Puri. One must try one's strength on such men and not on the novices in wrestling.

Chaitanya Deva was, as we all know, an incarnation of God. Well, what remains of his work now? How infinitely less valuable must be the work of him who is weak in spirit and has received no commission from the Lord?

How to receive a Commandment from the Lord.

Therefore I say (and the master sang, intoxicated with the wine of divine love):

SONG

Dive Deep

Dive deep, dive deep, dive deep, O my mind! Into the sea of beauty.
Make a search in the regions lower, lower down under the sea: you will come by the jewel, the wealth of *Prema* (intense love of God.)

Fear Not

'Fear not,' continued the Lord, at the end of the hymn, because I ask you to plunge, to dive deep into that sea. Fear not. It is the sea of Immortality.

Narendra and the Sea of Immortality

I once said to Narendra, who is here present, 'God is like a sea of liquid sweet. Would you not dive into this sea? Just think of a vessel with a wide mouth containing the syrup of sugar, and suppose you are a fly anxious to drink of the sweet liquid. Where should you sit and drink?' Narendra said that he would like to drink from the edge of the vessel, for if he came to a point beyond his depth he was sure to be drowned. Thereupon I said to him, 'You forget, my son, for diving deep into the divine sea, you need not be afraid of death. Remember *Satchidananda* Sea (the divine sea) is the sea of Immortality. The water of this sea never causes death. It is the water of everlasting life. *Be not afraid like some foolish persons that you 'may run to excess' in your love of God.*

From this sea of Immortality drink the *Chidananda Rasa*—the nectar of Absolute, everlasting knowledge and joy.

The Way to the Sea of Immortality

Yes, first see Him, realise Him, in this way; then shall you hear His voice. He will talk to you and, if He so wishes, will entrust you with His commission. *Infinite is the number of ways leading to the sea of immortality*. It is immaterial *how* you get into this sea.

A hope to All Religious Cults

Suppose there is a reservoir of nectar. It is open to you to walk slowly down the sloping bank from *any* point, get to the nectar and have a drink. You get immortal in any case. Again, what does it matter if one throws oneself into the reservoir or is pushed into it by somebooy? The result in either case is the same. You taste the nectar—the water of life—in either case. You become immortal.

Yoga or Communion

The ways are numberless; *Jnana*, *Karma*, *Bhakti*, all lead to God, other things remaining the same.

Yoga (communion with the Lord) is of three kinds: *Jnana-Yoga, Karma-Yoga* and *Bhakti-Yoga*.

1. *Jnana-Yoga.*

This is communion with God by means of *Jnana* (knowledge in its highest sense). The *Jnani's* object is to realise Brahman, the Absolute. He says, 'Not this.' 'Not this,' and thus leaves out of account one unreal thing after another until he gets to a point where all discrimination between the real God and the unreal ceases, and the Absolute is realised in *Samadhi.*

2. *Karma-Yoga.*

This is communion with God by means of *work*. It is what you are teaching.

Ashtanga-Yoga or *Raja-Yoga* is *Karma-Yoga* if practised

without attachment.[1] It leads to communion through meditation and concentration.

The doing of duties of householders (of the citizens)—doing them without attachment to the end that God may be glorified—is also *Karma-Yoga.*

Again worship according to the *Sastras*, silent repetition[2] of the name of God, and other *Karma* of the kind, is *Karma-Yoga* if done without attachment, for the glorification of God.

The end of *Karma-Yoga* is the same, *viz.*, the realisation of God, impersonal[3] or personal[4] or both.

3. *Bhakti-Yoga.*

This is communion by means of love, devotion, and self-surrender. It is specially adapted to this age.

This is the law for the present age.

Difficulty of Karma-Yoga

Pure work without attachment, as I have already said, is exceedingly difficult in this age. In the first place, there is, as I have already pointed out, hardly time in this age for doing the various works laid upon us by the holy books.

In the second place, you may form a resolution to work unattached, without expectation of any reward or fear of any punishment in this world or the next. But the chances are that, knowingly or un-knowingly, you get attached to the fruit of your work, unless indeed you are already a perfect man.

Difficulty of Jnana-Yoga

The path of absolute knowledge or communion by philosophy is also exceedingly difficult in this age.

[1] *Ashtanga-Yoga* (of *Patanjali*) means *Yoga* with eight members or steps, *viz.*, *Yama* (control over thought, word, deed), *Niyama* (rules for conduct), *Asana* (control over the posture), *Pranayama* (control over *Prana* or the breath of life.) *Pratyahara* (introspection), *Dharana* (concentration) *Dhyana*, (meditation), and *Samadhi* (God-consciousness.)

[2] Japa. [3] Nirguna. [4] Saguna.

In the first place, our life in this age resides, so to speak, in food.

Secondly, the term of human life in this age is far too short for this purpose.

Thirdly, it is almost impossible in this age to get rid of the conviction that the self is the same as the body,—which clings to us. Now, what is the conclusion which the *Jnani* must come to? It is this: 'I am not the body, gross or subtle. I am one with the Universal Soul, the Being Absolute and Unconditioned. Not being the body, I am not subject to the necessities of the body—*e.g.*, hunger, thirst, birth, death, disease, grief, pleasure, pain, etc.'

One subject to these necessities of the body and calling oneself a philosopher, is like a person suffering from intense pain caused by a thorny plant. It scratches and tears the hand and causes it to bleed. But he nevertheless says, 'Why, my hand is not at all scratched or torn. It is all right.'

Bhakti-Yoga: The Yuga-dharma

Hence the path of communion[1] by love, devotion and self-surrender to God is the easiest of all paths. It brings *Karma* (work) to a minimum. It teaches the necessity of prayer without ceasing. It is, in this age, the shortest cut leading to God.

Different Ways but The Same Goal

The meaning of this is that (1) discrimination between God, the only reality, and the unreal phenomenal universe, and (2) the doing of works, are far more difficult in this age than *Bhakti* as a method or path leading to God.

It is not meant that the goal is different.

The philosopher, indeed, wants to realise God Impersonal. What is meant is that such a person would, in this age, do better to follow the method of the *Bhakti-yoga*. Let him love, pray, surrender himself entirely to God. The Lord loves his devotee and will vouchsafe to him even the knowledge of the Absolute if he hungers and thirsts after it.

The philosopher will thus realise God, both Personal

[1]Bhakti.

and Impersonal. *Only let him, in this age, follow the method of the Bhakta.*

The *Bhakti-Yogi*, on the other hand, would be generally quite content with seeing, realising, the Personal God. The Lord would, however, make him heir to his infinite glories—grant unto him knowledge of both the Personal and the Impersonal. Both *Jnana* and *Bhakti* shall be his.

Can the Bhakta attain Brahma-Jnana?

For does not a person who manages to reach Calcutta succeed in finding his way to the *Maidan*, the Ochterlony Monument, the Museum and other places, and know which is which?

The important thing is to be able to come to Calcutta.

Do but come to my Divine Mother and you will get not only *Bhakti* but also *Jnana*, not only *Jnana* but also *Bhakti*—not only see Her in *Samadhi*, manifesting Herself in forms[1] Divine but also realise Her as the Absolute[2] in *Samadhi* in which all self in the devotee is effaced by my Mother and there is no manifestation of divine forms.

The true *Bhakta* says: Lord! Work with attachment I see, is dangerous, for just as a man sows, so must he reap. I see, again, that work without attachment is exceedingly difficult. Save me from the first, Lord, for else, I shall forget Thee. Deign to make less and less what work I have, until by Thy grace I see Thee and no work remains to be done. Till then, may it please Thee to grant that I may be blessed with that love, devotion and self-surrender to Thee which is the one thing needful. As for the little work that is left for my share, grown less and less by Thy grace, do Thou grant that I may have strength to do it without attachment. But until I am blessed with the vision divine and thus realise the true end of life, grant that my soul may not be disposed to look about for fresh work, unattached though it be—unless, indeed, I receive from Thee Thy commandment to do Thy work.'

The Bhakta's Attitude towards Karma: His Prayer

[1] Nirvikalpa. [2] Sakara Rupa.

Pandit : Please, Sir, how far did you go on pilgrimage?

Master (smiling): Well, I did go to some places. Hazra went farther, and higher up to Hrishikes on the Himalayas. I did not go so far nor so high up.

The Value of Pilgrimage

The vulture and the kite do, indeed, soar very high, but all the while their looks are fixed on the charnel-pits where the carcasses of dead animals are thrown.

What is the good of visiting places of pilgrimage,—once you are able to cultivate *Bhakti* (devotion to God)?

When on my pilgrimage I visited Benares, I was surprised to see that the grass there was the same grass as here, and that there were the same tamarind leaves!

Pilgrimages, without love and devotion to God, carry no reward. With devotion within your heart, it is not absolutely necessary that you must visit the holy places. You are very well off where you are.

Love of God is the one thing needful.

The charnel-pit is the world—which is another name for woman (carnality) and gold (riches, honours, fame, work with attachment, etc.)

The vulture and the kite are they that talk big and try to justify themselves by the doing of works enjoined by the holy books. All the while their mind is attached to the things of the world—riches, honours, sensual pleasures, etc.

Pandit : That is true, Sir, such pilgrimage is like setting at naught the jewel worn suspended on the breast of *Vishnu*, the second Person of the Hindu Trinity, and going about searching for other jewels.

Sri Ramakrishna : In order that your teaching should take effect you should take into account the time factor. Unless in the case of each individual, you do allow a certain period of time to go by, no teaching will bear fruit. Those whom you teach will not, as a general rule, be able at once

The Time Factor

to profit by your teachings unless their hour is come.

Spiritual awakening is very much a question of time. The Teacher is a mere help.

Doctors are of three classes.

Three Classes of Religious Teachers

There is one class of doctors who, when they are called in, look at the patient, feel his pulse, prescribe the necessary medicines, and then ask the patient to take them. If the patient declines to do so, the doctor goes away without further troubling himself about the matter. This is the lowest class of doctors. In the same way there are religious teachers who do not much care whether or not their teachings are valued or acted up to.

The second class of doctors not only ask the patient to take the medicine, but they go further. They reason with him in case he takes it not. In the same way, those religious teachers who leave no stone unturned to make other people walk in the ways of righteousness and of Truth by means of the arts of gentle persuasion must be said to belong to the next higher class.

The third and highest class of doctors will use force on the patient in case their kind words fail. They will go the length of putting their knee on the chest of the patient and forcing the medicine through his gullet. (*Laughter.*)

In the same way, there are some religious teachers who would use force, if necessary, on their disciples, with a view to make them walk in the way of the Lord. These belong to the highest class.

Pandit : So there are religious teachers, like doctors, of this highest class. Then, Sir, why do you say the time factor must be taken into account?

Sri Ramakrishna : There are doctors of the highest class. But suppose the medicine does not get to the stomach. The doctors then, with all their zeal, are quite helpless.

Fit Vessels to Receive the Truth

It is necessary to choose fit vessels as the receptacles for spiritual truths. I ask those who come to me, 'Have you got any guardian to take care of you?' For, suppose the father has left any debts. Suppose the would-be disciple has no one in the world to look after him. Then it would be next to impossible for such a person to fix his mind upon God. Do you hear, my child?

Pandit : Yes, Sir: I am all ears.

The conversation then turns on another subject, the grace of God.[1]

Master : Once a number of Sikh soldiers came to the Temple. They had a meeting with me just before the Temple of the Divine Mother. They said, 'God is very kind.' I asked, smiling, 'Is it indeed so?' They replied, 'Why, Sir, does not the Lord take care of His creatures, provide for their wants.' I said, 'The Lord is the *Father* of all. He *must* take care of His children—His own creatures. If He does not, who else is there to take care of them? Surely it is not the duty of people of the other quarter of the town to come and feed God's own creatures!'

Narendra : Then the Lord should not be called *merciful*?

Sri Ramakrishna : I don't forbid you to call Him so. You are at liberty to call Him by that name. I only meant to say that *the Lord is our own.*

Pandit : Priceless are these words!

Sri Ramakrishna (aside to a disciple) : You were singing.

Song for Worldly Objects

But your songs this day, were to me tasteless as if from want of salt. I could not enjoy them. Yours was the condition of a person looking for a situation through the recommendation of the master of the family. Hence I could not keep listening to the songs, but left the place.

The disciple blushed.

The Master here asked for a fresh glass of water. He

Purity

would not take the one already offered, which was therefore taken away. The Master, it appeared, looked upon it as unfit to be offered to the God in Him—

[1] Kripa.

being made impure by the 'feverish' touch of some wicked man.

Pandit (to Hazra) : You, gentlemen, the Master's constant associates, must always be in the midst of exceeding joy.

Master (smiling) : This day I have had the rare pleasure of looking at the moon of the second lunar day. I say moon of the second lunar day with a special meaning.

Sita said to Ravana, 'Thou art the full moon and my Ramachandra is the moon of the second lunar day.' Ravana was highly pleased until the sense was explained to him. Sita meant to say that the fortune of Ravana had reached its climax, and that now it must be on the wane like the full moon. Not so the fortune of Ramachandra which had reached only the second lunar day. His fortune like the moon of the second lunar day was not on the wane, but must ever grow day by day. Ramachandra must increase, but Ravana must decrease.'

Now the Master rising to depart, the Pandit and his friends bowed down before him. He then left the place, followed by his disciples.

SECTION IX

1884

SRI RAMAKRISHNA AT THE TEMPLE (DAKSHINESWAR)

Place—Dakshineswar Thakurbari, Calcutta.

Scene—The Master's room.

Date—3rd August, 1884, 2 p.m. to 9.30 p.m.

Present—Balaram, M., Rakhal, Bauls[1] from Shibpore and visitors from Bhowanipur, Hazra, Adhar, Ram Chatterji, etc., etc.

CHAPTER I

UNION WITH THE UNIVERSAL SOUL

The Master is seated on the lounge as usual with his face to the north. The western and the northern doors of his chamber look out on the sacred waters of the Ganges. The Bauls from Shibpore are seated on a mat spread on the floor of the room. They are singing hymns upon musical instruments—one of which was the well-known *Gopijantra* with one string, popularly called *Bong-bonga-bong*. They are seated with their faces towards the Master, that is towards the west. Others of the company are seated with their faces to the south and towards the Master.

One of the songs has a particular reference to the Six Lotus Wheels marking the different stages of progress towards union with the Universal Soul.

[1] A sect of devout Hindus: lit. mad for the Lord. These *Bauls* from Shibpore chant what is now known as Kali-kirtan.

At the end of this song, the Master Says:

The six wheels mentioned in the *Yoga* system of the *Tantras* correspond with the seven mental planes mentioned in the *Vedas*. When the mind is immersed in worldliness, it makes its abode in the planes of the anus, the sex organ and the navel successively.

The Six Wheels and the Seven Mental Planes

In the 4th plane the abode of the mind is the heart. The man is blessed with the vision of divine glory and cries out '*What is all this! What is all this!*'

In the 5th plane, the place of the mind is the throat. The devotee talks only on subjects related to God and gets impatient if any other subject comes up before him in the course of conversation.

In the 6th plane the mind is localised between the eyebrows. The devotee comes face to face with God; only a thin glass-like partition, so to speak, keeps him apart from the divine person. To him God is like a light within a lantern or the photograph behind a glass frame. He seeks to touch the vision, but he cannot. His perception falls short of complete realisation, for there is the element of self-consciousness retained to a certain extent.

In the last or the 7th plane it is perfect *Samadhi*. Then all sense-consciousness ceases and pure God-consciousness takes its place. In this state the life of the saint lingers for twenty-one days, after which he passes away. During these days he ceases to take any food. Milk, if poured into his mouth, runs out and never gets into the stomach.

The Master continues:

Some who may have got on to the seventh or the highest plane and have thus become lost in God-consciousness are pleased to come down from that spiritual height with a view to the good of mankind.

The Ego of Divine Knowledge

They keep the ego of knowledge or, in other words, the higher Self. But this ego is a mere appearance. It is like a line drawn across a sheet of water.

Hanuman was blessed with the vision of God both with form and without form. But he retained the ego of a servant of God.

Such was also the case with the Saints Narada, Sanaka, Sananda and Sanatkumara.

Here the question was asked whether Narada and others worshipped God as dualists and did not realise Him as God, the Absolute.

The Master says:

Narada and others had attained the highest knowledge. But still they continued like the murmuring waters of the rivulet to talk and to sing. This shows that they too kept this ego of knowledge.

They were knowing ones and also devotees. They talked and sang about the Lord with a view to the good of others.

A 'steam-boat' not only gets to its *own place of destination, but also* carries numbers of people on board to the same place.

Preceptors like Narada are like 'steam-boats.'

The Highest Teachers

The highest teachers may be divided into two classes:

First there are those that declare the Supreme Being as the formless one. Trailanga Swami belongs to this class. Generally speaking, holy men of this class are comparatively selfish, so to speak. They care only for the liberation of their own soul.

Those of the second class say that God is with form as well as formless, and that He manifests Himself to His devotees as a Being with forms.

Have you ever seen a water-passage running over with the water of the river with which it is joined?

The passage has sometimes no trace left, being entirely one with the river-water. But very often there may be noticed a slight movement in its water which proves its separateness from the river-water.

Pretty much the same is the case with the teacher belonging to the second class. His soul becomes one with the Universal Soul. *Still* there is this ego of knowledge *kept on*—a slight trace of individuality to mark his separate existence from the Deity.

Again, such a teacher may be compared to a jar or pitcher of water when it is filled to the brim. At the same time its contents or part of its contents may be transferred to another vessel. The disciple is the second vessel. The pitcher filled to the brim indicates the perfect state derived from the highest knowledge.[1]

Thus the ego of knowledge is kept for the purpose of teaching others the saving truths of religion.

Again, suppose a person digs a well. He is thirsty and drinks the water of the well. It is not unusual for such a person to keep with him the digging implements, that is, the hoe, the shovel, the spade, etc., for the sake of others who may want them for the same object. In the same way a teacher of the second class, who may have drunk the waters of everlasting life and may have thus quenched his spiritual thirst and come to the perfection of *Brahma-jnana*, is often anxious to do good to mankind. With this view he retains the ego of knowledge, the ego of Bhakti, the ego of preceptor.

Some persons eat mangoes and take away all traces of eating by wiping their mouth with a towel. These persons care only for their own selves. But there are others who are sure to share the mangoes with other people whenever they eat them.

This was precisely the mental attitude of the Gopis of Brindaban. They always desired to retain the power of *tasting* the love of Sri Krishna. To them He was the thing to be enjoyed, *i.e.*, spiritually. They wanted to be the persons enjoying. So sang Ram Prasad, 'I would much prefer to *eat* the sugar to *being* the sugar itself.'

Involution and Evolution

It is a case of involution and evolution. You go backwards to the Supreme Being and your personality becomes lost in His personality.

[1] Brahmajnana.

This is *Samadhi*. You then retrace your steps. You get back your ego (personality) and come back to the point whence you started only to see that the world and your ego or self were involved in the same Supreme Being, and that God, Man and Nature (or the world) are mere identities, so that if you hold to one of them you realise the others.

Call with *Bhakti* upon His hallowed name and *the mountain of your sins shall go out of sight*; just as a mountain of cotton will burn up and vanish if it but catches one spark of fire.

The Doctrine of Sin and Worship from Fear: Popular Christianity and Brahmoism

The worship from fear, that is, of hell-fire, is intended for the beginner. Some people talk of sin and sin only. Take popular Christianity and Brahmoism. Now these Christians and Brahmos as a general rule look upon the sense of sin as the whole of religion. Their ideal of a devotee is he who can pray, 'O Lord, I am a sinner: deign to forgive *my sins*.' They forget that the sense of sin marks only the earliest and a low stage of spirituality, which really consists in the love of God as our own father or mother.

People do not see the force of habit. If you say eternally, 'I am a sinner, I am a sinner,' you will remain a sinner to the end of the chapter.

One who says, 'I am bound to the world, I am bound,' will go on to be in bondage indeed for ever.

But that man is free who says, 'I am free from the bondage of the world, I am free.' Is not the Lord our own father?

Such is the great force of habit.

CHAPTER II

Intoxication with the Wine of Divine Love

Then turning to some of the company present who were singing, he said, "Will you sing songs which have for their burden the enjoyment by the human soul of God realised? Rakhal, (this he said to one of his young disciples present) do you remember the song sung the other day at Nobin Neogi's house, 'Be intoxicated with the joy of the Lord?' "

One of the company then said, 'Sir, may we be favoured with one of your songs?' The Master said, 'What shall I sing?—Well, I sing pretty much like yourselves. Very well, when the time comes I shall sing.'

So saying he remains silent for a while.

* * * *

The first five songs that he sings are about Sri Chaitanya Deva and Sri Krishna, that is, from the point of view of the Vaishnavas. Of the last three songs the burden is the Goddess of the universe. They were as follows:

SONG I

THE DEVOTEE AND HIS ECSTATIC LOVE FOR CHAITANYA DEVA, THE GOD INCARNATE

1. The waves of the love of Gour come dashing against my body. The swell of his sea of love causes the fall of the unrighteous: nay, the universe itself goes down.

2. I thought of stopping on the shore. But there is the alligator — the ecstatic love of Gour Chand which swallows me. Is there anybody that feels for me and will take me by the hand and drag me out of the water?

SONG II

THE DEVOTEE AND HIS ECSTATIC LOVE FOR CHAITANYA DEVA

1. Come, O my friend, look on the fair form of Gour! Behold, it is the lightning that has become one with the dark cloud![1]

[1] *Krishna* is the dark cloud; *Radha* is the lightning. The two have been made into one *viz. Gour Chaitanya.*

2. Here is a man of gold (so fair he is). The sea of his heart is moved incessantly into waves of tender feelings. The tenderness of his loving heart has softened and thus bent his fair body in three places. So my mind has been captured by the sight of Gour specially by his bewitching glances.

3. The body of my Gour is rubbed over with a mixture of curds and the red *alta* water. At the sight of this fair form my tender emotions (of love) are stirred up. The maker of this fair form is *Bhangad* (Siva) and the architect is Radha.

SONG III

DIVE DEEP

1. Dive deep, dive deep, dive deep, O my mind, into the sea of beauty.

Make a search in the regions lower and lower down under the sea; thou shalt come by the jewel, the wealth of *Prema* (intense love of God).

2. Within thy heart is Brindaban the abode of God who is love. Search and look; search and look; search and look. Thou shalt find it.

Then shall burn, without ceasing, the lamp of divine wisdom.

3. Who is that being that steered a boat on land — on land, on solid ground?

Says *Kabir*, 'Listen, listen, listen! Meditate on the hallowed feet of the divine preceptor.'[1]

SONG IV

THE MOTHER OF THE UNIVERSE AND THE DIFFICULTY OF REALISATION

1. Is it given to everybody to be blessed with such wealth as my Mother?

It is beyond the power of religious austerities ever practised by Siva to cause the mind to be immersed in the contemplation of Her hallowed crimson feet.

2. The wealth of princes, potentates and powers as of the gods of heaven, is beneath the contempt of him who meditates upon my Mother.

He is set afloat upon joy everlasting, once my Mother of the dark blue colour doth turn back and look at him.

3. The king of Yogis,[2] the king of ascetics[3] and the god[4] of heaven meditate in vain upon Her hallowed feet — so difficult is it to realise the blessedness that is there.

Kamalakanta is devoid of all virtues. But he still doth long for the vision of those blessed feet!

---

[1] Guru [2] Siva. [3] Mounis—Ascetics who observe a vow of silence.

[4] Indra,

SONG V

THE MOTHER OF THE UNIVERSE; LIBERATION AND LOVE OF GOD

1. What a nice machine has Mother of the dark blue colour made, what a nice machine has Mother made — the consort of the God of eternity!

What splendid tricks is She playing in the machine[1] which is but three and a half cubits in length!

2. Herself within the machine, She it is who holds in Her hand the string which does set it in motion; but the machine says, 'It is I that am moving of my own accord.' It knows not who causes it to move.

3. The machine that has realised Her, will not be required to be a machine any more. Mother Herself is bound to certain particular machines by the string of *Bhakti* (love).

The Master is singing of the Mother of the universe. At the end of the song, he is in *Samadhi*.

The eyes are fixed and half closed. The functions of the corporeal frame are suspended. Sense-consciousness has left him, giving place to pure God-consciousness.

CHAPTER III

THE MASTER'S SERMON

Pre-arrangement by God

Returning a little to his sense, he talks to the Divine Mother saying, 'Don't trouble me, O Mother! Come down to this place. Be still, O Mother. What Thou hast prearranged for every one—O Mother, shall alone come to pass! What shall I say to these people!'

[1] The body.

How To know God

Nothing can be achieved in the path of spirituality without discrimination between the Real (God) and the unreal or phenomenal universe; and without non-attachment to riches, honours, sensual pleasures, &c.

Non-attachment is of many kinds. One kind of non-attachment springs from the acute pain due to worldly misery. But the better kind arises from the consciousness that all worldly blessings, though within one's reach, are transitory and are not worth enjoying. Thus, having all, he has not anything.

Religious Awakening and the Time Factor

Everything rests upon time. For all religious awakening we must wait. At the same time the precepts of religious teacher should be listened to. One may be put in mind of these precepts on a future occasion and then one would probably cry out, saying, 'O! Yes! I heard this from such and such a person at such and such a time.' Another reason is,—our worldliness gradually wears off as the result of our listening to these precepts from day to day. Our worldliness is like the intoxication caused by wine which goes off gradually if repeated doses of rice-water are taken.

Limited Number of Seers

The number of those who attain divine wisdom is very limited. So in the *Gita*, 'Out of thousands only one doth strive for knowledge; and out of a thousand such people striving for knowledge only one doth succeed in reaching the goal.'

One of the company present, here quotes the text of the Gita.

Divine Wisdom and Non-attachment

The more is a person's attachment to the world, the less is he likely to attain divine wisdom. The less his attachment, the more is the probability of his getting such wisdom. Thus, wisdom may be said to vary directly as non-attachment to the world, its riches, its pleasures, &c., and inversely as attachment to the world.

Stages of Spirituality

Bhava is the state of being struck speechless at the thought of the Supreme Being (of whom the only things that can be predicated are Existence, Knowledge and Bliss Absolute). *Bhava* is the utmost point that can be reached by ordinary mortals.

Ecstatic love of God (Prema) is attainable only by a few. They are human beings with extraordinary original powers and entrusted with a divine commission. Being heirs of divine powers and glories, they form a class of their own.

To this class belong incarnations of God like Chaitanya Deva, and their worshippers of the highest order.

The two characteristics of this love are, first, the forgetfulness of the external world and, secondly, the forgetfulness of one's own body,—so very dear to one.

Bhava is like the unripe mango. *Prema* is like the ripe mango. This love is a string in the hands of the devotee which binds God. The devotee holds the Lord under his control, so to speak. The Lord must come to him whenever he calls out to Him.

In Persian books it is written that within the flesh are the bones, within the bones is the marrow, within the marrow is, *etc., etc.,* and that last and innermost of all is this love of God.

Krishna is called *Tribhanga Murari.* It is only a soft thing that is capable of changing its form. So this form of Krishna implies that he must have softened a little in some way or other. The softening in this case is accounted for by this love.

How to Pray

How to pray is the next question. Let us not pray for things of this world, but pray like the Saint Narada. Narada said to Ramachandra, 'O Ram, grant that I may be favoured with *Bhakti* (love, devotion and self-surrender) to the lotus of Thy feet.' 'Be it so, Narada!' said Ram. 'But wilt thou not ask for anything else?' Narada replied, 'Lord, may it please Thee to grant that I may not be attracted by Thy *Maya*, which so fascinates the universe.' Ramachandra said once more, 'Be it so, Narada; but wilt thou not ask for anything else?' Narada replied, 'No, Lord, that is all I pray for.'

Knowledge varies in degree and kind. There is first, knowledge belonging to men of the world—ordinary mortals. This knowledge is not sufficiently powerful. It may be likened to the flame of a lamp which only lights the inside of a room. The knowledge of a devotee is a stronger light and may be compared to the light of the moon which shows things outside of a room as well as those inside of it.

But the knowledge of the incarnation of God is still more powerful. It may be likened to a yet stronger light, the resplendent glory of the sun! Such light shows the minutest things both outside and inside of a room. Nothing is problematic to Him. He solves the most difficult problems of life and of the spirit as the simplest things in the world! His exposition of the most intricate questions in which man is interested is such as a child can follow. He is the sun of divine knowledge whose light takes away the accumulated darkness of ages!

Owner of both Divine Wisdom and Divine Love

Lastly, there is that unique composite light which may be called the Luni-solar Light—a light made up both of the light of the moon and of the light of the sun. To this composite light may be compared the unique wisdom of incarnations like Chaitanya Deva, who are marked alike by wisdom and love, strictly so called. It is unique like the sun and the moon appearing in the firmament at one and the same time.

The Worldly Man and His Hope

The man immersed in worldliness cannot attain wisdom divine. He cannot see God.

Does the muddy water ever reflect the sun or any surrounding object?

Is there no remedy for this state of things? Is there no hope for the worldly man? Yes, there is certainly.

If you drop a purifying agent, say, a piece of alum into muddy water, the water is purified and the impurities, all settle down at the bottom of the vessel. Discrimination of the real (God) from the unreal (*i.e.*, the phenomenal universe) and non-attachment to the world are the two purifying agents. Thus it is that the worldly man ceases to be worldly and becomes pure.

The Six Steps leading to Realisation of God

First Stage: The mixing in good company, *i.e.*, the company of holy men.

Second stage : Admiration for higher things, *i.e.*, things relating to the spirit.

Third stage : Single-minded devotion to one's ideal. The ideal may be one's spiritual preceptor. The ideal may be the Formless.

The ideal may be God Personal or any of His innumerable manifestations. It may be one's tutelary God or Goddess. The worshippers of *Vishnu* have this devotion to their tutelary God, *Vishnu* or *Sri Krishna*. The *Saktas* or the worshippers of *Sakti* (the Goddess that rules the universe) have this *Nishtha* for *Sakti* who is also known as *Kali*, *Durga*, &c.

Fourth stage : The state of speechless wonder at the thought of God.

Fifth stage : This stage is intensified when the feeling of devotion reaches the highest point after God vision. The devotee sometimes laughs, sometimes weeps, like a mad man. He loses all control over his body. *This stage is not attained by ordinary human beings who are not capable of conquering the flesh.* It is reached by incarnations of God alone who appear in this world for the salvation of mankind.

Sixth stage : *Prema* goes hand-in-hand with *Mahabhava*. *Prema* is the most intense love of God after realisation and is strictly the highest stage of spirituality. The two marks of this stage are, first, the forgetfulness of this world; second, a forgetfulness of the self which includes one's own body.[1]

[1]The technical names for these six stages of devotion in Indian philosophy

Chaitanya Deva who reached this stage was so much lost in the love of God that he often forgot himself and forgot the identity of the places where he had been before. Observing a forest before him, he so far forgot himself as to think that it was Brindavan. He looked at the sea while at Puri and took it for the Jumna. In this state he would throw himself into the sea and was on two or three occasions given up for lost by his friends and disciples. This stage leads the devotee to the goal, *viz*, to God. The devotee sees God. He attains the end of life. He is blessed with the vision Divine.

Here the Master said to the company present, 'If you have any question to put to me, you are welcome to do so.' But none present came forward to do so. And the Master went on saying:

Time Factor and Spiritual Discipline

Knowledge cannot be communicated all at once. Its attainment is a question of time. Suppose a fever is of a severe type. The Doctor cannot give quinine under such circumstances. He knows that such a remedy would do no good. The fever must first leave the patient, which depends upon time, and then the quinine would be useful. Sometimes the fever would go off without your having to give the patient quinine or any other medicine. Precisely the same is the case with man who seeks for knowledge. To him religious precepts often prove useless so long as he is immersed in worldliness. Allow him a certain period for the enjoyment of the things of the world; his attachment to the world will gradually wear off. This is exactly the time for the success of any religious instructions that may be given to him. Till then they would be as good as entirely thrown away.

Many come to me; and I have observed how *some* of them are anxious to listen to my words. But one or

---

are as follows:
[1] Sadhu-Sanga; [2] Sraddha; [3] Ishta-Nishta (including Guru-bhakti); [4] Bhava; [5] Prema; [6] Maha-bhava.

two of the company appear to be restless and impatient in my presence. They say to their friends in whispers, 'Let us go, let us go,—Well, if you mean to stay, we had better go into the boat and wait for you.'

It is difficult to drive nails into a *pucca* brick wall. It will break the head of the nails sooner than make any impression upon the wall.

It is idle to strike the crocodile with the sword. The chances are that the sword will not make a cut.

Therefore I say that the element of time is an important factor in all these matters.

Spiritual awakening is very much a question of time. The teacher is a mere help.

The meeting then broke up.

Karma

Master (to M.) : The fact is, a great deal of all this desire for knowledge or for freedom depends upon one's *Karma* in one's previous incarnations.

Disciple: Yes, sir, it is so difficult to understand one's *self*! We see the *self* only as it appears to us. Behind it there might be a hundred previous incarnations. We walk upon the floor of a house but we never stop to see how it is made and what kinds of things are beneath it.

The Master smiles at the disciple and leaves his seat. He comes out on the verandah next to the western door of his room, and for a time looks on the sun which is going down rapidly towards the horizon. He looks on the holy water of the sacred stream before him.

* * *

CHAPTER IV

Master and Disciple

A Revelation in the Flesh

A disciple is walking alone along the *pucca* embankment of the Temple on the side of the Holy Mother Ganges. He is watching Balaram and others getting into a boat to take them back home to Calcutta. It is a day in mid-summer; the sacred water is broken into waves. The day is drawing to its close. It is past five. The sky is cloudy and the clouds present a most charming sight, especially in the north. The disciple has before him in the foreground of the picture the *Panchabati* backed by a line of tall willow trees, with the silver stream flowing past on their right. In the background are the beautiful dark-blue clouds and also the dark stream underneath.

The disciple is looking on this charming scene. Suddenly his attention is arrested by the Master coming on from the south in the direction of the *Panchabati*, and those well-known Jhau trees.

As the Master smiled like a child five-years old and came up, the charming picture appeared to be more than complete! There is the universe on the one hand and the One Soul that on the other hand reflects that universe and sees it as it actually is. Yes, the disciple feels that in that presence he is as near the solution of the problem of life as can be. It is this presence which makes everything—the images of gods and goddesses—men, women, children—trees, flowers, leaves—every inch of ground in that Temple instinct with spirituality and full of the joy of the Lord. Yes, true enough he feels that it is the God-man before him that has thrown an irresistible charm over everything in that wonderful place—over every object, divine or human, animate or inanimate, seen by the outer or by the inner eye—from the dust under His hallowed feet to those sacred images worshipped in the Temple or perceived by looking within that other temple, the body of man, that veritable 'Revelation in the Flesh.' He feels like one spell-bound in that presence!

Said the Master to the disciple: 'Do you expect a shower? Well, get the umbrella for me, will you?'

He runs to the Master's room and presently comes

back with the umbrella. They have come to the foot of the *Panchabati.*

Master (to the disciple): Let me entrust you with this commission: you are to tell B. that when Rakhal leaves this place he must come and stay here for a day or two. Otherwise my mind shall be very unhappy. What sort of a boy do you find B. to be?

Disciile : He is remarkably mild and gentle.

Master : Is he *guileless* or not?

Disciple : To all appearance not perfectly guileless. But I think this may be explained. A person of a mild disposition keeps his thoughts and feelings to himself. He is never demonstrative.

By this time the Master has come back to His own quarters.

Before Hazra

A Doctor is present. This gentleman makes an excellent preparation of *Haritalabhasma* (calx of the sulphate of arsenic). Upon seeing him the Master says, 'His medicine suits me wonderfully. The man is a right man.' Thereupon Hazra says, 'Quite so, sir, but *samsar* (the world) is forced upon him. He cannot help it.'

House-holder and Ochre-coloured Cloth

Hazra commented rather severely on the ochre-coloured cloth worn by old Naba Chaitanya. A man of the world to wear a *gerua*! How shocking! The Master says, 'I really don't know what to say! There is, however, one consolation for me. I look upon all human beings,—in fact, all creatures—as incarnations of the Deity. I see God evolved into all things, God manifest in every thing—in man and Nature. I see God Himself has taken these multifarious forms that appear before our eyes in this universe!..

Narendra

Hazra: Narendra is once more involved in a law suit.

Master : Yes, but he believes not in the Goddess of the universe (personal God with forms).

Hazra : Precisely; he says, 'If I believe in *Sakti*, I should be setting a bad example to those that would follow me.'

Master : Well, what do you think is the extent of the good that he derives from here (*i.e.*, from himself).

Hazra : You love him.

Master (to M.) : Did you not meet him any of these days? Will you just see him at his house? O! Do bring him here along with you in a carriage. Will you?

Then turning to Hazra the Master says, 'What do you think of Bhabanath and his attachment to me? Is this not a case again of tendencies acquired in one's previous incarnations?

Talking of H. and Latu and referring to their habit of incessant meditation, the Master says to Hazra, 'What are all these? No end of meditation! What do you say?'

Hazra : Quite so. Had they been engaged in your service, that would have been a different matter altogether.

Master (pleading) : Well, possibly, their period of discipline being over, somebody else will take their place and serve.

What do you think of me? Do you not see that sometimes I have single-minded devotion to, say, the Goddess of the universe, and sometimes not ? Then I go in for all sorts of gods and goddesses and adore them with an equal degree of devotion! Sometimes again I meditate upon God the Absolute. I am sometimes a chaste wife and sometimes not! Is this not curious? Other people are actuated by a special feeling of their own. For instance, the ruling feeling with one person is the love of Krishna, of another is the love of Rama, of a third the communion with God the Absolute, and so on.

Hazra held his peace.

* * * * *

It was evening. After the usual prayers and other

religious exercises that are enjoined on the pious Hindu there was yet another meeting between the Master and the disciple above referred to.

Contradiction or Harmony?

The following dialogue then took place. The subject was the apparently contradictory systems of religious faith amongst the Hindus.

Disciple : Lord, is this a contradiction, some amongst the Hindus holding that Sri Krishna is identical with the Mother of the universe and others holding that Sri Krishna is God the Absolute and Radha is the Goddess who rules the universe, the creator, preserver and destroyer?

Master : The former view is that of *Devi Purana* Be it so, but there need be no contradiction; God is infinite. Infinite are the forms in which He manifests Himself! Infinite also is the number of ways leading to Him!

Disciple: Oh, I see! The end in view is how to get on to the roof of the house. The means may be different. It may be, Lord, as you often say, a single rope, a bamboo, a wooden ladder or a *pucca* staircase!

Master : Quite so. *That you see this at once is due to the special grace of God.* Without His grace doubt is never cleared up. The fact is, our attitude with respect to God should be like that of Hanuman who said to Ramachandra, 'Lord, I care not for the phases of the moon or for the appearance of stellar constellations on particular days. What alone I am concerned with is how to meditate upon Rama.'

The One Thing Needful-Bhakti

Suppose you go into a garden to eat mangoes. Is it necessary for you first to count the number of trees in the garden, which may be many thousands, or the number of branches of those trees, which may be tens of thousands, or lastly, the number of leaves, which may be hundreds of thousands? Certainly not. You should at once, on the contrary, proceed to *eat*. In the same way it is useless, to enter into all sorts of discussions and controversies regarding God which only cause a waste of time and energy. Instead of throwing away one's time in this way, one's present and most important duty—the duty that is nearest to one—is to love God—to cultivate *Bhakti* or devotion.

Disciple : I should greatly desire that my work in the world should become a little less than now. The pressure of work stands in the way of one's giving one's mind to God, does it not, sir?

Work In the World

Master : Oh yes, no doubt, that is so; but a wise man may work *unattached*, and then work would not do any harm to him.

Disciple : But, sir, that depends upon a tremendous power of will derived from the realisation of God; *i.e.*, called forth by God-vision. First the realisation of God; then, work without attachment. Is it not so, Lord?

Master : I must say you are right. But the probability is that you must have desired for these things in previous incarnations. Your duty now is to pray without ceasing for *Bhakti* or love of God so that the bondage of work shall gradually fall off.

Disciple (heaving a sigh) : It seems to me this is like locking the stable door after the horse has run away!

Master : Do you ever feel the joy of the Lord!

* * * * *

Master : Try to follow the precept that one should avail oneself of things that come naturally in one's way without having to put forth any effort for the attainment of those things. Take no thought for things of that kind, 'saving against the rainy day,' etc. etc.

Think Not of Morrow

Master : Are people drawn towards me by the attractive nature of what I say? What do they think of me? What do you feel when you look on me?

What thinkest thou of Me?

Disciple : Here I find in one and the same person the higher divine knowledge, the most intense love of God, the highest renunciation and with it a marvellous simplicity.

This simplicity is what keeps people back. The multitude turn away from such a simple and, what seems to them, such an ordinary man. But it is precisely this which causes a select few to be drawn towards you! To them the wonder is that it is possible for a person to keep up simplicity in spite of spiritual perceptions of a magnitude that rises above all human comprehension! Men-of-war have passed through the river and still it looks no better than a small creek or rivulet.

The Master on Himself—a Hint

Master (smiling) : There is a *Vaishnava* sect among the Hindus, hailing from *Ghosh Parah*. They say, 'You cannot get to be *Sahaj* (the pre-eminently-simple, namely, God) unless you have yourself become *Sahaj*.'

Master : Have I any egotism?

Disciple : Yes, a little; and that little has been, as you say, kept with a view: first, to the preservation of the body; second, the culture of *Bhakti*, or devotion to God; third, the desire to mix in the company of devotees; fourth, the desire to give instruction to others. At the same time, it must be said that you have kept all these after good deal of *prayer*. My idea, Sir, is that the natural state of your soul is capable of being described only by the word *Samadhi*. Hence I say that the egotism that you have is the result of *prayer*.

Master : Yes; *but it is not I that have kept it*—this self; *it is my Divine Mother*!

Disciple : The other day, you were talking to Pandit Sasadhar about Narada and his self. You said, 'One has to go to the Celestial Tree which grants all desires and then to pray; the boons that one will receive depends upon the kind of the prayer that one makes. God is the Celestial Tree.

Master : Yes. But it lies with my Divine Mother to grant the prayer.

* * * * *

The world is Terrible

Master : B. says, 'The world! Oh, Oh, how terrible!'

Disciple : Oh, that is, I am afraid, all hearsay. He has no personal experience, boy as he is.

Master : Yes, yes, that is so. How free from guile is N.!

Disciple : His very appearance is prepossessing. How attractive are his eyes!

Master : Not only the eyes, but taken all in all. At the proposal of his marriage, he said to his people, 'Why are you going to get me drowned? For, once married, it shall be all over with me!'

The Evils of Marriage

Later on the following conversation was held between Master and disciple. Rakhal was present.

Master (laughing) : People say it is exceedingly delightful to enjoy the company of one's wife after the day's hard work is over. (*Laughter.*)

Disciple : No doubt that is so in the case of those who look upon the wife as the greatest source of happiness. (Aside to R.) I am going through a cross-examination and the Master's questions are leading questions.

Master (laughing) : Mothers generally say, "If I can but procure for my child the 'Foot of a Tree,' the shelter where he is to take rest in the desert of this world, then my task is done." That 'Foot of the Tree' is said to be the wife! (*Laughter.*)

Disciple : There are parents and parents,—mothers and mothers. Surely parents that are *mukta* (liberated from the bondage of the world) would not think of giving their sons away in marriage. If they do so, they must be *mukta* (liberated) indeed!

The Master only laughed. Here the rest of the company left the room.

Master : What do you think takes place at the time of my *Avesha* (God-consciousness)?

Disciple : Your spirit, Lord, is then in the sixth *Bhumi* (plane) mentioned in the *Vedas*. Then you

Avesha: Blessed and Serene Mood

come down to the 5th plane when you begin to talk.

Master : I am only a humble instrument in His hands. It is He who is doing all these things. I do not know anything.

Disciple : This wonderful self-effacement! Hence it is, Lord, that all people are drawn to Thee.

Daya: Kindness to All

Disciple : You said that *Maya* is attachment to one's own relatives and friends, but *Daya* is love extending to all mankind—even to all God's creatures. I am afraid I do not see this clearly enough. Is it not the fact that *Daya* is a *pravritti* (*i.e.*, a feeling which makes a man cling to the world)?

Master : Why, *Daya* is not a bad feeling. It is elevating and leads one Godward.

Disciple : But is it not a fact that it belongs to the *pravritti-marga* (*i.e.*, the other way, which leads away from God)?

* * * * *

Disciple (humbly) : Sir, now I have a great desire to turn my exclusive attention to these things, and to this end should very much like that my work in the world should diminish.

Master : Oh yes, that is quite natural. I dare say the Lord will help you.

Nirakar or Sakar

Master : Do you believe in *Nirakar* or *Sakar* God with form or God without form?

Disciple : I go so far as the attributes. God has attributes; so far I see clearly enough. But is it not a fact that it is impossible to think of the 'Formless' without the help of forms? Anyhow we must go through forms or images.

Master (smiling) : So you see, I lay stress upon one's meditating on Personal God (God with form) as eminently favourable to the culture of *Bhakti*.

Disciple : Revered Sir, is Pandit Sasadhar making any progress in this direction (*i.e.*, in the path of *Bhakti*)?

Master : Yes, but he is drawn more to the path of

knowledge by philosophy. These men belong to a class of their own. They do not see that this way is exceedingly difficult.

No one spoke for some time. Was the Master all the while reading the soul of the disciple humbly sitting at his feet and looking up for strength and guidance into his benignant face, smiling and beaming with the joy of the Lord?

Renunciation

Master (encouragingly) : It is sufficient if one can give up the world from the mind.

Is not Outward Renunciation Necessary?

Disciple : This kind of teaching is, as it seems to me, intended for the weak. For men of the highest class it is *renunciation* in the strict sense of the word. *They must give up the world not only from the mind but also outwardly* !

Master : You have heard all about non-attachment that I was talking about?

Disciple : Yes, I understand by non-attachment not simply the want of attachment to things of this world. It is non-attachment *plus* something. *That something is the love of God.*

Master : You are quite right.

Disciple : Sir, what is God-vision?

God-vision

Master : God-vision cannot be made clearly intelligible to others. The state of things that comes about may, however, be described *to a certain extent.*

You have no doubt been to the theatre to witness a dramatic performance. Before the performance has commenced you must have noticed that the people are very busy talking to one another on a variety of subjects—politics, household affairs, official business, &c. But the curtain goes up and behold, mountains, cottages, rivers and men are suddenly presented to view! Instantaneously all noise, all conversation is at an end and each spectator is all attention to the novel scene that is being enacted before him.

Pretty much the same is the state of him who is blessed with God-vision.

Prema and the Man of the world

Disciple : *Prema*, as you have said to-day, is the string of love with which to bind the God of Love. With *Prema* (an intense love of God) one may be sure of seeing God as soon as one calls out to Him.

But the question is whether such Prema is within the reach of a man of the world (grihastha).

The Master was silent for a while.

* * * * *

Disciple : Haripada knows how to expound the *Puranas* like a professional Hindu Pandit. He knows for instance how to describe the life of Prahlada like such a Pandit.

Master : Oh, does he? The other day I noticed that his eyes were unusually worked up. Thereupon I asked him, 'Do you give yourself to excessive meditation?' He only held down his head. I said, 'Go not so fast; you must avoid extremes.'

It was about 9 P.M. Now entered Adhar Lal Sen, and a short while after there was a talk on the burning waters of Sitakund near Chandranath Hills in Chittagong. What seemed like tongues of flame were visible, it was said, from the surface of the water in the *Kunda*.

Master (to Adhar) : How do you account for this?

Here one of the disciples said to Adhar, 'It is phosphorus in the water, is it not?'

Adhar (to Master): It burns because of the phosphorus in the water.

Love for the Disciples

Master (to Adhar) : There is Ram here so kind. Otherwise there would have been nobody to call Harish and others (*i.e.*, the disciples) to dinner. They are so wrapt up in their meditation.

The Master had thus a good word to say by way of introducing Ramachatterji (the priest) to the favourable notice of Adhar, who was a Deputy Magistrate. Adhar often helped such men in a substantial way.

SECTION X

1885

SRI RAMAKRISHNA AT THE TEMPLE OF DAKSHINESWAR, WITH NARENDRA AND OTHER DISCIPLES

CHAPTER I

THE MASTER DESCRIBES THE PATH OF DEVOTION

(BHAKTI-YOGA)

Sri Ramakrishna is seated on the lounge, in deep *Samadhi*!

The disciples and other devotees are seated on the floor, where mats have been spread out. They all look on the Master. Amongst them are Mahimacharan, Rama (Datta), Manomohun, Nabai, M. and others. Later on comes in Narendra.

It is the first of March, Sunday, 1885, the full moon of Falgun. On this day, the festival of Doljattra is being celebrated.

The state of God-consciousness begins to leave the Master and he has the power of speech restored to him. But his mind is still in the God-world!

The Master speaks to Mahimacharan saying,—My dear sir, do tell me about the need for divine love. Do tell me how the love of the Lord is the one thing needful.

Mahimacharan (quoting *Narada-pancharatra*) : A voice from heaven said to Narada who wanted to practise austerities—

1. "If God is worshipped with devotion, what is the need for asceticism?

If He is not so worshipped, what again is the need for asceticism?

If the Lord is realised within and without, what is the need for asceticism?

If He is not so realised, asceticism would be of little avail.

2. Desist, O my child, desist from the practice of further austerities.

Go thy way at once to Siva—the ocean of divine knowledge.

From Him do thou learn how to love the Lord. Such love has been spoken of by the worshippers of God the Preserver—a love that never fails—a love that like a bill-hook cuts asunder the fetters of this world."

These words were heard by Narada when leading the life of an ascetic in a forest-retreat.

Master : This love for God is of two kinds. First, the love which is enjoined by the sacred scriptures. We are to worship in a certain way or repeat the name of the Lord so many times. All these belong to this kind of *Bhakti*. This is *Bhakti* according to the Law. It may lead to the knowledge of the Absolute in *Samadhi*. The self is thus merged in the Universal Soul never to come back. This is the case with ordinary devotees.

Chaitanya and Sri Ramakrishna

The case is different with divine incarnations— the Sons of God and those that are His own. Their love for God is not made up of mere formulae. It springs from within!

It wells up from the soul! Divine incarnations (like Chaitanya) and those that are nearest to Him have within their reach Absolute Knowledge in *Samadhi* and at the same time may come down from that height retaining their self and loving the Lord as father, mother, &c. Saying, 'Not this', 'Not this,' they leave behind them the steps of the staircase one after another until they get up to the roof. Getting up there, they say, 'It is this.' But soon they find out that the staircase is made of the same materials—brick, lime and brick-dust—as the roof itself. So they walk up and down, sometimes resting on the roof and sometimes on the steps of the staircase.

The roof symbolises the Absolute realised in *Samadhi* in which the self responding to the sense-world is blotted out. The staircase is the phenomenal world—the world of names and forms which, after the roof has been reached, is realised as the manifestation of the Absolute to the human senses.

Sukadeva was in *Samadhi* in which the self becomes one with the Absolute. To him the Lord sent Narada to ask him to read the word[1] of God before Raja Parikshit. Narada observed that the holy sage was seated like a stock or stone, absolutely dead to the world of senses. Narada began to play upon his lute, singing and praising the Lord in four verses. The first verse caused the hairs of Sukadeva's body to stand on end; the second, brought tears into his eyes. Then he could see, realise within himself, the spiritual form of the Lord. Finally, he came down from his spiritual height and held converse with Narada.

Thus Sukadeva had both transcendental knowledge and love for the Lord.

Hanuman realised God without form and God with form, and then passed his days in meditating upon a particular form of the Lord—the form of Ramachandra, a form made of spirit and bliss everlasting.

Much the same was the case with Prahlada and Narada. They realised the Absolute—they realised the spiritual forms of the Lord too, from another plane.

Prahlada realised, 'I am It' (God the Absolute). He also realised, 'I am Thy servant, Thou art my Lord.'

Narada passed his days in ecstatic love for the Lord.

This love solves the problem of life. So long as there is the self which says 'I', 'I,' the problem for *me* is 'How to live?' Shall I be content with a sensuous nature responding to a world of senses? No, let this self be the servant of the

[1]Bhagavata.

Lord—not the servant of the world and its so-called enjoyment! Thou art the Lord; and I am, O Lord, Thy servant. Not the enjoyment of the world and its pleasures, but the enjoyment of Bliss everlasting, the enjoyment of the never-failing joy of the Lord!

The Ego of Divine Love and the Problem of Life

Self or ego leads away from the Lord, but the ego of divine love—the ego of Godward knowledge—the ego of the child, leads to God. Sankaracharya retained after *Samadhi* the ego of Godward knowledge for the purpose of teaching mankind.

The self or ego of the child is not attached to things of this world. The child gets out of temper but soon there is not a trace of anger left in him. He builds a play-house for the dogs, but presently forgets all about this. His fondness for its playmates knows no bounds; but if he loses sight of them for some time, he forms new ties and forgets all about the old friends. The self of the child is thus unattached to anything. The self of divine love kept after *Samadhi*, in which it becomes one with the Absolute, solves the problem of life.

Another reason why *Bhakti* or love for God should be cultivated by men in general is that the ego cannot be shaken off. You may reason it away for a time but, behold! it comes up again; you cannot rid yourself of yourself, of the ego which says, 'I, I.'

The ego is like a water-jar, the Absolute is the shoreless ocean in which the water-jar is merged. You may reason that the Infinite or the Absolute is both within or without; but you cannot shake yourself free of the water-jar so long as you reason. The so-called Absolute is something relative to you so long as you reason. This water-jar that you cannot shake off is the self or ego of divine love. So long as there is the water-jar or ego, there are both I and Thou. Thus 'Thou art the Lord, I am the servant of the Lord'. *You may carry your reasoning to the highest point but the self or ego still remains.*

CHAPTER II

SRI RAMAKRISHNA TEACHES RENUNCIATION TO NARENDRA

Here Narendra comes in and falls at the feet of the Master. He speaks to Narendra, coming down from the lounge and taking his seat on one of the mats spread out on the floor. The chamber is by this time filled with the disciples and visitors from Calcutta and other places.

Master (to Narendra): Are you doing well, my boy? Is it true that you are a constant visitor at Girish Ghose's house?

Narendra : Yes, Sir, I do go to see him off and on.

Girish is a new disciple, having joined the Master in December 1884. The Master often speaks of the greatness of his faith—a faith which, as he often says, cannot be girt about with both the arms. And his longing for the Lord is even as intense as his faith. At home he always meditates upon God and is, as it were, drunken with the joy that the Lord alone can give. He is visited at his house by many disciples, specially by Narendra, Haripada, Narayan, Benode, and others. They have amongst them one theme alone for talk, *viz.*, the Master.

Girish is a man of the world—a householder. On the other hand, the Master sees that Narendra will renounce the world to do the work of the Lord. Narendra will renounce 'Woman and Gold.'

The Ideal Man or Sannyasin

Master (to Narendra) : Is it indeed true that you go often to see Girish Ghose at his house?

Well, one may wash ever so many times a cup which contains garlic: but the smell of the garlic will not leave the cup. Boys who have not entered the world and have not touched 'women and gold' are pure vessels—free from smell of any kind. Men that have been in the world for a long time are like vessels rubbed over with garlic.

They are again like mangoes pecked at and thus defiled by crows.

Again, young men who have not touched the world are like new earthen pots in which milk may be safely kept. On the other hand, worldly men are like earthen vessels in which milk was once turned into curds. In such vessels it is not safe to keep pure milk. The chances are that the milk will turn sour.

Knowledge or the love of God taught to pure young souls is like the pure milk which can be safely kept in new vessels. If taught to men of the world it is in very many cases thrown away like the milk kept in vessels which once contained curds.

The Imperfections of the House-holder

My dear boy, there are, indeed worshippers amongst men of the world who seek for the Lord. They form a class by themselves. Their mind is given to God and at the same time to the enjoyments of the flesh. In the Ramayana it is mentioned that Ravana was a type of this class of men. He wanted the good things of this world as well as God. He married the charming daughters of the Devas, the Nagas, the Gandharvas, the Asuras; at the same time he attained God in the end.

In the Puranas it is mentioned that the Asuras were given to the enjoyment of worldly pleasures; at the same time they attained God in the end.

Narendra : Girish Ghose now-a-days avoids the company of bad people.

Master : In a certain place there were seated some *sannyasins*, when a young woman chanced to pass by. All continued as before to meditate upon God, except one person, who looked on her with a glance of his eye. This man who had been attracted by female beauty had been formerly a householder and was the father of three children when he became a *sannyasi*.

If you rub garlic with a liquid into a solution and put it into a cup for a long time, would it not be hard to make the cup free from the smell of the garlic? Is it possible to make the *babuy* plant bring forth the sweetest mangoes?

Of course it is possible for a person who possesses occult powers to do this miracle. But it is not everybody that can attain these miraculous powers.

Yes, it is possible even for a man of the world to be pure like the young men who have not touched the world and who seek God alone, and for the *babuy* plant to bring forth the sweetest mangoes. But the power of doing these miracles must come down from the Almighty; and nothing is impossible with God. How rare, however, is such a gift from Heaven!

The thing is, you must give your whole mind to the Lord.

But a man of the world, a householder,—Oh, how he is troubled with many things! Has he indeed time enough to spare for the Lord?

A certain man wanted the services of a Pandit, well versed in the scriptures, through whom he could hear the word of God recited and explained every day. A friend of his said to him, 'Well I know such a Pandit; he is exactly the man we want; but there is one difficulty as regards this man. He has some land under cultivation, which he has to look after every day. There are four ploughs and eight bullocks always at work. Thus the difficulty is that he has no time to spare.' The man in search of a Pandit cried out, 'My friend, am I looking about for a learned Pandit like the one you have in view—a Pandit with ploughs and bullocks and arable lands to look after and with no time to spare? (*Laughter.*) No, no; I am in quest of a Pandit from whom I can hear the word of God!'

A certain king used to hear the word of God everyday recited by a learned Pandit. At the end of the lesson for the day, the Pandit used to say to the king, 'O, king, were you able to follow all this that I read before you?' To this question the Raja would only reply, 'My dear sir, it is for *you*, first of all, to understand the meaning of these holy texts!'

The Pandit thought over these words of the king everyday upon his return home. "Why does the king," thought he within himself, "say to me every day, 'Do *you* first understand the meaning?' " Being a devout Brahmana, he felt an awakening of the spirit within himself in the course of a few days. He realised that the worship of the Lord alone is the one thing needful. Being sick of the world and its pleasures, he gave it up. On the day he left his house in order to go into retirement, he sent a message unto the king, saying, 'O, king, I have indeed at last come to know the true meaning of the word of God (*i.e.*, give up everything for the sake of the Lord).'

That being my idea of men of the world, do you think I look down upon them? O, no. The knowledge of oneness tells me that everything is but a manifestation of God the Absolute on the plane of sense. Thus do I realise, actually see, that all women are so many forms in which the Divine Mother appears. So I revere all women alike—be it a woman of the lower class or an ideal wife who sets an example to others of conjugal love and devotion.

Alas, I look in vain for customers who want anything higher or better than *Kolai* pulse! Everybody runs after woman and gold! Very few do aspire for higher things!

They are attracted by female beauty,—by money, honours, titles,—not knowing that the blessed vision of the Lord—the divine beauty—will cause the highest place, even that of the creator, to appear as a thing not worth one's while to strive for.

A certain person said to Ravana, 'Why can you not approach Sita assuming the form of Rama—her beloved husband?' Ravana replied, 'My friend, if I once behold Rama in the recess of my soul—if I once meditate upon this divine form—Tillottama and other beauties would appear to me like ashes of the dead at the burning ghat. After that I can spurn the high place of the Creator, not to speak of women with all their charms!'

Verily these customers, every one of them, seek for *Kolai* pulse. It is given to pure souls alone, who have not touched the world, to love God alone—to have one aim,

—to have the mind fixed upon the Lord.

(To Manomohan, a householder and a disciple): I must say it, although you may take offence. I did say to Rakhal, 'My child, I should be better pleased to hear that you had plunged yourself into the Ganges and had been drowned, than if I ever heard that you had been mean enough to be anybody's servant for the sake of money or other worldly goods!'

The Service of the World and of Worldly Men.

(Rakhal is a young disciple now staying with the Master. He has married the sister of Manomohan.)

Turning again to Narendra the Master says:

A young Nepalese lady once came here in the company of Captain (Vishwanath). She played nicely on the *Eshraj* (a kind of violin) and chanted the name of the Lord at the same time. Her sweet voice drew quite a number into the room. On someone asking if she had married, she replied with some sharpness, 'I am the handmaid of the Lord! He is my Lord and Husband. Him alone do I serve and not any created being such as man.'

With 'Woman and Gold' always coming round about you, how is it possible to realise God? It is very hard indeed to live unattached in their midst. Hard is the case of the man of the world. In the first place, he is the slave of his wife; in the second place, he is the slave of the rupee; and in the third place he is the slave of him whom he serves for the sake of his living.

Akbar and the Fakeer

During the reign of Akbar there lived in a certain forest near Delhi, a *Fakeer* in a cottage. Many resorted to this holy man. But he had nothing with which to give them hospitality. He wanted money for this purpose and went for help to Akbar Shah, who was known for his kindness to holy men. Akbar Shah was then saying his prayers and the *Fakeer* took his seat in the prayer room. In the course of his prayers Akbar was heard to say, 'O Lord, do Thou grant unto me more wealth, more power, more territories.'

At once the *Fakeer* arose and was about to steal out of the room when the Emperor beckoned to him to be seated again.

At the end of the prayer, Akbar asked the *Fakeer*, 'You came to see me; how is it that you wanted to depart without saying anything to me?' The *Fakeer* said, 'The object of my visit to Your Majesty,—well, I need not trouble you with that.' On Akbar repeatedly pressing him to say what he wanted, the *Fakeer* at last said, 'Sir, many people come to me to be taught, but for want of money I am unable to see to their comforts; so I thought it as well to come to Your Majesty for help.' Akbar thereupon asked why he was about to depart without having told him the object of his visit. The *Fakeer* replied, 'When I saw that you were yourself a beggar, begging of the Lord wealth and power and territory, I thought within myself, 'Why shall I go a-begging of a person who is himself a beggar? I had better beg of the Lord Himself,—if, indeed, it is not possible for me to do without begging altogether!'

Narendra : Now-a-days, Girish Ghose thinks upon these matters alone.

Master : That is all right—as it should be. But why is it then that he calls names? My present nature cannot stand such rudeness. When there is a thunderclap the grosser objects are not so affected by it. But glass shutters move to and fro and make sounds! The *Sattva* element goes to make up my present nature. Hence it cannot stand noise and clamour. It was thus that my Divine Mother sent away Hriday who had latterly grown too rough for me.

(Smiling, to Narendra, after a while) : Do you agree with what Girish Ghose says (as to God being incarnate in man)?

Does God Incarnate Himself?

Narendra : He says, indeed, that he believes in divine incarnation. His faith being so deep-rooted, I thought it as well not to say anything the other way.

Master : How great is his faith ! Do you not think so?

The Master is seated on the mat spread on the floor.

Close to him is M.; in front of him is Narendra; the other disciples and Calcutta-visitors are seated round about. All look on the Master.

He is seated still for a while looking on Narendra with love unspeakable. He says unto him, 'My child, O! You cannot attain the end of life without renunciation of 'Woman and Gold'!

Saying this he becomes filled with divine fervour. He looks on him with love and sings:

SONG

1. Afraid am I to speak the word unto Thee: equally afraid am I,—if I do not speak it.

The fear that ariseth in my mind is that I may lose Thee—yes, be robbed of Thee, my wealth, my treasure!

2. Knowing well Thy mind, we shall teach Thee the holy name, that is to bring Thee to the Beloved.

It is now for Thee to get ready to receive that Name which has enabled us on many an occasion to steer the boat safe to land.

The Master is afraid lest Narendra ceases to be his own—lest some man plucks him out of his hand! Narendra is in tears as he hears the Master singing.

A visitor who has come to see the Master for the first time is seated near him and watches everything. He says to the Master,—

'Sir, if 'woman and gold' are to be given up, how should the householder, the man who has a family to bring up, solve this problem?'

Master : Well, Sir, you are at liberty to live with your wife and children and do your duty as a house-holder. What has passed between ourselves does not concern you.

Mahimacharan, a householder who has heard everything, sits speechless, holding his peace.

Master (smiling to Mahima) : Go on ahead. And halt not on the way. Go deeper into the forest, you shall get

The Problem For the Householder

sandal-wood. Go yet deeper, you shall come upon a silver mine! Do not stand where you are; but go on ahead. Yes, deeper still, and you shall come upon a gold mine! Move on still further, and you shall be placed in the midst of diamonds and rubies and sapphires! Yes, go on ahead.

Mahima : We ought to move on indeed. But alas! something holds us back, and keeps us from moving forward. Some unknown force holds the reins and pulls us back.

Master (smiling) : Why, my dear Sir, let the reins be cut asunder by the sword of His holy name! The name of the Divine Mother, the Consort of Eternity, is capable of cutting in twain the bonds of death!

Since his father left the world Narendra has been put to great trouble. He has passed through many a trial and suffering. The Master looks on Narendra from time to time. He says smiling on him with love and the light of sympathy beaming from his eyes,—'Have you already turned out to be a *Chikitsaka*, a physician of many years standing?'

The Master quotes the proverb, saying,

'A *Vaidya* is a physician who has succeeded in killing a hundred patients!

A *Chikitsaka* is he who has despatched a thousand at least unto eternity!' (*Laughter.*)

Narendra has had already enough of the bitter cup. Does the good Master refer to this?

Narendra smiles and holds his peace.

CHAPTER III

The Master with His Disciples

It is afternoon. The disciples and other devotees are waiting about in the Temple garden. The Master converses with M. He talks of the younger disciples.

Master : Everybody except Paltu says, 'I am getting on well with my meditation' How is it that Paltu cannot do so and fix his mind on God?

M. : He has so many things to read for the examination. That probably stands in the way of concentration.

Shadows of the World and Narendra

Master : What do you think of Narendra? Is it not the fact that there is no guile in him?

M.: Yes, that is so, Sir.

Master : Yes, the death of his father has left his family almost helpless.

Master : He has to think a good deal about his family. Thus, the light within him is a little hidden under the shadows of the world. This state of things, however, will not last long.

The Master now and then steps into the corridor where Narendra is talking with a *Vedantin.* He watches Narendra talking.

The disciples have come back into the chamber. The Master asks Mahimacharan to recite a Sanskrit prayer from the Sacred Books.

Mahima quotes from *Mahanrivana Tantra saying:*

'In the lotus of my heart do I worship God the Absolute whom *Hari* (God, the Preserver), *Hara* (God, the Destroyer) and *Vidhi* (God, the Creator) all desire to know, and upon whom the *Yogis* always meditate with a view to realisation.

He removes all fear of birth and death. He is Absolute Existence and Intelligence.

He contains within Himself the seed of the multitudinous worlds.'

Message of Hope to the Householder

The Master is deeply touched as these and other holy texts are being chanted by Mahima, who then proceeds to recite a prayer to Siva composed by Sankaracharya. In it the Lord of the world is asked to save the devotee from being drowned in the sea of the world. The world is also represented in this prayer as a place of misery—a deep dense wilderness in which one loses the way and cannot find the way out.

Now Mahimacharan is a man of the world and a householder.

Sri Ramakrishna (to Mahima) : Why do you say that the world is a well in which men are drowned, or that it is a deep dense forest in which one must lose one's way? Why do you say it is a place of misery and nothing more? These epithets are all very good from the standpoint of a beginner. Surely they are all quite out of place on the lips of him who clings to the Lord in weal and in woe. Away with all fear —when it is the Lord that guides your feet! Then cry out with joy like another devotee, also a householder:

"Verily is this world a mansion of joy.
Let me pass my days eating, drinking and rejoicing.
Janaka the royal sage, how great was his power? Was there anything in which he was found wanting — spiritual or temporal?
Ah! No, he did give his mind to God and at the same time drink out of his cup of milk!'

Whom to fear? The Lord is your friend; hold him fast and He will lead you by the hand. Never mind that it is 'a deep dense forest overgrown with weeds and thorns!' Put on a pair of shoes and the thorns will not prick your feet or cause them to bleed. Away with fear. In this play of 'hide and seek', touch the Holy Person of the grand dame, our Divine Mother, who leads the play unattached. Once you touch Her Person, you are spared the necessity of taking any further part in this exciting play. Yes, you shall have no longer to run about excited and to be in bondage like the thief of the play.

Janaka, the royal sage, you know, wielded a couple of swords. One was the sword of true knowledge, the other the sword of work. He who is expert in handling the swords has nothing to fear.

* * * * *

The Master remains sitting on the lounge. M. is seated on the floor close to him.

Master (aside to M.) : What he has said has drawn my

mind, as it were, away,—from lighter matters.

(The Master here speaks of the first prayer chanted by Mahimacharan addressed to God the Absolute.)

Now they are singing forth the name of the Lord and dancing with joy. The Master joins the disciples. He is filled with deep devotional feelings and sings and dances with the devotees.

The singing over, the Master says to the disciples, 'The chanting of the Lord's name with love is the one thing needful; all the rest is of little value! *Bhakti* is the reality; all else is unreal!'

* * * * *

They are seated on the floor talking. Narendra and Ram (Datta) are engaged in hotly discussing a point. Ram has come to see the Master after his recovery from a recent illness.

The Master watches them talking and raising their voice in the course of the discussion.

Master (aside to M) : I, for my part, do not like such discussion. (Aloud to Ram) : Stop, you are not perfectly restored to health!—Very well, go on softly, and do not get excited.

(Aside to M.) : All this is not at all to my liking. I used to cry to my Divine Mother, saying, "O, Mother, one man says, 'It is thus, It is thus,' another man says, 'It is something else.' Reveal unto me, good Mother, what the truth is!"

SECTION XI

1885

SRI RAMAKRISHNA AT THE HOUSE OF BALARAM, A DISCIPLE, WITH NARENDRA (SWAMI VIVEKANANDA), GIRISH, BALARAM, CHUNILALL, LATU, M., NARAYAN AND OTHER DISCIPLES

CHAPTER I

THE MASTER TEACHES THE DISCIPLE

Wednesday, the 11th of March, 1885, or the 29th Falgun of the Bengali year is the 10th day of the dark fortnight of that month. On this day Sri Ramakrishna has come to the house of Balaram, one of his disciples. He arrived from Dakshineswar at about 10 o'clock in the morning, and has had his dinner there.

Lord bless you, Balaram! It is your house which the Master has chosen to make his chief 'vineyard' to-day! It is here that he has bound devotee after devotee by the ties of divine love! It is here that he has so often danced and sung the name of the Lord at the head of his disciples! It seems as if another Gouranga is setting up a fair in the house of his disciple Sribash for the 'buying and selling' of divine love.

How great is the Master's love for his disciples! There at the Temple of the Mother, alone he cries like a child! He longs to see them! Sleepless at night he says to the Divine Mother, 'Oh, Mother! Deign to draw him into Thy fold! He is so devoted to Thee, poor boy! Oh, how I long to see him! Mother, bring him here or take me to the place where he is.' Is this the secret of his coming to Balaram's house so often? He says indeed to everybody, 'Balaram is a true Bhakta; he daily worships the Lord of the universe, his household God; his offerings are therefore always acceptable.' But whenever he comes to his house he says to Balaram, 'Go and invite my Narendra, Bhabanath, Rakhal, Purna, Narendra junior, Narayan and other disciples. Offering food to them is the same thing as offering it to God Himself. These indeed are not ordinary men. They are parts of the divinity manifest in the flesh.'

It was at Balaram's house that there was so much dancing and singing at the time of the car-festival. Many a time have the devotees met here 'at the Durbar of God's love.'

M. is a teacher in a neighbouring English school. He had heard that Sri Ramakrishna was at Balaram's house. Being a little free from work, he came down there at about noon to see the Master. He bows down and salutes his feet.

The mid-day dinner is over and the Master is in the drawing-room taking rest. The young disciples are seated round him. From time to time he is taking out *cabab*, and other spices from a small pouch.

Sri Ramakrishna (affectionately to M.) : You are here! Is there no school to-day?

M.: Sir, I have come directly from the school; I have just now nothing of importance to attend to there.

A devotee : No, Sir, he is playing truant and has kept away from school. (*Laughter.*)

M. (to himself) : Ah me! It is, indeed, as if some invisible power has drawn me to this place!

The Master then grew a little thoughtful. He then bade M. take his seat near him and talked with him on various subjects.

He said to him, 'Wring the wet towel here for me, would you? and put the coat in the sun.' Again, 'My legs and feet are aching, will you rub them softly a little?' M. does not know how as a disciple he is to serve the Master. So the gracious Master teaches him. M. eagerly sets about doing the Master's bidding. He strokes his hallowed feet gently with the palm of his hands and fingers, while the Master teaches him.

Sri Ramakrishna (to M.) : Tell me M., what you think of this. For some days, a strange state of things has been going on. It is now beyond my power to touch any metal. Once I put my hand to a metallic cup; do you know what came of this? I felt as if the sting of some horned fish had been thrust into my flesh. The pain was very acute. But, you know, one cannot do without a washpot. So I thought of carrying it to the foot of the willow-tree. I wrapped it in my towel and then tried to take it up. As soon as I touched it, the same acute pain came back. It was indeed terrible. At last I was forced to pray unto the Divine Mother, saying, 'Oh Mother, forgive me this time; I will never do so any more.' Do you not think that this is a warning from Mother that I should stand apart absolutely from all sorts of enjoyments?

Intense Renunciation

M. : I dare say, revered Sir, that is the true explanation.

Sri Ramakrishna (to M.) : N. junior often comes to see me. Do you not think that his people will take him to task for this? Oh! He is a nice boy, so pure! The fact is, he is absolutely free from carnality.

N. Junior

M. : Yes, revered Sir, he is indeed a young man of no ordinary calibre.

Sri Ramakrishna : That is so. Furthermore, he says, 'The word of God, if it once reaches my ear, becomes stamped upon my mind.' Again 'In my infancy I used to cry for the Lord. I was so much troubled at heart because I could not see Him.'

In this way the Master talked on about the young devotee, when one of the disciples cried out saying, 'Well Mr. M., when do you go back to school?'

Sri Ramakrishna : What o'clock is it?

A disciple : It is just ten minutes to one.

Sri Ramakrishna (to M.) : You had better go back;

it is late already. You are on duty. (To Latu.) Well! Where is Rakhal?

Latu : He is gone home.

Sri Ramakrishna : Is it possible? How is it he did not see me when he left!

CHAPTER II

IN THE AFTERNOON WITH DISCIPLES

After school M. called again. The Master, he is pleased to see, is seated in the midst of his disciples in Balaram's drawing-room. On his face is a sweet smile, the reflection of which was caught by the faces of the disciples. M. salutes the feet of the Master, who beckons to him to be seated by his side. Girish (Ghosh), Suresh (Mittra), Balaram, Latu, Chunilall and many other disciples are present.

Sri Ramakrishna (to Girish) : You had better argue the point with Narendra. See what he has got to say.

The Doctrine of Divine Incarnation

Girish : Narendra says, 'God is infinite. We cannot even say that all that we see or hear—be it an object or a person—is a part of God; much less God Himself. A part of infinity cannot be conceived.'

Master : God is indeed infinite. But He is omnipotent. He may so order that His divinity as love may be manifest in the flesh and be among us as God-incarnate. Divine incarnation is a fact. Of course, one cannot make this perfectly clear by means of words. It is a fact to be seen and realised by the spiritual eyes. One must see God to be convinced of this.

By analogy we can at best faintly apprehend the matter. Suppose, one touches the horn of a cow, or her feet, or the tail, or the udder: would this not be the same as touching the cow herself? For us human beings the chief thing about the cow is the milk, which comes from the udder. Well!

The milk of divine love streams to us from God-incarnate.

Girish : Narendra says, 'Is it possible to know God, to hold the divine idea within the compass of our small poor brain? God is infinite!'

Perception of the Infinite

Master (to Girish) : That is indeed true. Who can know God? It is not given to us, nor is it required of us to *know* Him fully. It is enough if we can see Him—feel that He is the only reality! It is enough if we can see God-incarnate.

A person, suppose, goes up to the holy river Ganges and touches the water. He would say, 'I have been blessed with the vision and touch of the holy river.' Surely it is not required of him to touch the river from Hardwar to Gangasagar, from its source to the mouth! (*Laughter.*)

If one touches your feet, surely that would be the same as touching you.

A person walks up to the sea and touches the water. Surely it is the same thing as touching the sea.

Fire is latent in all objects. But in the constitution of wood it is to a greater degree than in other objects.

Girish (smiling) : I for my part am in quest of the *fire.* Therefore all that I care for is a place where I can get the *fire.*

Master (smiling) : Well! Wood, as made by God, has more of this element than other objects. Do you seek God? Well, seek Him in man! His divinity is manifest more in man than in any other object. Look around for a man with a love of God that overflows—a man who yearns for God—a man intoxicated with His love. In such a man has God incarnated Himself.

(To M.) : God indeed is in all things; only His power is manifest in them to a greater or less degree. God-incarnate is God's power (divinity) most manifest in the flesh.

Girish : Narendra says, 'It is beyond the power of word, thought or the senses to know Him—beyond the power of thought—beyond the reach of mind.'

Master : That is not quite so. It is true enough that the conditioned mind cannot realise Him. But He can be realised by the pure mind, which is the same thing as the pure reason, which is the same thing as the pure or unconditioned soul. He cannot indeed be sensed by the finite reason or by the finite, relative, conditioned mind, which has a sensuous nature, and is thus marked by an attachment to 'Women and Gold' (carnality and worldliness). The mind may get rid of its sensuous nature, be purified by culture, and be once more free from all worldly tendencies, desires, and attachment, and thus be one with the Unconditioned Soul.

Was it not thus that the sages of old saw God? God, the Unconditioned Spirit, they saw by means of the purified mind (the mind stripped of its sensuous nature) which they found to be the same as the Atman or the Unconditioned Soul within.[1]

Girish (smiling) : Narendra has been beaten by me.

Sri Ramakrishna : Oh no! On the contrary he says, 'Girish (Ghosh) believes in the incarnation of God! His faith is firm as a rock; surely it is not proper for one to meddle with such a faith!'

Girish (smiling) : Sir, we are all talking away; our words flow like water, but your M. here sits with his lips closed. What in the world does he think of? Do be good enough to throw light upon this point. (*Laughter.*)

Master (smiling) : Beware of the following: (1) of him whose words flow like water; (2) of him the door of whose heart is closed to you; (3) of the devotee who shows off to the world his devotion by the sacred *Tulsi* leaf stuck into the ear; (4) of the woman who wears a long veil; (5) of the tank covered with scum, the cold water of which is so injurious to health. (*Laughter.*) I must say our M. here is no such thing—rather let us say, the depth of his soul has made him speechless. (*Laughter.*)

Girish : Sir, will you kindly repeat the proverb?

Chunilall: Guardians of boys are beginning to talk

[1] Compare Kant's exposition of the Transcendental Reason or the Faculty of the Unconditioned.

about M's conduct as Headmaster. Our friend N. junior is a pupil of his; so are Baburam, Narayan, Paltu, Purna, Tejchandra. The guardians complain that it is M. who brings these boys to our Master, so that they neglect their studies. They hold M. responsible for all this.

Master : Oh dear! Who will believe all that they say against him?

Just at this moment Narayan comes in and falls at the Master's feet. Narayan is of a fair complexion, 17 or 18 years old. He is a student and a beloved disciple of Sri Ramakrishna. The Master is so much attached to him that he sometimes cries before the Divine Mother in his anxiety to see him.

He looks upon the boy as Narayana (God) Himself.

Girish (at the sight of Narayan) : Hallo! Who sent you word that the Master is here? M., I am afraid, is going to do it for everybody! (*Laughter.*)

Sri Ramakrishna (laughing) : Pray, hold your tongue! People are already speaking ill of him (M.).

* * * * *

The conversation next turns upon Narendra.

A disciple: He does not come to us now-a-days as often as he used to do before.

Master : It is no wonder that he does not come to us. Wonderful is the thought of bread and butter ! It makes even such a great poet as Kalidas (author of Sakuntala) lose his wits! (*Laughter.*)

Balaram : He is a great friend of Annada Guha, grandson of the well-known Shiboo Guha. He always walks with him.

Master: Yes, they meet generally at the house of a friend of theirs who is employed in some Government office. They hold prayer meetings as Brahmos there.

Balaram (smiling): Brahmans generally say that Annada Guha is very conceited.

Acceptance of gifts and Loss of Independence

Sri Ramakrishna : Pay no heed to what the Brahmans say. You know their ways ; he who gives good gifts to them is a good man; the rest of mankind are bad! (*Laughter.*)

CHAPTER III

SINGING THE NAME OF THE LORD WITH DISCIPLES

Sri Ramakrishna expresses a desire to listen to the chanting of hymns. Balaram's drawing-room is filled with visitors. Every one watches the Master, eager to hear whatever may fall from his lips and mark what he is going to do next. Tarapada is invited to sing. He sings a song describing the sports of the 'Shepherd of Men,' Sri Krishna.

SONG

1. Have mercy on my miserable self, Oh God, Thou who used to go about in the groves of Brindaban! Thou charmer of the mind, Thou who used to play on the sweet flute while incarnate in Brindaban.

2. At Brindaban, Thou didst pass Thy days in boyhood. Thou didst kill the dragon. Oh Lord! Thou sayest, 'Fear not.' to the weary and heavy-laden that pray for Thy help in their trouble! How beautiful art Thou with Thy loving eyes looking askance and with the peacok's feather dancing on Thy forehead. Thou bringest joy unto the heart of the greatest of the lovers of God. It was Thou who didst lift up the hill on Thy arm. It was Thou who didst pull down the pride of Kamsa; it was Thou who didst once enjoy the company of Thy great devotees, the Gopis, during that manifestation of the highest divine love, at Brindaban.

Oh Thou of the dark complexion, so beautiful, with wild flowers decorating Thy person!

(Oh my mind say, 'O Sweet Lord!' say, 'O Sweet Lord!').

Sri Ramakrishna (to Girish) : What a charming song! Did you compose it?

A disciple : Yes, Sir; he has composed all the songs in the drama called Chaitanya-lila.

Master (to Girish) : This song is grand! (To the singer.) Can you sing about Nitay (Brother of Chaitanya)?

He sings about Nitay preaching the love of God taught by Chaitanya.

SONG

ECSTATIC LOVE OF GOD

1. Come those that want the love of God once taught at Brindaban by the most beloved of the Lord.

The high tide of that love flows past, and is not going to last for a long time! Have a care!

2. Do you not see this love streaming out in a hundred different directions? He who wants it shall get as much as he pleases.

3. Radhika is made of this love, pure and simple. She it is to whom is given to deal out this love.

Now therefore say, 'O sweet Lord' at the call of this love.

Oh! This love makes one's heart intoxicated with this joy of the Lord. It makes it dance with this joy.

4. Say, say, 'O sweet Lord' at the call of this love.

Oh come! Oh come!

SONG

GAURANGA (CHAITANYA) GOD-INCARNATE

1. Lord of fair complexion! what divine idea has brought peace unto Thy life when Thou goest about in the guise of Gauranga?

Oh! Thou art immersed in the sea of the divine love.

That sea has been broken into waves by the strong wind of enthusiasm that is blowing. It is not too much to say that many will bid adieu to the honour of their families for Thy dear sake and join Thee.

(O Lord, Thou hast taken my mind!)

2. It was Thou, O Lord, who didst when incarnate as Sri Krishna, tend the cows at Brindaban! It was Thou who heldst between Thy fingers that enchanting flute of Thine which once shook the minds of the Gopis!

It was Thou who once didst raise on Thy arm the hill of Govardhan and so didst keep Brindaban from destruction! O, it was Thou who didst fall at the feet of the Gopis to atone for the offence of wounding their dignity, and hadst the moon of Thy fair face swimming in tears of repentant love!

('O Sweet Lord! Thou hast taken my mind!)

Everybody presses M. to sing. M. is shy and asks in whispers to be excused.

Girish (to the Master, smiling) : Sir, we cannot with all our combined efforts make M. sing a single song! (*Laughter.*)

Sri Ramakrishna (annoyed) : He will no doubt show his teeth at school! Strange that all his shyness springs up at the time of chanting the name of the Lord!

M. looks blank for some time.

Suresh (Mitra), another disciple, is seated at some distance from the Master. Sri Ramakrishna smiles on him affectionately and points to Girish.

Sri Ramakrishna (to Suresh) : Do you talk of the wild life that you once lived? O, here is one who is very much more than your match! (*Laughter.*)

Suresh (laughing) : That is indeed true, revered Sir! He is my *dada* (respected elder brother) in that respect. (*Laughter.*)

Girish (to Master) : I never paid attention to my studies in my boyhood. How is it, revered Sir, that people do insist on calling me learned in spite of all this?

Sri Ramakrishna : Mahima Chakravarti has gone through a pretty large number of the sacred books.

(To M.) : Is it not so, M.?

M.: Quite so, revered Sir.

Girish : What do you speak about, Sir? Is it *learning*? Then excuse me, please, I am not the person to stand in awe before it.

Master (smiling) : Do you know what I think of it? Books—sacred scriptures—all point the way to God. Once you know the way, what is the use of books? Then the hour comes for the culture of the soul in solitary communion with God.

A person had received a letter in which he was asked to send certain things to his kinsmen. He was going to order the purchase of the things when, looking about for the letter, he found it was missing! He searched for a long time. His people also joined him in the search. At last the letter was found and his joy knew no bounds. With great eagerness he took it up and went through its contents. It ran as follows: 'Please do send five seers of sweetmeats and one piece of cloth.' When he knew the contents, he threw the letter on one side and set forth to get the things wanted.

How long then does one care for such a letter? So long as one does not know its contents. The next step is to put forth one's efforts to get the things desired.

Similarly the sacred books only tell us of the way leading to God, that is, of the means for the realisation of God. The way being once known, the next step is to work one's way to the goal. Realisation is the goal.

What is the use of mere book-learning? The Pandits may be familiar with plenty of sacred texts and couplets. But what is the good of repeating them? One must realise in one's soul all that is mentioned in the scriptures. Mere reading shall not bring knowledge or salvation, so long as one is attached to the world, so long as one loves 'woman and gold' (*i.e.*, carnality and worldliness.)

In the almanac it is recorded that the rainfall will reach 20 adas (measures of capacity). But wring the almanac, not a drop will come out! Not a single drop—although you may want it very much! (*Laughter.*)

Girish (smiling) : Revered Sir, what do you say about the almanac? Will not a single drop come out of it? (*Laughter.*)

Master (smiling) : Oh, the scholar will talk very big, but he will have his eyes all the time from his high place upon 'woman and gold' or, in other words, on sensual pleasures and the 'almighty dollar.'

The vulture soars high up in the sky but its gaze is fixed on charnel-pits—places where the carcasses of dead animals are thrown. (*Laughter.*) Oh, they have a keen eye from their high place on those pits and carcasses below!

On Narendra

Master (to Girish) : Narendra is a young man of a very high order. He is in for everything—singing, playing on musical instruments etc., on the one hand, and the study of the various branches of knowledge on the other. He possesses the virtues of temperance and truthfulness and, what is more, is already beginning to know that God is real, that things of the world are of a fleeting nature, and that one should not be attached to them. Many and various are the good qualities that he has.

(To M.) : Well! Do you not think he is very good?

M. : Quite so, revered Sir; he is indeed, as you have described him.

Sri Ramakrishna (aside to M.) : Just look at his (Girish's) devotion to the Lord and his faith in Him, which is as firm as a rock!

M. looks on Girish with wonder. Girish has been coming to the Master only a very few days. But M. sees in him a familiar friend and brother—his own flesh and blood—'One of the brilliant gems strung together with one and the same thread in a necklace!'

* * * * *

Narayan said, 'Revered Sir, shall we not have the pleasure of listening to your songs?'

SONG

The Beloved Mother of the Universe

1. Oh my soul! Do thou clasp to thy heart my beloved Mother. Let thee and me alone have the privilege of looking on Her...

Let Her be seen by none else, by none else!

2. The desires—oh, get out of their way, my soul; and then let us enjoy Her presence alone: only let us have the organ of speech (the tongue) for our sole companion that we may cry out unto Her, saying 'Mother, O Mother!'

3. There are the desires; there are those which point to us the path leading to worldliness: oh, do not let them come near us!

Let the eye of wisdom that leads godward keep watch and keep us away from evil.

The Master then sings another song as if he were placed in the position of the weary and heavy-laden men of the world, who bend under the weight of their trials and sufferings.

SONG

The Mother and Weary Children

1. Oh Mother! Thou art made of bliss everlasting!; why then is it denied unto me?

2. My soul, oh, good Mother! knows not anything but the lotus of Thy hallowed feet.

Why then does the ruler of death, the king of justice, find fault with me? Tell me what answer to make to that dreaded king?

3. It was my heart's wish, oh Mother! to repeat Thy sacred name and go my way across this sea of the world. But not even in my dream had I the least idea that I should be drowned by Thee in this shoreless ocean.

Day and night, oh Mother! Thou Consort of the God of Eternity! have I been repeating Thy sacred name, which brings salvation unto Thy weary children. But alas! My endless troubles will never leave me; I only regret that if I die in this miserable plight, no one else will ever take Thy name.

The Master next sings about the joy of the Divine Mother, the manifested energy of the Absolute. He sees with his own spiritual insight the joy that the Mother, the Personal God (who creates, preserves and destroys), feels in communion with the Impersonal or the Absolute.

SONG

The Great Mystery: The Personal-Impersonal Ecstasy

1. In the company of the Absolute, oh Mother ! Thou art always immersed in sportive joy.

2. Thou art deep drunk with the wine of that joy. Thou art reeling but Thou dost not lose Thy footing! The Absolute, Thy husband, lies down and moves not.[1]

3. Thou standest on His breast and lookest as if Thou hast lost all control over Thyself.

The universe quakes under the weight of Thy feet. Mad are Thy looks, as well as of Thy Consort.

* * * * *

[1] Does this mean that we receive no message from the Absolute and that the personal side of God is the only actor before our eyes?

The disciples listen to the songs in deep silence. What strikes them is the change that has come over the Master. He is beside himself with the joy of the Lord—intoxicated with the unbounded bliss.

The song comes to an end. The Master says after a while, 'I am sorry I could not sing well to-day; I have caught cold!'

CHAPTER IV

At the Close of Day

It is evening. The shadows of eternity have fallen on the ocean-breast, and on the deep dense forest, and on the summits of mountains that kiss the firmament on high. They have cast a gloom on the boundless expanse round about and on the solitary bank of the undulating river that sends forth the never-ceasing sound of its many waters. At the sight of this sacred, solemn gloom, little, puny man cannot help being in another state of mind. The sun, he was only a few moments back giving light to all nature, inanimate as well as animate! Whither is he gone? The question puzzles the child—a being who is new to the world! It appeals no less to the holy man, for he has the soul of a child. He feels that he is always in the presence and care of his Divine Mother. It is evening! What a miracle! And wrought by what a wonderful being! The birds come together and sing on the boughs of trees. Human beings too do the same thing—those amongst them in whom the spirit within has waken up. They sing the name of the Lord.

It is evening. The disciples would not leave their seats. With their heads upraised and with eager ears they listen to the sweet name of the Lord chanted by the Master—sweeter, as repeated by him, than any they have ever heard before!

Yes, they have never heard another child calling out so sweetly to its Mother, saying, 'Ma, Ma!' It seems as if drops of nectar fall from the Master's lips. The infinite sky, the heaven-kissing mountain, the deep blue ocean, the boundless expanse, the deep, dense wilderness—what is the use now to go amongst them in quest of the Divine Father and Mother of the universe? What is the use now of fixing one's attention on the 'cow's horns' or her feet or other parts of her body? The Master has spoken of the udder of the cow to-day—from which to draw the milk of divine love! Is it indeed given to me to behold the vision of God-incarnate in this very room? What else could have brought to the hearts of the disciples—those that are weary and heavy-laden—the peace that passeth all understanding and the joy that is of the Lord? What else could have made this vale of tears flow over with joy? Is it possible that the man before me is God-incarnate? Whether he is so or not, my mind and heart and soul are his own—to deal with just as he pleases! He is already the Polestar of this enigmatical life! It is for me now to watch how in his great soul the Supreme Being, the Cause of causes, is reflected!

Thus did some of the disciples think within themselves. They felt they were blessed as they heard the Master chant the name of the sweet Lord God,[1] the name of the Father who takes away all trouble, all sin and iniquity—and the name of the Divine Mother.

How to Pray

The chanting of the names being over, the Master prays unto the Mother. It seems as if the god of love has taken a human body in order to teach man how to pray. He says, "Ma, I throw myself upon Thy mercy—may the lotus of Thy feet ever keep me from whatever leads Thy children away from Thee! I seek not, good Mother, the pleasures of the senses! I seek not fame! Nor do I long for those powers which enable one to do miracles! What I pray for, O good Mother, is pure love for Thee—love for Thee untainted by desires, love without alloy, love that seeketh not the things of the world, love for Thee that welleth up unbidden out of the depths of the immortal soul! Grant likewise, O Mother, that Thy child, bewitched by the fascinations of the world-system[1] may not forget Thee—forget Thee, entangled in this charming net of the world that Thou hast woven under him, made of 'Woman and Gold!' O, grant that he may never be charmed into loving these! O, good Mother, seest Thou not that Thy child hath none else in the world but Thee! O, I know not how to chant Thy name! Devoid am I of deep devotion,—of knowledge too, that leadeth unto Thee—devoid of genuine love, for Thee! O, vouchsafe unto me that love out of Thy infinite mercy!"

This evening prayer—is it called for in the case of this God-man?—for him who chants the name of the Lord day and night?—for him out of whose hallowed mouth there flows a never-ceasing stream of prayers unto the most high? Is it then that the Master observes these forms with a view to teach mankind how to live and pray?

*   *   *   *   *

Girish has invited Sri Ramakrishna to his house. He must come that very night.

Master : Do you not think it will be late?

Girish : No, revered Sir; you will come away as early as you please. As for myself I shall have to go to the theatre —they have quarrelled amongst themselves and I shall have to make it up.

Going downstairs from the first floor he has become like another being. He looks as if he were lost in the thought of God; he looks as if he has drunk deep! He is followed by his disciples Narayan and M. A little behind came Ram, Chuni and others.

Yes, lost ! It seems as if sense-consciousness were beginning to leave him. Narayan comes forward to hold him by the hand lest he should miss his footing. The Master seems annoyed.

A short while and he says to Narayan with great tenderness, 'If you hold me by the hand people will say, he is a drunkard! Let me walk on without any help.'

He crosses the next turning at Bosepara just a little away from Girish's house. What is it that makes him walk so fast? The disciples are left behind. Who can tell what divine idea has found its way into his heart?

What is it that makes him walk like a mad man? Is it because he is thinking of that Being who in the Vedanta is said to be beyond the reach of word and thought? Just a little while ago at Balaram's house he declared that the Being is *not* beyond the reach of the purified supersensual mind, that He may indeed be *realised* by the pure mind, which is the same thing as the pure reason,—which is the same thing as the pure soul! Or it may be that he is just at the present moment beholding that Being as a reality!

Is this realising 'Whatever is, is God?'

Ah! Here is Narendra coming! Many a day hath the Master cried, saying, 'Narendra, Narendra, Narendra,' like one gone mad! But now Narendra is here before him and yet he exchanges no word with him! Is this what people call *Bhava* (God-consciousness)—a state into which Gauranga (Chaitanya) is said to have been constantly thrown? Who is there to look through the mystery of God-consciousness?

He has come up to the end of the lane leading to Girish's house. The disciples all walk after him.

Now he turns to Narendra, and speaks, 'Is it well with you, my boy? Till now I had not the power to talk to you.' Every word that falls from his lips is charged with uncommon tenderness and affection.

He has not as yet come up to the door of the house. All at once he stops. He looks at Narendra and says, 'One word—this is one of the two (the human soul?) and this is another (Cosmos?).'

Was he indeed looking on the soul and the world? If so, in what light? He was looking on speechless!

One or two words have dropped from his hallowed

lips—like some solemn texts from the inspired scriptures, the Vedas—like unto the blessed word of God!

Or was it as if one had gone to the shore of the infinite ocean and stood there mute, looking on the boundless expanse! And had heard one or two echoes from the never-ceasing voice that comes up from the eternal deep?

CHAPTER V

All About God-incarnate

At the door stands Girish. He has come to greet the Master. The Master comes up, the disciples coming after. At the blessed sight, Girish falls at his feet upon his face like a rod! Blessed indeed is the sight, and the disciples behold it with awe and admiration.

Girish rises at his bidding. He receives on his head and person the dust of his hallowed feet. He leads the way to the reception-room where the Master and the disciples take their seats. The disciples are eager to sit close to the Master. They long to drink the nectar of the words that bring everlasting life.

On Newspapers

He is about to take his seat, when he finds a newspaper lying by his side. Newspapers have concern with worldly-minded men and deal with worldly matters,—with gossip, and with scandals. Hence they are unholy objects—in his eyes. He makes a sign and the paper is put away. Upon this he takes his seat.

Nityagopal bows down and salutes his feet.

Master (to Nitya) : Well! And then?

Nitya : Yes, revered Sir, I was unable to come to Dakshineswar. I was unwell. There was pain all over the body.

Master : Are you keeping well now?

Nitya : Not very well, I am sorry to say.

Master : You had better remain one or two notes below the highest in the gamut!

Nitya : Company does not agree with me. They say of me all manner of things. That puts me into fright. At other times I am quite free from fear, and I feel the strength of the spirit within me.

Master : That is only natural. Who is the constant companion?

Nitya : Tarak. At times even he does not agree with the state of my mind.

Master : Nangta[1] used to say that he had at his monastery an ascetic who had acquired some miraculous powers. He used to go about with his eyes fixed on the sky. His companion Ganesh Gorgy left him and he became disconsolate!

By this time a change has come over the Master. He remains speechless for a while!

Getting back into consciousness he says, 'Thou hast come, hast thou? Well, I am here too!'

Who will pretend to fathom this mystery? Is this the language of the gods?

Among the disciples who sat on this occasion at the feet of the Master were Narendra, Girish, Ram, Haripada, Chuni, Balaram, M. and many others.

Narendra does not believe in the incarnation of God. On the other hand Girish has a burning faith that God incarnates Himself from age to age in this world of ours. The Master wishes that they should argue the point before him.

Sri Ramakrishna (to Girish) : I should like to see you both talk over the matter in English. (*Laughter.*)

They talk—not, however, in English but in Bengali with a few sprinkling of English words. Narendra says, 'God is infinite, it is beyond our power to conceive Him by means of our little intellect. God is in every human being. It is not the case that He is manifest only in one particular individual.'

[1]*Nangta*:—The Sannysin (Tota Puri) who taught Vedanta philosophy to Sri Ramakrishna for about a year.

Master (affectionately) : I quite concur. He is in every object, in every human being; only there is a difference in the manifestation of divine energy in those objects. Sometimes the divine energy manifesting in certain objects leads one away from God. It is then called ignorance. When it leads Godward it is called knowledge. Again the manifested energy is greater in some 'receptacles' and less in others. Thus it is that all men are not equal.

Ram : What is the use of all this idle talk?

Master (sharply) : No, no; there is a good deal of meaning in all this.

Girish (to Narendra) : How do you know that God does not take a human body, and thus incarnate Himself?

Narendra : Surely God cannot be realised by words or by the mind!

Master : Quite so; not by the finite conditioned mind. But He can be realised by the pure mind freed from its sensuous nature by means of culture and *sadhana*. Then this very mind becomes the same as the pure reason or the faculty of the unconditioned, which is the same thing as the pure unconditioned Soul. In this wise did the holy sages realise the pure unconditioned Soul.

Girish (to Narendra) : Do you not see that if God would not incarnate there will be none else to make all these things clear and solve all these problems? God incarnates Himself and becomes man in order to teach what is true knowledge, what again is true devotion or the love of God. Who else is there to teach?

Narendra : Why! He will certainly teach me from within the heart!

Master (affectionately) : That is indeed so. He will teach as the ruler of the heart within.[1]

The discussion grows warm. It turns on matters too high for human comprehension. Infinite—is it divisible? What does Hamilton say as to the limits of human know-

[1] Antaryamin.

ledge; and Herbert Spencer—and Tyndal—and Huxley?

Master (aside to M.) : I for my part do not like these things. God is beyond the power of reasoning. Something more; I see that whatever is, is God. Then what is the good of reasoning about Him? I do actually *see* that *whatever is, is God.*

Master : It is He who has become all these things! It is this and it is also that which seems to contradict this! There is a stage at which the mind and the determinative faculty are lost in the Absolute—the Absolute which cannot be conceived as made up of parts. At the sight of Narendra my mind gets lost in the Absolute;—what, pray, do you say to this?

Girish (smiling) : I hope, revered Sir, you do not think as though we understood everything besides that! (*Laughter.*)

Sri Ramanuja and His Doctrine of Visishtadwaitam

Master : Then at the end of the *Samadhi* I must come down two notes at least below the highest note in the scale before I can utter another word!

Vedanta has been explained by Sankara. Another point of view is that of Ramanuja, who put forward the doctrine of qualified non-dualism.

Narendra (to Master) : Sir, may I ask what is meant by Visishtadwaitam.

Master (to Narendra): There is this doctrine the view of Ramanuja, *viz.*, the Absolute must not be considered apart from the world and the soul. The three between them form one—three in one and one in three!

Let us take a Bel fruit. Let the shell, the seeds and the kernel be kept separate. Now suppose somebody wanted to know the weight of the fruit. Surely it would not do now to weigh the kernel alone of the fruit. The shell, the seeds and the kernel are all weighed in order to get the real weight of the fruit. No doubt we reason at the outset that the all-important thing is the *kernel*, and not either the shell or the seeds. In the next place we go on reasoning, saying that the shell and the seeds belong to the same substance to which the kernel belongs. At the first stage of the reasoning we say, 'Not this,' 'Not this.' Thus the Absolute is not soul (not the finite individual soul). Again, it is not the world either. The Absolute is the only reality, all else is unreal. At the next stage we go a little further. We see that the kernel belongs to the same substance as that to which the shell and the seeds belong. Hence the substance from which we derive our negative conception of the Absolute is the identical substance from which we derive our conception of the finite soul and the phenomenal world. Your 'Relative,' must be traced to that very Being on which your Absolute rests. Hence, as Ramanuja says. the Absolute is qualified by the finite soul and the phenomenal world. This is the doctrine of qualified non-dualism or Visishtadwaitam.

CHAPTER VI

God-Vision

Master (aside to M.) : I do see that Being as the Reality before my very eyes. Why then should I reason? I do actually see that it is the Absolute who has become all things about us; it is He who appears as the finite soul and the phenomenal world! One must have an awakening of the spirit within to see this Reality.

How long must one reason or discriminate, saying, 'Not this,' 'Not this,'? Why, so long as one is unable to see Him as the Reality. Of course it would not do for a person merely to say, 'I have seen beyond the possibility of a doubt that it is He who has become all.' Mere saying is not enough. By the Lord's grace the spirit must be quickened. Spiritual awakening is followed by *Samadhi*. In this state one forgets that one has a body; one loses all attachment to things of the world—'Woman and Gold;' one likes no other words than those relating to God; one is sorely troubled if called upon to listen to worldly matters.

The spirit within being awakened, the next step is the realisation of the Universal Spirit. It is the spirit that can realise the spirit.

God-Incarnate and Revelation

(To M.) : O, I have observed there is a good deal of difference between the mere intellectual comprehension of God by reasoning or discrimination and the actual realisation through meditation in solitude; and again between these on the one hand and the realisation through His grace. If out of His abundant grace He makes us realise what is God-incarnate, then all reasoning would be quite thrown away—it would need nobody to explain what is an incarnation.

Let me make this clear to you. A person, suppose, is in a dark room. He rubs the matches on the side of the box and all at once a light is struck! If the Lord is gracious enough to strike the light for us and dissipate the darkness of ignorance, then it is that all doubts shall cease for ever! This sort of disputation shall never carry us far.

Upon this the Master invites Narendra to be seated by his side. He makes many kind inquiries about him and caresses him.

Narendra (to Master) : Why, revered Sir, I did meditate in solitude on the Divine Mother for three or four days together, but nothing has come of it.

Master : All in good time; do not be impatient. Mother is not a different Being from God, the Absolute. The Mother is the Personal side of God the Absolute. When thought of apart from His works the Supreme Being is called God the Absolute. Again, when we think of God as creating, preserving, and destroying, *i.e.*, in relation to His works, we call the same Being the Personal God, the Divine Mother.

God Impersonal and Personal

The same Being to whom you apply the name of *Brahman* in the *Vedanta*, I call by the name of Mother.

God the Absolute or Impersonal and God Personal

are the same, just as fire and its burning power are the same —in the sense that the one cannot be thought of without the other. If you postulate the Personal you must postulate the Impersonal: if you talk of the Impersonal you must already have taken the Personal for granted.

It is getting late. Girish must go out to the theatre— of which he is the manager. He says to Haripada, 'Be good enough, my brother, to call a cab;—I shall have to go to the theatre.'

Master (laughingly, to Haripada) : Mind, a cab; see that you bring one! Don't forget. (*Laughter.*)

Haripada (smiling) : No, revered Sir. Am I not going on that errand? (*Laughter.*)..

Girish (to Master) : I am afraid I must leave you, revered Sir, and go out to my place of business, the theatre, unfortunate that I am!

Master : No, you must serve both parties. Janaka served God, being unattached to the world. He looked to the interests of both, this world and the next. He drank of the 'cup of milk' but did not forget the soul.

Girish : I am thinking, revered Sir, of giving up the theatre and of making them over into the hands of the younger fellows.

Master : No, no; it is all right, as it is. You need not have any such idea. You are doing good to many.

Narendra (softly): Just a moment ago he was calling Him God-incarnate! I suppose, he must now leave his God-incarnate to Himself and be off to the theatre and mind his own business!

CHAPTER VII

The Master in Samadhi

The Master has Narendra seated by his side. He fixes his eyes on him. He moves down to sit closer to him.

Narendra does not believe that God incarnates Himself. But what does that matter? The Master's love for him is still as great as ever!

Touching his person the Master says to him, 'Dost thou feel that thy dignity has been wounded? Be it so; we too are of the same mind with thee and feel for thee.'

Did the Master see with his inner eye that after all, Narendra was right in declining to admit that God could incarnate Himself? Is He not our own father and mother? Why does He not then strike the light in the inner chamber of the soul and give us the power of beholding the blessed vision as God Incarnate? Is not His own child justified in having a sense of wounded dignity upon being denied the inheritance of true knowledge, which he may well claim to be his own by the right of birth?

Disputation and Realisation of God

(To Narendra) : So long as one goes on questioning and reasoning about God, one has not seen Him as the Reality. You two were engaged in disputation. That, however, was not to my liking.

How long will there be noise in a house where a feast is given to a large party of men. Why, so long as they have not commenced to eat. When dishes are served and the guests fall to, three-fourths of the noise is gone. Then the courses of sweetmeats—the more they are dealt out, the more does the noise subside; when the turn comes for the curds (the last course) only one sound is heard, *soop-sup*. The feast over, the next thing for the guests is to go to sleep!

The nearer you come to God the less are you disposed to question and reason. When you come up to Him, when you behold Him as the Reality,—then all noise—all disputations are at an end. Then it is the time for sleep, *i.e.*, for enjoyment which comes in *Samadhi*, in which one is in a state of communion with the soul divine.

Saying this, the Master gently strokes Narendra's

person, touches his sweet face and caresses him saying.

'HARI OM,' 'HARI OM,' 'HARI OM.'

'GOD THE ABSOLUTE'

Why is he doing all this? Does the Master behold the vision divine manifest in Narendra? Does he behold the real man in the apparent man before him? Is this the same as seeing God in man?

What a miracle passes before the eyes of the disciples! Look on the Master, and see how his sense consciousness begins to leave him! Look again, and see it has left him altogether! Is this the trance with semi-outer-consciousness spoken of about Gouranga (Chaitanya), God of love incarnate at Nadia! Even now, the Master's hand continues to rest on Narendra's body! Is he actually engaged in serving God (Narayana) manifest in the man before him and touching His feet? Or, is he breathing into him the inspiration,[1] the power that comes from above?

Look ! Yet other changes come over the Master! Behold what he says to Narendra with folded hands! 'A song (do thou sing): then I shall be restored—how else shall I be able to stand on my legs?—my Nitye![2]—O!' He is deep drunk, intoxicated with the wine of divine love, the love for Gouranga (God-incarnate),

A short while and he is speechless again—speechless like a marble statue! Drunk with the joy of the Lord the Master goes on saying—

'Take care, Radha, lest thou should fall into the Jamuna. O! Thou art mad with ecstatic love for Him who hath incarnated Himself at Brindaban, the Lord Sri Krishna!'

[1]Sakti-Sanchara.

[2]Nitye or Nityananda, brother in the Lord of Sri Chaitanya. He was full of the madness of love for Chaitanya whom he regarded as God-incarnate.

Once more in deep *Samadhi*! Getting back to sense-consciousness he repeats portions of a well-known song of Radha:

"O my friend, how far is that blessed woodland, the land where is to be seen my own beloved one?
Behold, here comes the fragrance from the blessed person of my beloved!
I am unable to take any step forward, oh my friend!"

Now he has lost all sense of the world—he does not bear in mind anything or any person in his present state—Narendra is seated before him, but apparently he does not see him. He has lost all consciousness of time and place! The mind, the heart and the soul have all become absorbed in God!

Behold, he stands up saying, 'Deep drunk with the wine of divine love, with love for the fair Lord!' A few moments and again he takes his seat.

He says, 'Yonder is a light coming this way—but I cannot even now say where the light comes from.' Now Narendra begins to sing:

SONG

GOD-VISION

1. Oh Lord! Thou hast blessed me with Thy vision and so hast removed all my sorrows.
A charm hast Thou thrown over my soul!
2. Beholding Thee the seven worlds forget their grief!
What to speak of my poor self so mean and unworthy!

Listening to the song the Master has once more lost all sense of the outer world! His eyes are closed. His body and limbs are still! He is in a deep *Samadhi*.

* * * * *

The *Samadhi* over, he exclaims, 'Who is it that will take me home to the Temple?'

A child looking for a companion! Left alone, it sees nothing but darkness round about.

It is getting late. It is the night of the 10th day of the dark fortnight in Falgun. The Master has set his face to go to the Temple at Dakshineswar. He is seated in the cab which will take him there. The disciples all stand on either side of the carriage to see him off. Even now he is deep drunk with the joy of the Lord!

The cab rolls away. The disciples look on for a few moments and then go their ways each to his own home.

SECTION XII

1885

SRI RAMAKRISHNA AT SYAMPUKUR (CALCUTTA) WITH THE DISCIPLES; AND ISHAN, Dr. SARKAR AND OTHERS

CHAPTER I

Is God with Form or without Form?

It is the fourteenth day of the light fortnight after Durga Puja; Thursday, 22nd October 1885. The Master is at Syampukur (a district in Calcutta) and is under the treatment of Dr. Sarkar and other physicians. This day besides Dr. Sarkar, Girish (Ghosh), Ishan (Mukhopadhyaya), M., and many other disciples and *Bhaktas* are present.

Sri Ramakrishna talks pleasantly with a smiling face to everybody; Ishan, Girish and the Doctor take part in the conversation.

*   *   *   *   *

Doctor : Knowledge (of God's works) makes one speechless; his eyes are closed and he is in tears! Here comes the love of God.

Sri Ramakrishna: The love of God is like a lady and so has access even to the *zenana* (harems), Knowledge (derived by reasoning) can go only up to the outer apartments (quarters reserved for men) and cannot get any entry into the inner apartment.

Doctor : That is indeed true. But women of questionable character should not be admitted into the *zenana*,—for instance women of the town. Hence the need for knowledge.

Every fool should not be allowed to get in because he says 'I love God'.

Sri Ramakrishna : If a person is sincere and yearns for God, he is sure to realise Him in the end, whether he knows your philosophy or not. If in his search after the Lord he comes into a wrong path, the Lord will lead him forth to the goal, provided he thirsts after Him. A certain devotee went out on a pilgrimage to Puri; but not knowing the way he went due west instead of south. In his longing to see the holy image he asked people which way he should go. They said, 'Go thy way towards the south. Thou hast lost sight of the right road leading to the Temple.'

Doctor : Well, the man in his ignorance did lose his way.

Master : People talk of errors and superstitions and pride themselves upon book-learning. But the sincere devotee finds the loving Lord ever ready to lend him a helping hand. It matters not that he has been for a time walking along a wrong path. The Lord knows what we want, and in the end fulfils the desire of our heart.

Is God with form or without form?

The question was asked whether God is with form or without form.

Sri Ramakrishna: God is with form as well as without form.

A certain monk went to the temple of Jagannath at Puri. He had doubts as to whether God is with form or without form. When he saw the holy image he desired to examine this. He passed his staff from the left to the right in order to feel if it touched the image. For a time he could not see anything or feel with the staff! So he decided that God is without form. But when he was about to pass the staff from the right side to the left, it touched the image! So the *sannyasin* decided that God is both with form and without form.

But it is very difficult to realise this. He that is without form—how can he be with form? This question naturally arises in the mind.

Doctor : He has made forms; hence He is with form.

Again, He has created the mind, which has no form. Hence, He, the creator, is without form. Thus it is possible for Him to be both with form and without form.

Master : Unless one realises God one is not able to comprehend all this. For the sake of those that love the Lord, He manifests Himself in various ways and in various forms.

A dyer had his own way of dyeing cloths. He would ask the customer, 'In what colour do you want your cloth dyed?' If he said red, the dyer dipped the cloth in his tub and brought it out saying, 'Here is your cloth dyed red.' Another wants his cloth dyed yellow. The dyer dips it in the same tub, brings it up, and behold, the cloth is dyed yellow. In the same way, when another colour is wanted—blue or orange or violet or green—the same tub is used with the like result.

A customer who was watching all this came up to the dyer and said, 'My friend, I am not fond of any one colour. I rather like your own taste. I want the dye in which you have dyed yourself.' (*Laughter.*)

The Lord manifests Himself, as with form or without form, with particular reference to the need of the devotee. The manifested vision is relatively true, that is relatively to different men who are, in the first place, limited, conditioned beings, and, in the second place, placed in the midst of the different things about them. The divine dyer alone knows in what colour He has dyed Himself. Verily He is not bound by any limitation as to form or manifestation or the negation thereof.

A man said to his friend, 'My friend, I went to the foot of the tree up there and saw a beautiful animal of red colour.' His friend said, 'O, I have seen it, too. You say it is red. But, no, it is green.' A third man said, 'No, no, I saw it too, I saw it yellow.' Others testified that they were sure that the colour was orange, blue, green and so forth. From words they were about to come to blows, when another man joined them. He heard everything and bade them hold their peace, saying, 'Behold, I abide at the foot of the tree, and I know the animal very well. Every one of you is right; for it is a chameleon, which changes its colour every moment. It is now red, now green, now yellow, now blue and so on. What is more, I see that sometimes it is *colourless.*'

He who has left all for the sake of the Lord—who lives under the tree of life and watches—to him is it given to know what the Lord is like. He knows that the Lord manifests Himself in diverse forms to His devotees. The chameleon,—now he is red, now yellow, now orange, now green! and now absolutely devoid of colour! He is the Omnipotent Being, creating, preserving, and destroying—possessed of Attributes, the thought of which strikes us dumb. But that is only as He manifests Himself to man. He is, again, the Absolute of whom nothing can be predicated, like the chameleon which is devoid of all colour.

Yes, He is both *with* form and *without* form, as you say. Just think of a shoreless ocean. When it is very cold, the water near the surface congeals into ice. And the ice takes different forms in different places. But when the sun is up and shines upon the ice, it melts away into formless water again.

The shoreless ocean is God. The intense cold is the soft, cooling influence of devotion or the love of God. The ice appearing under different forms is God, manifesting Himself, as it were, to the devotees under the cooling influence of deep devotion. The melting away of the ice under different forms is the disappearance of the spiritual forms (in which the Lord manifests Himself) under the burning rays of the the sun of knowledge Absolute realised in *Samadhi.*

Doctor: When the sun is up, the ice indeed melts. And what is more, the water changes into invisible vapour. This we know from science. Do you not think, Sir, this will carry the analogy a little farther?

Master: The meaning of the analogy is that reasoning as to the real and the unreal, we come to the conclusion that God the Absolute is Real and the phenomenal universe is unreal. The latter includes all things that have name or form—material or spiritual. This is the conclusion of Vedanta philosophy. Reasoning on this line and realising in the *Samadhi* which follows, the knowing one says, 'God is not a person'—for that would be limiting God. Nothing can be predicated of God the Absolute. The conditioned self is effaced in *Samadhi*. Thus there remains no individuality to predicate about the Absolute. The Absolute is realised then only as Absolute Consciousness.

Hence *Bhakti* (the devotional feeling) is like the cooling light of the moon. Absolute knowledge is like the sun with its burning rays. It is said that in the extreme north and in the extreme south there are seas where water changes into masses of ice which stop the course of ships.

Doctor: You see, Sir, man has his progress stopped in the path of devotion unaided by reasoning.

Master: His course, indeed, is stopped—were you to carry the metaphor further on. But surely no harm is done by that. For that ice is nothing else but the congealed form of the formless water of that ocean of the Absolute: God *Satchidananda*. So he also realises God but in a different aspect. If you like the path of knowledge or philosophy better, you may reason, 'The Absolute is the only Reality, and the world with names and forms is unreal.' The ice will then melt away under the powerful rays of the sun of true knowledge, leaving the shoreless unbounded ocean for you to realise!

* * * * *

CHAPTER II

How to Control the Desires and Passions

Sri Ramakrishna (to Doctor): The following are among the persons who do not get a knowledge of God:

First, he who is proud of his learning: second, he who is proud of his wealth. You may say to such a person, 'There is a holy man in a certain place, will you come to see him?' But he is sure to make excuses and say that he cannot come.

He thinks he is too big a man to pay a visit to such a person.

'Pride comes of ignorance.'

* * * * *

The question is how may pride, covetousness, lust, anger and other passions be controlled. Girindra Ghosh of Pathuriaghatta (a district in Calcutta), said, "It is not possible for one to entirely rid oneself of the passions. Hence let us give them a different direction. In the place of sensual pleasures let the object of our desire be God Himself. Let us enjoy the ecstasy of divine bliss. Let us be proud that we are the sons of God—the servants of the Most High. Let us be proud of having believed in the name of the Lord and say, 'I have taken His hallowed name and I am already free from sin, free from bondage, and I care not for salvation. The things of this world are not, indeed, mine—money, honours, my family and the rest—but the Lord is mine and those that love the Lord.'

"Do I covet riches or titles? No, what I covet most and long for is the vision divine.

"In this way the six passions may be turned Godward."

Doctor : It is hard to control the passions. They are like restive horses. They must have their eyes covered by blinders. In some cases their eyes should be entirely shut out from the outside world to keep them from stumbling or going astray.

Master : Should one be blest with God-vision, one's passions are unable to do evil.

Perfect men like Narada or Prahlad, do not need any such blinders over their eyes. The child who holds the father by the hand and walks in the field along the balk does, indeed, run the risk of letting go his father's arm and falling into the ditch. It is quite otherwise with the child whose arm is held by the father. Verily he never falls into the ditch.

Doctor : It is not right for the father to hold the child by the hand. That would stand in the way of self-help.

Master : Those that have seen God have rid themselves of the lower self. They act with their higher self, which is one with the Lord. They feel that it is not they who help themselves but the Divine Mother. All their strength comes from Her. Apart from the Divine Mother they are as good as non-entities. The child feels strong only in the presence of its Mother.

Doctor : Unless one covers their eyes the horses will not move a single step. Is it possible to realise God, unless, one's passions are kept under control?

Master : You speak of the path of knowledge or discrimination. Yes, that path also leads to God. The knowing one says, 'One must be first pure if one desires to see God. One must first control one's passions. First self-discipline, then knowledge of God.'

Path of Knowledge

There is another path leading to God — the path of devotion. Once there is in the human soul the love of God, once the chanting of His holy name fills the devotee with joy, no effort is needed for the control of the passions. Such control comes of itself.

Path of Devotion

When a man is troubled with grief, can he be in a mood to enter into a quarrel or to join a feast or to give his mind to sensual pleasures? Can a moth ever seek darkness after having seen the light once?

Doctor (smiling) : No, it does not;—it is rather ready to rush into the flame, and perish there.

Master : No, that is not so; the true worshipper of God does not meet death like the moth. The living light to which the devotee is drawn does not burn and cause death. It is like the light coming from a gem, shining yet soft, cool and soothing. It does not burn but gives peace and joy.

Difficulty of the Path of Knowledge

The path of knowledge leads, indeed, to God, but it is very hard. It is easy enough to say with the knowing one in so many words and to reason thus: 'I am not the body or the mind or the determinative faculty; I am not subject to disease or grief or want of peace; I am above happiness and misery; I am not bound by the senses—my true self is God, of Whom the only thing that can be predicated is Absolute Existence, Absolute Knowledge and Absolute Bliss.' It is easy to say all this, but hard to realise.

The hand is torn and scratched by thorns; it is bleeding; surely it does not lie in one's mouth to say, 'Why, my hand is not at all torn, nor does it bleed, and nothing is the matter with me!' One must actually burn, in the flame of knowledge, the thorn of ignorance which leads away from God and causes all the ills that flesh is heir to.

Book learning and Divine Wisdom

Many think that knowledge (of God) cannot be attained without the study of books. But higher than reading is hearing; higher than hearing is seeing (or realisation). Hearing from the lips of the preceptor makes a greater impression than the mere reading of books. Seeing makes the greatest impression. Better than reading about Benares is hearing about the place from the lips of one who has visited it; better even than hearing is seeing Benares with one's own eyes.

At a game of chess the onlookers can tell what is the correct move, better than the players. Men of the world think they are very clever; but they are attached to things of this world—money, honours, pleasures, etc. Being actually engaged in the play, it is hard for them to hit upon the right move. Holy men who have given up the world are not attached to it. They are like the onlookers at a game of chess. They see things better than men of the world.

Doctor (to a disciple) : Had he (Sri Ramakrishna)

only read books he could not have attained such wisdom. Faraday communed with Nature and could thus discover many scientific truths. Mere book-learning could not have placed such knowledge within his reach. A close observation of Nature helped him a great deal. Mathematical formulae only throw the brain into confusion and stand very much in the way of original research. This gentleman here (*i.e.*, the Master) is so wise because he is a child of Nature.

Sri Ramakrishna (to Doctor) : There was a time when I lay down on the ground at the foot of the *Panchabati* in my yearning for the Divine Mother. As I lay down, I used to cry and pray to my Divine Mother for more light, saying, 'O Mother, letters have I never known; do Thou grant that it may be given unto me to know and to realise that which is attained by those that work unattached without looking for the fruits of their actions; also to know and to realise that which is attained by Yogins by means of concentration, and lastly, to know and to realise what the knowing ones know by means of discrimination.'

Books have I never read. It is my Divine Mother who hath revealed unto me these things and many more things!

Ah me! What a state of ecstasy it was! In such a state sleep leaves one.

And the Master sang:

SONG

1. My sleep hath been broken. I am not going to sleep any more.
Any way I am now awake.
Having got Thee, O sleep of communion, O Mother,
Into sleep have I lulled sleep for ever.

2. An excellent theme have I got to think upon.
From the land where there is no night,
Hath come unto me a citizen with that theme.
Worship at stated hours by day or by night hath for ever become barren unto me.

* * * * *

I have never read the books. But see how people make much of me! That is because I chant the holy name of my Divine Mother.

Sambhu Mallik used to speak of me, saying, 'Here is Santiram Singh quite able to beat anybody although sword or shield he hath none.' (*Laughter.*)

The conversation next turned on the performance of a play by Girish (Ghosh) called the 'Life of Buddha.' The Doctor had been invited by the author to see it. He had been very much pleased with the performance.

Doctor (to Girish) : It is most wicked of you to draw me to the theatre every day.

Sri Ramakrishna (to M.) : I can't make out what he says.

M. (smiling) : The Doctor says that the play has proved to be a great attraction for him.

CHAPTER III

Divine Incarnation

Sri Ramakrishna (to Ishan) : He (the Doctor) does not believe in divine incarnation. What have you got to say to him on this matter?

Ishan : Sir, what shall I say? To question and reason on such matters is not to my liking.

Sri Ramakrishna (sharply) : Why? Will you not say the right thing, if necessary?

Ishan (to Doctor) : It is our pride which causes the want of faith. Ramachandra was a human being only in appearance. In reality He was the Supreme Being. Out of His body has come forth the infinite universe with the boundless firmament, the sun, the moon and the stars, the deep blue ocean and the snowcapped mountains!

Sri Ramakrishna (to Doctor) : This much is hard to

understand. How can the human being (the divine incarnation) who appears to view with all his limitations be the same as the Infinite, Eternal, Supreme Being? One who has realised God knows that God the Absolute appears to us as the phenomenal universe—as man and Nature. He *appears* as man with his limitations; but really He has no limitations. For instance, it cannot be said of Him, that because He has taken a human shape He is not outside of that shape. He may be here and at the same moment He may be elsewhere. One who has seen God sees all this, and believes. The ordinary man with his ounce of reason cannot see this. Can a pot with a capacity of only one seer of milk ever hold four seers!

Human Being as Divine Incarnation

Hence in these matters one must put faith in the words of those who have seen God. Such men only meditate upon God. If you seek legal advice will you not consult lawyers who are in the profession? Surely you will not take the advice of the man in the street!

* * * * *

Criterion of Truth: Science of Phenomena or Science of Realities; Physical Science or Transcendental Perception

Ishan (to Doctor) : May I ask why you think that God does not incarnate Himself as a human being? It was only a moment ago you admitted that God may be with form as well as without form, and said that nothing is impossible with God.

Sri Ramakrishna (smiling) : My dear Sir, the fact is, such a thing is not declared in his books on science. (*Laughter.*) It is not set forth there in so many words that God may come down into this world as a human being for the salvation of mankind. That being so, how can he believe? (*Laughter.*)

Let me tell you an amusing story. A person called upon a friend and reported to him saying 'Haven't you heard the latest news? Well, I was yesterday passing along the street when down came the house belonging to the

Mukherjis with a terrible crash.' The friend cried out, 'Is that so? But let me consult the newspaper and see if this is true.' He read the newspaper, but there was nothing about the coming down of the house. Upon this, he coolly said to the other, 'I can't put faith in your words. It is not so stated in the paper here.' The first replied, 'But I saw it with my own eyes!' The man still would not believe, and said, 'Well, there is nothing set down in the newspaper about it; how can I believe it?' (*Laughter.*)

People do not see that science deals only with the conditioned knowledge. It brings no message from the Land of the Unconditioned. Such message has been brought by holy men who have seen and realised God like the *Rishis* of old. It is they alone that are competent to say 'God is thus and thus.'

The Doctor is speechless and makes no remark.

Girish (to Doctor) : You must confess that Sri Krishna was God-incarnate. I will not let you regard Him as a *man*. You must say that He was either God or a demon.

Child-like Simplicity and Faith in God

Sri Ramakrishna : Verily one must be free from guile like the child in order to have such faith in God. The Lord is far away from the duplicity of the world. Worldliness (love of money, honour, sensual pleasures) brings on doubt and scepticism — and the pride of learning, the pride of wealth and the rest.

(To the disciples) : He (the Doctor) is, however, free from guile.

Girish (to Doctor) : Do you not think, Sir, that it is not given to a man of duplicity to attain knowledge?

Doctor: Certainly; that is not possible.

Sri Ramakrishna: How child-like was Keshab (Sen)! Well, once he went into the Temple. At about four in the afternoon, he was going round to the guest-house there; he asked if the guests, holy men and poor men, were soon going to be fed. Like a child he had no idea that it was late in the day and that the guests for that day had already had their dinner.

Knowledge relating to God keeps pace with faith. Where there is little faith it is idle to look for much knowledge. The cow which comes to be over-nice in matters of eating is not liberal in its supply of milk. But the cow to whom all kinds of food are welcome—herbs, leaves, grass, husks, straw—and eats them up with great appetite, gives an abundant supply. Her milk comes down from the udder into the pail in torrents. (*Laughter.*)

Faith like that of a child is the one thing needful. Such faith leads one to God. Mamma has said pointing to a stranger lad, 'He is thy dada (brother).' At once the child believes in it absolutely and looks upon the boy as his own brother. Again mamma has said, 'There is a hobgoblin in that room.' The child is absolutely sure that there is such a terrible thing in that room.

He that believes like the child receives the grace of God. The calculating intellect of the worldly weighs things with an eye to worldly loss and gain. Man's limited reasoning does not see far enough. It has no right of entry into the land of the gods. It is faith—the faith of a child—which leads you forth into that land.

Doctor (to the disciples) : It is, however, not right for the cow to eat up all sorts of things. I once had a cow which went in for all sorts of food. I was taken very ill, I was at a loss to account for my illness. At last I came to know that the root of all this evil was the cow, which had been eating the refuse of corn and such-like things for some days. (*Laughter.*) The result was that I had to go up to Lucknow for a change. I got well, but at the cost of Rs. 12,000 (*roars of laughter*).

Well, it is not so easy to see the relation between cause and effect. In the family of the Pikepara Babus a child, seven months old, was taken ill with whooping cough and I was called in for treatment. I tried my utmost to trace the disease to its cause, but in vain. At last it came to my knowledge that the ass which supplied the milk for the child had got drenched in the rains!

Sri Ramakrishna (to the disciples, laughing) : Now see; as if some one said, my coach stopped a few moments under the tamarind tree and so I have got acidity. (*The Doctor and others all laugh.*)

Doctor : The captain of a ship had a bad head-ache. The doctors on board held a consultation and had a blister applied to the side of the ship! (*Laughter.*)

Company of the Holy Men

Sri Ramakrishna (to Doctor) : The company of holy men is always needed for one who seeks God. A man of the world is always subject to chronic disease. Holy men should be consulted as to the remedy. Merely hearing them as they teach is not quite enough for one's purposes. Medicine must be taken into the system and strict rule should be observed in matters of diet.

Doctor : Yes, it is the diet which, more than anything else, causes the cure.

Sri Ramakrishna: Doctors are either first class, second class or third class. Holy teachers are, like doctors, divided into three classes.

The third class doctor feels the pulse and says, 'You should take medicine.' He then goes away, not caring whether the patient takes his advice or not.

The second class doctor reasons with the patient and uses sweet words to induce him to take the medicine.

The first class doctor is ready, in case the patient hears not his word, to put his knee on the chest of the patient and force the medicine down his throat! (*Laughter.*)

Doctor (laughing) : Under certain kinds of treatment the doctor need not use force and put his knee across the chest of the patient. For instance, Homeopathy. (*Laughter.*)

Sri Ramakrishna (smiling) : That is true; but the patient need not be afraid even if such a doctor uses force and puts his knee across his chest.

The Strict Discipline of Monastic Life.

Renunciation of 'Woman and Gold' has been laid down only for those that lead a monastic life. Monks must not so much as look at the pictures of women. Even the *thought* of spiced pickles causes the mouth to water—not to speak of the sight or the touch of those dainties!

But this hard rule is not meant for men of the world like you;—it is intended purely for monks. For your part you may go amongst women with a mind unattached and fixed upon God. That your mind may be thus unattached and fixed upon God it is good that you should often retire into solitude—a place away from either men or women—a place where you may be left absolutely to yourself, praying to the Lord with a yearning heart for true knowledge—a place where you may stay for at least three days, if not more, or for at least one day if not for three.

Your path, again, as a married man is to live with your wife just as brother and sister, after one or two children are born to you, and to pray to the Lord constantly that both of you may have strength to live a perfect life of spirituality and self-control.

Girish (smiling to Doctor) : My dear sir, you have been staying on here for three or four hours! I wonder when you are going to see your patients. (*Laughter.*)

If you go on in this way you may ruin your practice.

Doctor : Talk not of practice or of patient! Your Paramahamsa will make me lose my all! (*Laughter.*)

Sri Ramakrishna (smiling to Doctor) : Well, there is a river called *Karmanāsa*—which means that it puts an end to all work. If you take a plunge into that river you shall run a great risk. After the bath you shall lose all power of doing any work whatsoever. (*The Doctor and others all laugh.*)

Doctor (to M., Girish, and other disciples): My friends, do regard me as your own; not as a professional man, whom you wanted for his advice, but as your own kith and kin.

Pure and Selfless Love of God

Sri Ramakrishna (to Doctor) : Let me tell you of one thing. It is possible to have a love of God which is pure and selfless. Blessed is he who has such love for the Lord! Prahlad had such a love.

A devotee of this class says, 'O Lord, I pray not for wealth or fame, pleasures of the flesh or for any other blessings that the world can give. Do Thou grant that I may love Thee with a love which seeketh not the things of the world, but Thee alone.'

Doctor : Yes, Sir, I often see people bowing down before the image of Kali. These worshippers all seek some worldly object;—some pray for means of living, some for the healing of some disease, and so forth.

Doctor (to Sri Ramakrishna) : It is not right for you, ill as you are, to hold converse with anybody. Of course, you must make an exception in my favour. (*Laughter.*)

Sri Ramakrishna (smiling) : Will you be good enough to see that I am healed? You see how I cannot repeat and glorify the name of the Lord!

Doctor (smiling) : What is the need for repeating His name? Meditation is quite enough for our purposes.

Sri Ramakrishna : What do you say? You want me to be narrow and one-sided? I eat my fish dressed into various dishes—fish in curry, fish fried, fish with tamarind, cutlet, *pillau*, and so forth. I long to worship the Lord in as many ways as I can, and still my heart's desire is not fulfilled! I long to worship Him with flowers and fruits and other offerings, to repeat His sacred name by myself; to meditate upon Him, to chant His hymns, to dance in the joy of the Lord!

Doctor : Well Sir, I too do not like to be narrow or one-sided.

Belief in Divine Incarnations

Master : Amrita, your son, does not believe in Divine incarnation. Well, it matters not. Those that believe that God is without form will see Him—as well as those who believe that He is with form. The two things needed are faith and self- surrender. Man is liable to error at every step. In any case he cannot hope to be absolutely free from error. Do you want to put four seers of milk into a water-pot which can hold only one seer?

But you must cry to the Lord with a longing yearning

heart, whether you believe that God is with form or without form. The Lord is the Ruler of the soul within, and shall grant your prayer if your cry goes forth unto Him from the inmost recesses of your heart, whether you believe that the Lord is with form or without form.

The cake made with candy will taste equally sweet whether it be straight or oblique when taken up into the mouth. (*Laughter.*)

Amrita, your son, is a good lad.

Doctor : Oh, he is a disciple of yours!

Sri Ramakrishna (smiling) : There is not a fellow under the sun who is my disciple. On the contrary, I am everybody's disciple. All men are sons of God—servants of the Lord. I too am a son of God and His servant. Uncle moon is every body's uncle ! (*Laughter.*)

(The Master here refers to one of the popular folk-tales current in Bengal, which speaks of the moon as the maternal uncle of everybody.)

SECTION XIII

1885

THE MASTER AT SYAMPUKUR, CALCUTTA, WITH HIS DISCIPLES

Sri Ramakrishna with Narendra (Vivekananda) Sarat (Saradananda), Kali (Abhedananda), Rakhal (Brahmananda), M., and other disciples at Syampukur, Calcutta.

CHAPTER I

In Ecstasy

It was about half past five in the afternoon on Tuesday. 27th October, 1885. The great national festival Durgapuja had been celebrated only a few days back. It was so difficult for the disciples to join the festivities with their whole heart. How could they rejoice when the Master was suffering from a serious malady?

The Temple of Kali at Dakshineswar, where he ordinarily resided, was not within easy reach of Calcutta physicians. So the Master had been staying for the last three months at Syampukur and was now under the treatment of Dr. Sarkar. The hint thrown out by the Doctor that the disease was past all human remedies, proved a heavy blow to the poor disciples. It was so hard to believe that the Blessed One was soon to leave them like orphans thrown adrift upon the wide world, scattered abroad like sheep having no shepherd. It was so distressing to think that the days of rejoicing, coming one after another, which they had passed with him, were numbered. They shed tears in solitude. Hoping against hope, they yet prayed for his recovery. They served him with body, mind and soul, nursed him, attended to his smallest wants day and night. To the younger disciples, headed by Narendra, this great and unique service for the Master led the way to the great renunciation of the world of which they are the most glorius examples in the present day. For, was not Sri Ramakrishna their living Ideal, a unique example before their very eyes—who had given up the world and its so-called pleasures for the sake of God?

Strange that in spite of the serious illness, people poured in to see, even only to catch a glimpse of the God-man of whom they had heard so much. They felt that truly it was peace and joy to come into the presence of Sri Ramakrishna. 'Oh how kind, how loving!' was the universal observation. Anxious for the welfare of the meanest among them, he would talk to them of God—of His Heavenly Mother—in the midst of intense physical sufferings! At last the physicians left a strict injunction with the disciples not to allow people to see him and engage him in conversation. Dr. Sarkar, who would stay with the Master for hours together (sometimes six or seven hours continually) would say to him, 'Take heed how you talk to anybody; the only person you may talk with for a length of time is myself,—in whose favour you may thus make an exception.' The fact was that the Doctor had been charmed with his company as well as with words 'sweet as honey' that fell from his lips.

Besides Vivekananda and the Doctor there were present on this particular occasion, Girish Ghosh, the great Bengali dramatist and poet, Doctor Docouri, Narendra (junior), Rakhal, M., Sarat and many others.

The Doctor felt the pulse and prescribed the necessary remedies. There was then, for a while, a talk with reference to the course of the disease; after which the Master took the first dose of medicine as directed.

Dr. Sarkar rising to depart said to Sri Ramakrishna, who was talking to Syam Babu, 'Now that you have got Syam Babu to talk to, will you allow me to bid you good-bye?'

Sri Ramakrishna : Would you like to hear some songs?

Doctor : I should like very much; but your feeling would be terribly worked up, and you will shoot up into all sorts of antics. One's feelings must be kept under control.

The Doctor took his seat once more. Narendra poured out his charming melodies to the accompaniment of the *Tampura* and *mridanga* (musical instruments).
He sang :

SONG

God and His Work

1. Wonderful, infinite is the universe, made by Thee! Behold, it is the repository of all beauty.

2. Thousands of stars do shine—a necklace of gold studded with gems! Innumerable are the moons and the suns!

3. The earth is adorned with wealth and corn; full indeed is Thy storehouse. O great Lord, innumerable are the stars which sing, 'Well done, Lord! Well done!' They sing without ceasing.

He sang again :

SONG

The Mother of the Universe

1. In the midst of the dense darkness, O Mother, breaketh forth a flood of light, Thy wealth of formless beauty. To this end is the Yogi's meditation within the mountain cave.

2. In the lap of darkness infinite and borne on the sea of great *Nirvana* the fragrance of peace everlasting floweth without cessation.

3. O Mother, who art Thou, seated alone within the Temple of *Samadhi*, assuming the form of the Great Consort of the Lord of Eternity and wearing the apparel of darkness? The lotus of Thy feet keepeth us from fear! In them doth flash the lightning of Thy love for Thy children. From Thy face of spirit is poured out laughter loud and terrific.

Doctor (to M.) : It is dangerous to him—this singing! It will work upon his feelings with serious results!

Sri Ramakrishna (to M.) : What does the Doctor say?

M. : Sir, the Doctor is afaid lest this singing should

work upon your feelings and bring on *Samadhi.*

Sri Ramakrishna (to the Doctor, with folded hands): No, Oh no; why should my feelings be worked up? I am very well!

But as soon as these words were uttered, the Master, who was already losing sense-consciousness, went right into deep *Samadhi.* His corporeal frame became motionless! The eyes moved not! He sat speechless like a veritable figure of wood or stone! All sense-consciousness had left him! The mind, the intellect and the heart, had all stepped out of their wonted course towards that one object, the Mother of the universe!

Again did Narendra pour out of his sweet throat, melody after melody.

He sang :

SONG

The Lord My Husband

1. What an enchanting beauty is here! What a charming face! The Lord of my soul hath come to my (humble) abode!

2. Behold! The spring of my love is running over (with joy)!

3. O Lord of my soul, Thou who art made of love alone, is there any riches that I can offer to Thee? O, accept my heart, my life, my all, yes Lord! My all deign to accept!

And yet again:

SONG

Nothing Good or Beautiful without the Lord

1. Gracious Lord, what comfort can there be in life, if the bee of my soul is not lost in the lotus of Thy feet for evermore!

2. What is the use of countless heaps of wealth if at the same time Thou the most precious of all gems art not kept with care?

3. The tender face of the child I do not wish to see if in that face, beautiful

like the moon as it is, I cannot see (the image of) Thy loving face.

4. What a thing is moonlight! It would indeed appear to be made of darkness absolute, if, when the outward moon appears in the heavens, the moon of Thy love riseth not also in the firmament of the soul at the same time.

5. Even the holy attachment of chaste wife would be full of impurities, if the gold of her human love is not set with the priceless gem of Thy love divine.

6. Lord, scepticism about Thee, the offspring of infatuation, is like the never-ceasing bite of the poisonous snake.

7. Lord, what more shall I say to Thee! Thou art the (priceless) jewel of my heart, the abode of joy everlasting!

Listening to the song—specially to the portion referring to the chaste wife and the child, the doctor cried out, 'Ah me! Ah me!'

Narendra sang again :

SONG

THE ECSTATIC LOVE OF GOD

1. O! How long shall I have to wait for the coming of that madness of love for God, when having nothing else in the world to wish for, I shall chant the name of Hari (God) and there shall flow from my eyes a stream of tears of love.

2. When shall my life, my mind, be made pure! O when shall I go forth on pilgrimage to the *Brindaban* of love! When shall darkness of my eyes be driven away by the collyrium of knowledge divine!

3. When shall the iron of my body be turned into gold at the touch of the divine touch-stone! O when shall I see the vision of a world made up of God alone!

4. When shall my desire for doing good works be a thing of the past! When shall my sense of caste and family distinction be gone! O when shall I be placed beyond fear, anxiety, and the feeling of shame! When shall I be free from pride and slavish obedience to custom!

5. With the dust of the feet of *Bhaktas* (true lovers of God) rubbed all over my body, with the scrip of renunciation placed over my shoulders, O when shall I drink the water of ecstatic love with the palm of both my hands from the river of divine love!

CHAPTER II

THE ABSOLUTE

In the midst of the songs Sri Ramakrishna has come to himself again. The music ceased. Then followed more of the conversation, so charming alike to the learned and the illiterate, to the old and the young, to men and to women, to great men and to small men! The whole company sat mute and looked in silence on his divine face.

Is there any trace now of that serious illness from which he is suffering? Joy is there on the face radiant with celestial glory!

Turning to the Doctor, Sri Ramakrishna began the conversation.

Sri Ramakrishna : Do give up shyness, Doctor. One should not be shy in taking before others the name of the Lord, or in dancing with joy while chanting His sweet name. Do not care for what people say. The following proverb is very edifying—

'Shyness, contempt and fear—

These three remaining, one cannot be perfect.'

The shy man thinks, 'I am such a big man! If this finds its way into big people's ears what would they say!' O, what a shame if they say, 'Doctor, the poor fellow, has been dancing. He must have lost his head!'

Doctor : That is not my line at all. I don't care what people may say.

Sri Ramakrishna (smiling) : On the contrary, you do care for it very much. (*Laughter.*)

The Realisation of the Absolute

Sri Ramakrishna: Get to the other side of both knowledge and ignorance. Ignorance is the consciousness of many, *i.e.*, the knowledge of diversity without knowing the Unity, without the knowledge of the one God. The egotism due to erudition proceeds from ignorance. The conviction that God is in all objects—that there is unity in variety—is called knowledge of oneness. Knowing Him intimately is realisation.

Suppose your foot is pricked with a thorn. Well, you want a second thorn to take it out. When the first thorn is taken out you throw away both. So, in order to get rid of the thorn of ignorance, you bring in the thorn of knowledge. Then you throw away both ignorance and knowledge with a view to the complete realisation of the Absolute. For the Absolute is beyond knowledge as well as ignorance.

Lakshman once said to his divine brother, 'O Rama, is it not strange that a God-knowing man like Vasishta Deva should have wept for the loss of his sons, and would not be comforted?'

Thereupon Rama replied, 'Good, my brother, bear in mind that whoever possesses relative knowledge of unity (God) must at the same time have relative ignorance also.'

He is not in the nature of things free from ignorance as to God, for knowledge and ignorance in this case are as correlatives. For a knowledge of unity in the universe presupposes a concurrent knowledge of diversity. One who feels the existence of light has also a feeling as to the existence of darkness.

The Absolute is beyond knowledge and ignorance, beyond sin and virtue—good works and bad works—cleanliness and uncleanliness—as understood by the limited faculties of man.

With this Sri Ramakrishna repeated the following song of Ramaprasad:

SONG

The Science of God-vision

1. Come, oh my mind, let us go out for a walk: oh, thou shalt pick up four fruits at the foot of that wish-yielding tree, my Mother, the consort of the Eternal.

2. Thou hast two wives, attachment (which leadeth thee to things of the world) and non-attachment (which leadeth thee Godward, away from the things of the world). Now, when thou dost go out for a walk, take non-attachment along with thee as thy companion.

Non-attachment hath a son called discrimination of the real from the unreal. Him thou shouldst ask for information about the real.

3. The offspring of attachment, thy first wife, thou must try to bring to reason, taking care always to keep at a safe distance from them.

If they refuse to listen to reason, thou shouldst, oh my mind, cause them to be drowned in the sea of knowledge.

4. When shalt thou sleep in the chamber of Spirit with cleanliness and uncleanlines both by thy side?

For as soon as these co-wives are made friends, thou wilt see my Mother of the dark-blue colour (the Mother of the Universe.)

5. Keep the two goats of merit and demerit fastened unto the post of inconsequence.

Then sacrifice them with the sword of knowledge thus giving them liberation.

6. Thy father, oh my mind, is egotism and thy mother is ignorance; both of whom thou must send away.

If ever thou feelest drawn towards the pit of infatuation, then hold on to the prop of patience.

7. *Prasad* saith, "Oh my mind, in this way wilt thou be able to face the account."

In this way wilt thou be entitled to be called 'my darling', 'my pet'; 'the god of my father,' and a 'mind after my mind.'

God the Absolute Beyond Speech and Mind

Syam Babu : Sir, may I ask what remains after you have thrown away both the thorns as you call them—knowledge and ignorance?

Sri Ramakrishna : Well, what remains, as you say, is the eternal absolute pure consciousness as has been described in the Vedas.[1] But how can I make it clear to you? Suppose some one asks you what is the taste of clarified butter. Is it possible to make the matter perfectly clear to him? The utmost that one may say in reply to such a question is, the taste of the butter is precisely like the taste of butter! (*Laughter*.)

A girl who was unmarried once asked a friend, "Your husband is come, do tell me what sort of joy you feel whenevery you meet him?' Thereupon the married girl said, 'My dear, you will know everything when you have got a husband of your own; how can I make it clear to you now?'

In the *Puranas* we are told that the Mother of the universe incarnated Herself as the daughter of Himalayas. Just after she was born the king of the mountains was blessed with the vision of the various manifestations of the Omnipotent Mother. Then, said he, 'O Mother, let me see God the Absolute, about whom there is so much in the *Vedas*.'

[1]Nityasuddhabodha-rupam.

The Child-incarnate thereupon said, 'Father, do you wish to see God, the Absolute? Well, in that case you must live in the company of holy men—men who have given up the world. . Then only can I fulfil the desire of your heart. What It is, cannot be told in words.'

Some one has well said, 'All things, with the sole exception of God the Absolute, have become defiled like leavings of food.' The idea is, that the Sacred Scriptures of the world, having been read and recited with the aid of the tongue, have become defiled like the food thrown out of the mouth. But there has been as yet in this world no created being who has been able to express by word of mouth the nature of the Absolute. Thus the Absolute is not defiled by the mouth, so to speak.

There is joy unspeakable in the company of the Lord. Words of the mouth cannot describe it. He alone knows, who has felt it.

CHAPTER III

Book-Learning and Egotism

Addressing the Doctor, Sri Ramakrishna went on saying, "Unless one gets rid of egotism, one cannot look for the wisdom of life.

"Then shall I be free
When 'I' shall cease to be."

'I' and 'mine' is ignorance. 'Thou' and 'Thine' is knowlege. The true devotee says, 'Lord, Thou art the only active agent. I am only an instrument in Thy hands! I act as I am made to act by Thee. Thine are all these riches, the house, the family, everything! Nothing is mine. I am only a servant. Mine is only to serve according to Thy bidding.'

Strange that conceit must have a hold on those who have anything to do with books. Once Kalikrishna Tagore had a talk with me on God. He said to me, 'Sir, I am quite aware of all that you say. I have read them in the books.' Well, thereupon I said to him "My dear sir, a person who has visited Delhi does not make much of his travels and say, 'I have been to Delhi, and brag of it. A *Babu* (a well-to-do and highly respectable gentleman) does not himself say, 'I am a *Babu*.' " (*Laughter.*)

Syam Babu : Sir, Mr. Tagore has great respect for you.

Sri Ramakrishna : My dear Sir, how shall I describe the vanity of a sweeper woman who was once serving at the Temple at Dakhineswar? She had a jewel or two on her person. This, I suppose, had filled her with vanity; so she once cried out at the sight of the persons crossing her way, 'Hey! get out of the way, you people!' (*Laughter.*)

Such was the sweeper woman. It is needless to speak of the vanity and the conceit of other and bigger people!

Sin and man's Responsibility

Syam Babu :Sir, on the one hand, we are told that man is punished for his sins; and on the other hand that God is the actor, men being humble instruments in His hands. How can we reconcile the two views?

Sri Ramakrishna: How you talk like 'a gold merchant'[1] who weighs things with his delicate balance!

Narendra : What the Master means to say is that you are talking like one who has too much of a calculating turn of mind.

Sri Ramakrishna : I say Podo, eat the mangoes! What is the use of thy counting how many hundreds of mango trees there are in the garden, how many thousands of branches, how many tens of millions of leaves, and so on? You are here to eat the mangoes. Do eat them and go your way.

(To Syam Babu) : You have come into this world as a human being, with a view to attain God by means of devotion and piety. Your duty is to try your best to acquire love for the lotus feet of the Lord. Why trouble yourself about

[1]Suvarna vanika.

this and that and a hundred other matters? Would philosophical discussions make you wiser than before? Do you not see that four ounces of wine are quite capable of making you intoxicated? That being so, there is no use in your calculating how many barrels of liquor there are in the tavern, getting intoxicated being your only object!

Doctor: Quite so, Sir. What is more, the liquor in God's wine-shop is beyond all measure. It can never be exhausted.

Sri Ramakrishna (to Syam Babu) : Furthermore, why do you not execute a power of attorney in favour of the Lord? Let all your cares and responsibilities rest on Him. A person of high character, suppose, is entrusted by you with certain duties. Surely, such a person is not capable of doing you wrong. The question whether a sinner will be punished hereafter or not may well be left to Him.

Doctor : It is He alone who knows what He is going to do. Human calculation cannot go far enough. The Lord is above and beyond all human calculation,

Sri Ramakrishna (to Syam Babu) : How very fashionable this sort of talk has grown amongst you Calcutta people! They speak of the absence of the principle of equality in God's dealings with man! Why should God, they complain, make some people happy and others unhappy! These fools only see God's nature to be the same as their own.

Is Fame or Popularity the End of Life?

Hem used to come to the Temple at Dakshineswar in company with his friends, the Jambazaar Babus. Whenever he had occasion to meet me he used to say, 'Well Mr. Bhattacharya, there is only one thing worth having in this world, *viz.*, honour. Is it not so?' *Very few see that the end of human life is to see God.*

The Subtle or Fine Body

Syam Babu : Sir, we hear a good deal of the 'astral' body we posses—the subtle body[1] as different from the gross[2] body. Can any person

[1]Sukshma Sarira. [2]Sthula Sarira.

show that my double (the subtle body) actually leaves the gross body and goes elsewhere?

Sri Ramakrishna : A true devotee would not care to show you all this. He cares not the least whether some fool will regard him with respect or not. To have some big people hover about him is the last thing he wishes for.

Syam Babu : Will you please say, Sir, how you know the subtle body from the gross?

The Gross Body. the Subtle Body. the Body of Ecstasy and the Great Cause or the Unconditioned

Sri Ramakrishna : The five elements make up the body. The subtle body is made up of the *manas* (feeling and volitional aspect of mind), the *buddhi* (the determinative faculty), *ahamkara* (the egoism or the sense of I) and the *chitta*? (the memory). The inner body which feels the beatitude of God-vision is called the body of ecstasy, or the *Karana sarira.* The *Tantras* call it *bhagavatitanu.* Beyond all these is *mahakarana,* the Great First Cause—the Unconditioned—which cannot be expressed by words!

CHAPTER IV

THE IMPORTANCE OF PRACTICE

Sri Ramakrishna : What is the use of merely listening to lectures? The real thing is practice.

You say the words *siddhi, siddhi* (hemp leaves) repeatedly. Will that give you intoxication? You may pound the drug to a paste and smear your whole body with it. Will that make you intoxicated? No, you must swallow a little of it.

There are threads of various counts such as, No. 40, No. 41, and so on. Well, you do not know one number from another unless you are in the trade. It is by no means hard for those in the trade to differentiate a thread of a particular number from another number. That being so, I say, do practise a little. That done, it would be easy for you to have correct idea as to the gross body, the subtle body, the *Karana* (the causal body) and the *Mahakarana* (the Great First Cause or the Unconditioned).

Devotion to God, the One Thing Needful; How to Pray

When you pray, ask for *Bhakti* to His lotus feet. After Ahalya[1] was made free from the curse called down upon her by her husband, Ramachandra said, 'Do ask for a boon from me.' Ahalya said, 'Oh Rama, if Thou wilt give me a boon, do Thou grant that my mind may ever be on Thy feet, which are beautiful like lotus. O, I may be born amongst swine, but that will not matter then!'

For my part I pray for devotion alone to my Divine Mother.

Putting flowers upon Her lotus feet, with folded hands I prayed saying, 'Mother, here is ignorance, here is knowledge. Oh! Take them; I want them not; grant that I may have pure love alone. Here is cleanliness of the mind and the body; here is uncleanliness; what shall I do with them? Let me have pure love. Oh! Here is sin, here is merit; I want neither the one nor the other; let me have pure love alone. Here is good, here is evil; Oh! Take them! I want none of them! Let me have pure love alone. Here are good works, here are bad works. Oh! Place me above them, I want them not; grant that I may have pure love alone.'

If you take the fruit of good works, you must take the fruit of bad works also. If you take the fruit of merit, you must take the fruit of sin also. Knowlege of the one[2] implies a knowledge of the many, *Ajnana*. Taking cleanliness[3] you cannot get rid of its opposite, uncleanliness. Thus knowledge of light implies a knowledge of darkness, its opposite. A knowledge of unity implies a knowledge of diversity.

[1]Ahalya—wife of the great sage Goutama. She was a devoted wife, but the villainy of her seducer, who personated her husband, made her unchaste. Hence the curse, the effect of which was, it is said, that she was turned into stone. The touch of Ramachandra made her human once more.

[2]Jnana. [3]Suchi.

Blessed is that man who loves God! What matters it if he eats the flesh of swine? On the other hand, let a man live upon sacred food;[1] but if he is attached to the world and does not love God, then--

Doctor : Woe unto him! What good shall he gain? But Buddha once ate swine's flesh. What do you think was the immediate result? Why, *colic*! Now the poor man took to opium as a remedy. You know what is the secret of *Nirvana* and all such nonsense—the man remained stupefied with opium, and in such a state had no sense-consciousness. This was your so-called *Nirvana*!

This remark of the Doctor on Buddha's *Nirvana* gave rise to loud laughter. The conversation went on.

The Worldly Man and Work without Attachment

Sri Ramakrishna (to Syam Babu) : To lead the life of a householder is by no means wrong. But take care that you work without attachment, with your mind always pointing to the feet of the Lord. Suppose a person has a carbuncle on the back. Now this man may talk as usual. Perhaps he attends to his daily work. But pain constantly puts him in mind of the carbuncle. In the same way, although you are in the world you should turn your mind constantly to the Lord.

A woman secretly carries on an intrigue with her lover. Live in the world like that woman, doing your many duties, with your soul secretly yearning for the Lord. She thinks of her lover all the time that she does her household duties.

(To the Doctor) : Do you follow this?

Doctor : Never having had such feelings as those of the woman, how can I follow?

Syam Babu : My dear Doctor, excuse me, but you do follow a little, do you not? (*Laughter*.)

Sri Ramakrishna : More especially as he has been in the business for a long time. Is not that so? (*Laughter*.)

Theosophy

Syam Babu : Sir, what do you think of Theosophy?

[1] Havishyanna—rice cooked with clarified butter, etc., and offered to the Deity.

Sri Ramakrishna : The long and short of the matter is that people making disciples belong to an inferior order of men. Again, those that seek for occult powers, also belong to an inferior class; such powers, as for example, that of getting across the river Ganges on foot or of reporting here what another person is talking about in a far off country. It is by no means easy for such people to get pure love (Bhakti) for the Lord.

Syam Babu : But, Sir, the Theosophists seek to put Hinduism once more on a firm basis.

Sri Ramakrishna : That may be. Well, I am not well posted as to their views or doings.

Syam Babu : Questions like the following are dealt with in Theosophy: What regions is the soul bound for after death—the lunar sphere or the stellar mansions, and so forth?

Sri Ramakrishna : But let me give you an idea of *my* way of thinking. Somebody put it to Hanuman, the great lover of God, 'What day is it of the lunar fortnight?' Hanuman replied, 'My dear fellow, excuse me. I know nothing about the days of the week, the day[1] of the lunar fortnight, or the stars telling of one's destiny on a particular day. That is not my line. I meditate on God and on God alone.'

Syam Babu : Sir, the Theosophists believe in *Mahatmas*. May I ask whether you hold that *Mahatmas* are real beings?

Sri Ramakrishna: If you care to take my word for truth, I say 'Yes.' But will you be good enough to let these matters alone? Come when I am better. Do but have faith in my words, and I will see that you find peace. Do you not see I don't take either money or clothes or any other thing? In some theatrical representations respectable visitors are expected to encourage the actors by money gifts during the acting. *Here* people are not called upon to make such gifts. This is why so many come here. (*Laughter.*)

(To the Doctor) : What I have got to say to you is this—but do not take offence: you have had enough of the

[1]Tithi.

things of the world—money, fame, lectures and so on. Now give your mind a little to God, and come here now and then. It is good to listen to words relating to God. Such words enlighten the soul and turn it to God.

CHAPTER V

Incarnations of God

A short while after, the Doctor stood up to say good-bye. But Girish came in and the Doctor was so glad to see him that he took his seat again. Girish, stepping forward, saluted the Lord and kissed the dust of His hallowed feet. The Doctor watched all this in silence.

Doctor : So long as I am here Girish Babu will not be good enough to come. He must come just as I am about to go away. (*Laughter.*)

There was then a talk about the Science Association and the lectures delivered there. Girish took an interest in these lectures.

Sri Ramakrishna (to the Doctor): Will you take me one day to the Association?

Doctor : My dear Sir, once you are there you will lose all sense-consciousness at the sight of the glorious and wonderful works of God—the intelligence shown in those works—the adaptation of means to end!

Sri Ramakrishna : O! Indeed?

Doctor (to Girish) : Do every thing else, but pray do not worship Him as God. By so doing you are only bringing ruin upon such a holy man!

Worship of The Spiritual Preceptor

Girish : Sir, there is, I fear, no help for it. He who has enabled me to get across this terrible sea of the world and the no less terrible sea of scepticism—O, how else shall I serve such a person? There is nothing in Him that I cannot worship.

Doctor : I myself hold that all men are equal. A grocer's child was once brought into our place for treatment. Its bowels moved. Everybody put up the ends of their cloth to their nose, I did not. I sat by the child for half an hour. I did not put up the cloth to my nose even when the scavenger passes by with the tubs on his head. No, that is for me impossible. The sweeper is by no means less a human being than I am. Why shall I look down upon him? As to this holy man here, do you think I cannot salute and kiss the dust of his feet? Look here. (The Doctor salutes and kisses the dust of the Master's feet.)

Girish: Oh, Sir, the angels of heaven are saying, 'Blessed, blessed be this auspicious moment!'

Doctor : You seem to think that saluting one's feet is something like a marvel! You don't see that I can do the same in the case of everybody. (To a gentleman seated near) Now, Sir, oblige me by allowing me to salute your feet. (To another) And you, Sir. (To a third) And you, Sir. (The Doctor salutes the feet of many.)

Narendra (to the Doctor) : Sir, we look upon the Master as a person who is like God. Let me make my idea clear to you. There is a point somewhere between the vegetable creation and the animal creation where it is difficult to say whether a particular thing is a vegetable or an animal. Much in the same way there is point somewhere between the man-world and the God-world where you cannot say with certainty whether a person is a human being or a God.

Doctor : Well, my friend, matters relating to God cannot be explained by analogy.

Narendra : I say not God, but God-like man.

Doctor : You should not give vent to feelings of reverence like that. Speaking for myself, no one has been able, I am sorry to say. to judge my inward feelings. My best friends often regard me as stern and cruel. Even you, my good friends, may beat me some day with shoes and turn me out.

Sri Ramakrishna (to the Doctor) : Now, don't say so, Doctor! These people love you so much. They watch and look for you as ladies come together in the bride-chamber looking for the coming bride-groom ! (*Laughter.*)

Girish : Sir, every one here has the greatest respect for you.

Doctor : (Sorrowfully) : My son—even my wife—looks upon me as hard-hearted—and for the simple reason that I am by nature loath to give vent to my feelings.

Girish : In that case, Sir, don't you think it would be better to throw open the door of your mind—at least out of pity for your friends. You well see that your friends do not understand you.

Doctor : Shall I say it? Well, my feelings are worked up even more than yours.

(To Narendra) : I shed tears in solitude.

The Teacher and the Atonement

Doctor (to Sri Ramakrishna) : Well, Sir, may I say that it is not good that you allow people during *Samadhi* to touch your feet with their body?

Sri Ramakrishna : Surely you do not say that I am conscious of this?

Doctor : You feel that that is not a right thing to do, don't you?

Sri Ramakrishna : What shall I say as regards the state of my mind during *Samadhi*? After the *Samadhi* is over I sometimes go so far as to ask myself, 'May this not be the cause of the disease that I have got?' The thing is, the thought of God makes me mad. All this is the result of madness. There is no help for it.

Doctor (to the disciples) : He expresses regret for what he does. He feels that the act is sinful.

Sri Ramakrishna (to Narendra) : Well, you have a keen insight. Do explain it all to him.

Girish (to Doctor) : Sir, you are quite mistaken. He is by no means sorry that his feet touch the persons of the *devotees*. No, it is not that. His body is pure, sinless, purity itself. He is good enough, in his anxiety for their spiritual welfare, to allow His hallowed feet to touch the body of the *devotees.* As a result of his taking their sins upon himself, his own body, he sometimes thinks, may be suffering from disease. You may think of your own case. You were once taken ill with colic, as you once told us, as the result of hard study. Well, did you not at that time express your regret that you had sat up reading till very late hours at night? Does that prove that reading till very late hours at night is bad? The Master may be sorry from the point of view of a patient. He is by no means sorry from the point of view of a Teacher of God anxious for the welfare of humanity.

The Doctor was rather put out of countenance and hung down his head.

Doctor (to Girish) : I confess I am beaten. Now give me the dust of your feet.

(To Narendra) : This matter apart, I must admit the acuteness of his (Girish's) intellectual powers.

Narendra (to Doctor) : You may view the question another way. You sometimes devote your life to the task of making a scientific discovery—and then you do not look to your body, your health and so forth. Now, the knowledge of God is the grandest of all sciences. Is it not natural that the Master has risked his health for this purpose, and, may be, has ruined it?

Doctor : Religious reformers without a single exception —Buddha, Jesus, Chaitanya, Muhammad —all were at the end filled with egotism. They all declare, 'What I say—that alone—is absolutely correct; nothing else!' How shocking!

Incarnations of God

With this the Doctor stood up to depart.

Girish (to the Doctor) : Sir, don't you think you are running into the same error? You point out they were all egotists,—all of them, without exception, egotists! You find fault with them and, don't you think, the same charge may be laid at your door?

The Doctor was silent.

Narendra : We offer to Him worship *bordering* on divine worship.

SECTION XIV

1886

SRI RAMAKRISHNA AT COSSIPORE GARDEN WITH NARENDRA (VIVEKANANDA), RAKHAL, M., GIRISH AND OTHER DISCIPLES

CHAPTER I

Divine Incarnation for the Sake of Those that Love the Lord

Sri Ramakrishna is staying with his disciples in the garden at Cossipore. He is lying very ill in the large room upstairs.

It is evening. Narendra and Rakhal are gently stroking his feet with the hand. Mani is also seated near the Master who beckons to him to join in the service and relieve one of the two brothers.

It is Sunday, 14th March 1886, second Chaitra, ninth day of the light fortnight of Falgun. It is the Sunday after his birthday anniversary, which came off on the preceding Sunday at the garden. Last year the anniversary was celebrated with great rejoicing at the Temple at Dakshineswar. This year the Master is very ill and his disciples are sorely troubled in spirit. God indeed was worshipped as usual on that day and the usual offerings were made to Him. But there was no feast made in which the public could take part.

The disciples are all present in the garden watching and nursing their beloved Master. Our Holy Mother is also here,—night and day she is engaged in the blessed service of her Lord. Most of the younger disciples are here. They have practically left their homes and have thrown themselves heart and soul into this noble work—that of ministering to Him—from whom they have learnt the true meaning of life in this enigmatic world.

The older disciples, many of whom have entered the world, come to see the Master almost every day. Some of them come to stay for two or three days at a time.

He is very ill to-day. It is midnight. The garden and the house are bathed in the moonlight. But the hearts of the disciples know no peace, for it is feared that He, who has solved the problem of life for them, is about to leave this world!

There is perfect silence. All nature is still, save for the rustling sound of the leaves which slightly move in the gentle breeze of spring that blows from the south. In the midst of this stillness is the Master lying in his chamber upstairs, sleepless! One or two disciples are seated near, watching. At times he seems to fall asleep. Or is it that he has passed into that blessed state of communion in which the mind remains unmoved in the midst of the greatest sorrow and sufferings?

M. is seated by his side, dumb, bewildered at the sight of sufferings unspeakable—a sight which would rend the heart of the most hard-hearted. At the bidding of the Master, he comes still nearer. He says to M., in broken words, 'Lest you and your brothers here shall go about weeping, I do suffer so much! If you all say, 'Your sufferings of the flesh are terrible—let the body be given up'—if you will say it—then this body may be laid aside!'

M. is speechless and looks bewildered!

It is the moment of agony with the disciples; their hearts are rent asunder. He who is their father, their mother, their leader, their protector, their master, their all, speaks these words! What are they to say in reply? 'Is this another Crucifixion,' thinks one of them to himself, 'another sacrifice for the sake of mankind and specially for the sake of those who in the absence of their Shepherd will be like so many scattered sheep?'

* * * * *

It is the dead of night. The Master gets worse. Is there no help?

A message is sent to Calcutta friends. Doctor Upendra and Kaviraj Navagopal come up with Girish from Calcutta at the dead of night.

The disciples are with the Master. He seems a little better.

He says, 'The sufferings are of the flesh; that is as it should be—for the body is made of the five elements,—yes, it comes from matter.'

Turning to Girish, he says—'What do you think I always see in this state? Well, it is the spiritual forms of the Lord. Many and various are those forms! Amongst them do I behold also this form here; in which too the Lord hath manifested Himself.'

(By 'this form' the Master means his own form.)

CHAPTER II

God-vision of Sri Ramakrishna

It is between 7 and 8 o'clock the following morning, Monday, 15th March. The Master has rallied a little. Softly he talks with the disciples. He is seated reclining on pillows. At times he expresses his thoughts by means of signs.

Narendra, Rakhal. M., Latu, Sasi, Gopal (senior) —are seated before Him.

The disciples sit mute; their heart knows no peace. They call back to their mind the state of the Master on the previous night, and look grave.

God Manifests Himself as Man and Nature

Master (to M.): Do you know what I see! I see Him as All. Man and other creatures,—they appear as veritable figures skin-bound,—with the Lord within,—shaking the head or moving the hands and feet!

I had once a like perception: One Substance, I felt, had taken the forms of the cosmos with all living creatures; like a house of wax, with gardens, roads, men, cows, and the rest, all made of wax and nothing but wax!

I see, I realise, that all the three come of one Substance, —the victim to be sacrificed, the block for sacrifice, and he who cuts down the victim for sacrifice.

[Does the Master say that he offers himself as a sacrifice for the sake of mankind and that it is the Lord that manifests Himself as the victim for sacrifice?]

Saying this the Master cries out in a feeble voice, 'Ah me! Ah me! What a vision!'

The state of God-consciousness once more! The Master has soared high above the sense-world! The state of ecstasy is not good for him,—so think the disciples. But they know not what to do.

He comes back again to the ordinary state of consciousness. He says, 'Now I am free from suffering of any kind. I am as well as ever.'

The disciples see that he has passed into a state which is beyond joy and grief, happiness and misery.

Latu hangs down his head which rests on the palm of his hand, as he watches the Master with a sorrowful heart.

The Master lifts up his eyes and looks on the disciples. His heart overflows with the unspeakable love that he bears towards his darlings—a love that the world cannot give—a love that passes all human understanding.

Rakhal and Narendra! How he fondles them! He strokes their faces and caresses them as if they were children five years old!

A short while after, he says to M. in a sad tone,—'Were it given to this body to stay on in this world for a few days more, the souls of many people would have been waked up!'

With these words he remains silent for a time. He continues, saying,

'BUT IT HATH BEEN ORDAINED OTHERWISE!'

The disciples wait for his next words. The Master says again, 'Yes, such is not the will of the Lord; here is one in whom there is no guile, one that knows not letters; and people may take advantage. He may give away God's best gifts to those that are not worthy and know not the value of devotional exercises, in this age of sensuality and mammon-worship.'

Does the Master mean that the Son of God, the divine incarnation, is the embodiment of God's love for mankind, and that the world cannot be kept going if all human beings who are expected to work for the perpetuity of the species came to realise God through His Son, and thus bring a cessation to it?

Rakhal (affectionately) : Do speak to the Lord, Sir, so that Thy body may remain in this world for some time more.

Sri Ramakrishna : The Lord's will be done!

Narendra : Thy will has become one with the will of the Lord!

The Master holds his peace as if thinking within himself.

Sri Ramakrishna (to Narendra, Rakhal and others): Well, nothing comes of my speaking to the Lord about it. His will shall be done.

I now see that I and my Divine Mother have become one once for all. Radha said to Krishna, 'O Beloved, abide Thou within my heart and appear not any longer in Thy human form'. But she soon yearned to see Krishna in human form. Her heart struggled and panted after the Beloved. But the Lord's will must be done, and Krishna did not appear in human form for a long time.

Rakhal (aside to the disciples): The Master speaks of Chaitanya.

M. (to himself) : One with His Divine Mother! One with the Undifferentiated! Now it is so hard for him to continue as a separate personality! The Son merged into the Mother! Is this the meaning of the Master's words?

CHAPTER III

A Message from the Beyond

The disciples sit still. The Master looks on them with affection. He puts his hands upon his heart and will speak.

Sri Ramakrishna (to Narendra and other disciples): Here (that is, within himself) there are two Persons. One is the Divine Mother—

The disciples wait for the rest of his words.

He continues:

One is the Divine Mother, the other person is Her devotee. It is the second person who has been now taken ill. Do you understand this?

The disciples sit still and do not utter a single word.

Sri Ramakrishna : Alas! To whom shall I speak all this? And who is there to understand me?

A short while and the Master continues:

The Lord comes with His disciples as a Divine Incarnation. He takes a human body; His disciples go back with Him to the Divine Mother.

Rakhal : Therefore, Sir, you must not go before us and leave us behind.

The Master smiles with love unspeakable beaming from his eyes. He says on:

A band of *Bauls*[1] comes into a house all on a sudden; they chant the name of the Lord and dance with joy! That done, they leave the house at once! As abrupt in going as in coming! And the people know them not!

The Master and the disciples smile..

The Master continues:

[1] *Bauls* are a sect of Hindus who renounce the world and are filled with the madness of Divine Love.

Taking human body, one cannot avoid suffering.

I sometimes say to myself, 'May the Lord grant that I may not be sent unto this world any more!'

But there is one thing to be taken into account. The rice and *dal* to be had in one's home ceases to interest one if one is invited to the Lord's feast.

M. (to himself) : Does the Master mean that the Son of God who is the embodiment of God's love is ever fond of abiding with His own, *viz.*, those that love the Lord, and Lord alone? The ambrosia that He distributed at His feast, was it not the love of the Lord?

Master : He takes the human body for the sake of the pure souls that love the Lord alone.

The Master looks on Narendra with ineffable tenderness!

Paths of Knowledge and Love of God

Master (to Narendra) : Once an outcaste was carrying basket-loads of raw meat hung to a sling on his shoulder, when he met Sankaracharya (the Hindu saint and reformer) passing by after bathing in the holy waters of the Ganges. It chanced that he touched the person of the holy man. Sankara got offended and cried out, 'Thou hast touched me, sirrah'. He replied, 'My good Sir, neither have I touched thee, nor hast thou touched me! Do thou reason with me and say whether thy true Self is the body or the mind or the determinative faculty and tell me what thou art truly. Thou knowest that the true Self is not attached to any of the three Gunas that constitute the world *Viz.*, *the Sattva* (rhythmic matter), *Rajas* (vibratory matter), and *Tamas* (inert matter).'

The Absolute,—do you know what It is like? It is like the air, which carries odours, be they good or bad, but itself remains unaffected by them.

Narendra : That is indeed true, Sir.

Master : The Absolute is beyond all attributes,—beyond whatever is connected with the world-process.

The world-force either leads Godward or away from God. Woman and gold lead us away from God. Knowledge, renunciation, devotion, etc. lead to God. Sankara never parted with the latter. He retained the *ego of the preceptor*! You and the others here feel concerned for me; this concern comes out of the latter and it leads to God.

If one takes the help of that part of the world-force which leads to God, one may realise the Absolute. Reaching the roof some like to come again down the staircase; they retain the love for Personal God even after realisation of the Absolute. They do so for setting an example to mankind; and also for enjoying the sweetness of divine love and the company of those that love the Lord.

Narendra and other disciples remain silent. After a while Narendra speaks.

Narendra and Renunciation

Narendra : There are people who get very much annoyed with me at my pointing out the need for renunciation.

Master (softly) : One *must* renounce—give up the world for the sake of the Lord.

The Master looks grave,—gently touches his own person and draws the attention of Narendra and other disciples, saying, 'Suppose, there are two things in a line, one after the other, in such a way that you cannot get at the second object without putting the first and nearer object on one side. In that case if you want to take the second and more distant object, must you not put the first aside?'

Narendra : Precisely so, Sir!

Master (softly to Narendra) : When you see everything as the manifestation of the Lord, can you see anything but the Lord? Where is your world or family then,—standing by itself?

Narendra : Assuredly not. *The world must be renounced.*

Master : If you see the Lord alone, surely you cannot see anything else,—one's family and kinsmen and so forth!

But one needs giving up from the mind. Those that come here,—none of them is of the world.

(Smiling) : Some amongst them chanced to have a fancy for women. (Rakkal, M., and others smile.) That is all. They are in the world but not of the world. Their desire to enjoy the company of women has been fulfilled and they can now give their whole mind to God.

Narendra and his Heroic Spirit

Tenderly does the Master look upon Narendra. He is filled with joy as he casts his eyes upon him. He turns to His disciples and says, 'marvellous!'

Narendra (smiling to Master): What is marvellous, Sir?

Master (smiling) : The progress that is being made towards renunciation.

The Master means the renunciation of Narendra.

Narendra and other disciples hold their peace and look on the Master.

Here Rakhal speaks.

Rakhal (smiling to Master) : Narendra is now beginning to understand you well.

The Master smiles and says:

'Yes, that is so. What is more, I see there are many more here who are beginning to understand (To M.) : Is it not the case?'

M.: Yes, Sir, that is indeed so.

The Master looks for a time on Narendra and M. He beckons to Rakhal and other disciples, pointing to them. First he points to Narendra and then to M.

Rakhal sees his meaning and speaks.

Rakhal (smiling to Master) : You mean, Sir, that Narendra has the spirit of a hero, while M. has the spirit of *Sakhi* (a lady friend). (*Laughter.*)

(By *Sakhi* Rakhal means one who like the *Gopis* of Brindavan worships the Lord of the universe as the bridegroom).

The Master smiles.

Narendra (smiling) : M. here, is a man of few words—and shy. Is it thus that you call him a *Sakhi?*

Master (smiling to Narendra) : Well, what do you think is the nature of my feelings?

Narendra : Why, Sir, you are everything! A hero who has cut his way to the Reality with the sword of discrimination and with a strength which the world cannot give! You have the feelings of a *Sakhi* too—love unspeakable, the ecstasy of divine love which is called up by the divine lover alone. You are a hero, *Sakhi*—and everything else—in your yearning for the Lord!

A Revelation

The Master has all his feelings stirred up. He lays his hand upon the heart and speaks.

Master (to Narendra and other disciples) : *I see—I realise—that all things, every conceivable thing—comes out of this*!

He asks Narendra by signs, 'What do you understand?'

Narendra : Every conceivable thing, that is, all created objects come out of Thee!

Master (rejoicing, to Rakhal) : Do you see how he understands?

He asks Narendra to sing. Narendra will renounce the world and is filled with the spirit of renunciation. He sings:

SONG

Transitory is human life like drops of water dancing on lotus leaves.
Hence the need for the company of holy men that have renounced the world.
One instant spent in their company does take a person like the ferry-boat across the Sea of the World.

Here the Master interrupts Narendra, saying, 'What is it that you sing? These are common-place things—and meant only for the beginner.'

Narendra now sings of the Lord as the divine lover whom the devotee longs to see.

SONG

1. O, my friend! whither is gone the Divine Lover of *Braja*? Dost thou not see that separation from Him will kill me?

2. Artless daughter of a milkman that I am, He hath forgotten me and hath made love to others more beautiful than myself!

Who did know, my dear friend, that a Lover so tender, so divine would go abegging for external beauty!

3. Fool was I to have forgotton myself at the sight of His heavenly beauty and to have held His feet fast to my throbbing bosom! O, now I must consign this body to a watery grave in the Jamuna! Or do thou get me poison and let me thus put an end to a miserable existence!

4. Or let me have some creeper from the woods to fasten round my neck; let me thus die by hanging to a young Tamal tree dark brown like Him;

Failing all this let me repeat night and day the sweet name of the Beloved, *Syam, Syam, Syam, Syam*, and stop not until this miserable body ceaseth to breathe.

The Master as well as his disciples are all deeply touched with the sweetness of the song. Tears of love divine stand on the eyes of the Master and of Rakhal.

Narendra is filled with ecstasy, places himself in the position of a *Gopi* of Brindavan (a female lover of the Lord) and sings again:

SONG

O My Beloved! O Beloved mine!
What do I say to Thee, O what do I say,
(Foolish woman that I am and never a favourite of Fortune)
Thou art the mirror to be held by my hands, Thou art the flower for my head!
O, I shall make Thee a flower, wear Thee among my hairs!
I shall hide Thee, hide Thee, O my Beloved, under the braided hair
Worn under the hair, no one shall find Thee!
O, Thou art the cooling collyrium for the eye,
Thou art the betel leaf chewed with nuts and sweet fragrant spices for the mouth.

I shall make Thee, O my Beloved, my *Syam*, collyrium for the eye and thus wear Thee!

They shall think I have painted my eyes with the dark-brown pigment and shall not find Thee!

Thou art the cool fragrant sandal paste for the body and the necklace for the neck!

I shall cool, O my Beloved, my body, mind and soul with Thee, my dark-brown sandal paste.!

And I shall make Thee my necklace and wear Thee round my neck and on my bosom and next to my heart.

To the body Thou art the life! To the house Thou art the one thing that one cannot do without.

To me, O my Beloved, Thou art verily what wings are to the bird,—what water is to the fish.

INDEX

A

Abhedananda, (See Kali).
Absolute (Brahman) unattached, '61: Our 'Absolute' implies the relative, 81-82, 288; is beyond speech and mind, 288-289; not defiled by mouth 290-291; *vide* Brahman.
Adhar, 7, 198.
Adwaita and Visishtadwaita, a reconciliation 119; philosophy 76; vide Vedanta.
Adwaitin, his problem, 76; and ordinary men, 78, 115.
Agnosticism in the West, 182.
Ahalya, 295.
Ajnana, 86.
All ways lead to God, 190; lead to the same Goal, 192.
Analogies, the use of, 70.
Anur, the place of the Master's first God-vision, 2.
Ashtavakra Samhita, 155.
Atonement and the Guru, 301.
Avesh, 218.
Avidya, 61, 68.

B

Baburam, 7, 244.
Bad men how to deal with them, 38.
Badge of authority, 188.
Bel tree, place of Sadhan, 19.
Balaram, 55, 91, 198, 238, 241, 256.
Bankim Chandra Chaterji, 7.
Become as a child, 173.
Bejoy (Goswami), 111, 113, 131.
Benode, 227.
Bhagavandas, 8.
Bhagavat Gita, 60.
Bhakta, can he get a knowledge of the Absolute of Brahmajnan? 80, 185; his wish, 84 various classes of Bhaktas, 149; and the Lord's Drawing-room, 114 or the Dualist, 115; and Karma, 194; his prayer, 193.
Bhakti Yoga, 175, 191; the Yuga-dharma, 192.
Bhakti the one thing needful, 215, 272, 295; and asceticism, 223.
Bhavanath, 170, 239.
Body, gross body, subtle body, the body of ecstasy, 293; and soul, 114.
Bondage, the cause of 44.
Book-learning, the value of, 59, 248; and Divine Wisdom, 273; and egotism, 291.
Brahman is the Unconditioned, 61; Unattached, 61; Unspeakable, 62; unfathomable by Conditioned Knowledge, 63; beyond Desa, Kala, Nimitta, 62; beyond all predication, 64; and Sakti, —One and the Same, 70; is not beyond the Purified Supersensual Mind, 254; *vide* Absolute.
Brahmacharya, 64.
Brahmananda(See Rakhal).
Brahmoism and Christianity, 202.
Brahmo-Samaj, 125; and Janaka, 128, and One thing Needful, 179 and Motherhood of God, 147; and God's Works, 138; schism in, 177 and prayer, 153.

C

Caste system, 94.
Chaitanya Deva, 60, 110, 189, 207, 210; and Sri Ramakrishna, 224, owner of Divine Wisdom and Love, 268.
Chandramani Devi, Sri Ramakrishna's Mother, 1.
Charitable and other works, 181.
Charity, and Self-love, 181.
Child-like simplicity and faith, 277.
Christianity, 125.
Chunilal, 7, 238, 241, 253, 256.

Commandment, God's 133, 186; How to receive it from God, 189.
Commissioned Teacher and his Nature, 187; and the wisdom of life, 187.
Communion by Love, 184 (see Bhakti-yoga.)
Company of Holy Men, 124, 291; and the giving up of the world, 279.
Contradiction of Harmony, 215.
Cosmos made up of Satva, Rajas, and Tamas, 254.
Cossipore Garden, 302.
Creation, 120.
Creeds, room enough for all, 131.
Criterion of Truth, 276.

D

Dakshineswar, 4, 155.
Daya, 156, 219.
Dayananda Saraswati, 8, 154.
Debendra, 7.
Desires and passions, how to control them, 270.
Devotion to God, 280; its effect on work, 233.
Disciples how to choose them, 53, His own, 53, 7, 8; with his, 98, 130, 223, 234, 266, 137, 167, 211, 221
Discrimination and Dispassion, 36, 80, 185, 186; after True Knowledge, 66, 108.
Disputation and Realisation, 262.
Diversity, 43.
Dreams, God-vision in, 102.
Dualist, 115, 200.
Duty of a father, 30.

E

Ecstatic Love, 237.
Ego—of Knowledge, 199; of a Servant, 200; of Bhakti 201; of Love and the Problem of Life, 225, of the Preceptor, 309.
Egoism and Altruism, 179.
Egotism, 172.
Energy, the Omnipotent, 144.
End of Life or the One Thing Needful, 104, 107, 215, 293.
England and America 174.
Environment, the Power of 124.
Equal—are all men equal? 43, 71.
Evil, Problem of, 43, 61.
Experience for a Teacher, 185.
External World, what is it? 76.

F

Faith—power of, 45; and Self-surrender, 281; efficacy of, 83; its omnipotence, 87; the One Thing Needful 278.
Fame, desire for it condemned, 153, is it the End of Life? 172, 293.
Family Life with Discrimination, 128, 129.
Fear not, 180, 189, 288,
First Seek God, 107.
Fit vessels 195.
Forms of the Deity, 75.
'Free, I am' cherish the idea, 156; curse of service, 170, 231.

G

Gadadhar, name of His Childhood, 2.
Ganga Mata, 8.
Gardener, the Divine, 151.
Gifts, 244.
Girish, 7, 227, 232, 238, 253, 307; and Doctor, 298; and Vivekananda, 299.
Goal of the Vedantin, Union, 63.
God—is God with or without Form? 31, 269; how to see Him, 36: His Name enough to save; sinner 45; the only proof of, 69; is He partial? 71; God Personal and God Impersonal, 65 Personal God a necessity, 77, 85; Identity of Personal and Impersonal, 89. Personal God can give Knowledge of the Absolute, 81; Chanting God's Name, 101, 102; is anything impossible with Him 100; the One Thing Needful, 107; in the

Temple of the Heart, 107; God with different names, 115; One God, 118; the Only Master, 131, 132, 144; the Absolute and the Mother the same 152; He does everything, 117; the Absolute and the Creator, One and the same, 162, 178; is Love 206; how to know God, 206; Does God incarnate himself? 232; is not beyond the purified Mind, 254; God in everything, 252.
God-Incarnate and Revelation, 260.
God-in man, 143.
God-vision, 84, 142, 220, 259; Signs of God-vision, 187; in dreams, 102.
Good and Evil, 61.
Grace, 277.
Guilelessness, 170.
Guru is only a spiritual awakener and help, 195.
Guru and Atonement, 300.

H

Hanuman, 45, 225, 297.
Hari (Turiananda), 7.
Harmony of Creeds, 215; of Religions, 9, 138.
Hazra, 145, 213.
Hope to all Religious Cults, 190.
Hospital, the Lord's, 150.
Householder, his imperfections, 227; the Problem of Life solved for, 34, 109 124, 129, 181, 233; Message of Hope to, 235.
How to Pray, 252, 295 .

I

Ideal Man, or Sannyasin, 227; never lose sight of the Ideal, 176.
Identity of God, Soul and Nature, 76; of the Mother with the Soul and Cosmos, 79.
Ignorance, 31, 88.
Illusive power of Maya, 67, 68.
Image worship, 31, 34.
Images, the Divine Presence in 157.
Immortality of the Soul, 143; Sea of, 189.
Impersonal and Personal, 69; Identity of, 89, 260.
Incarnation, 144, 241, 257, 298, 302, 306; and Revelation, 260; does God Incarnate Himself as Man? 232, 242, 275; is it necessary to believe in it? 281.
Independence, 244.
Infinite, 242.
Intoxication with Divine Love, 203.
Involution and Evolution, 201.
Ishan, 266, 275.

J

Jairambati, birthplace of the Holy Mother, 4.
Janaka and Brahmo Samaj, 128.
Jnana yoga, 62, 190, 192, 272, 273.
Jnanin like a Steam Boat, 200.

K

Kali (Abhedananda) 7, 283.
Kalipada (Ghosh), 7.
Kamarpukur, His Place of Birth, 1.
Karmà, 159, 193, 211; and the Divine Mother, 79; *vide* Work.
Karma Yoga, work without attachment 174; difficult in this age, 174, 190, 191.
Kedar, 7,45, 47.
Keshab Chandra Sen, 6,29,147, 152, 153; and Sri Ramakrishna, 140, 141.
Khudiram Chatterjee, His Father,1.
Kindness to all, 219.
Kingdom of Heaven or Social Reforms? 108.
Knower and Lover, 161.
Knowledge of Oneness, 288, Knowledge which leads Godward, 58; True Knowledge, 181.
Krishna Kishore, 8; his faith, 94, 125, 156.

L

Latu, 7, 98, 141, 214, 238, 241.
Learning without Discrimination, 186.

Lectures and Social Reforms, 107; Value of Lectures, 32, 184, 188.
Liberated, 43.
Liberated Soul and Divine Mother, 122.
Life. End of, 135, enigma of 121; Problem of, 85.
Logic, Induction and Deduction, 47.
Lord, nothing is good or beautiful without the, 286.
Lord's Drawing-room, 114.
Lord's Hospital, 150.
Love—of one's own is Maya, 156. love of God and Renunciation, 178; communion by 184; its effect on Discrimination, 185; madness of, 168.

M

M. his first meeting with the Master, 25, 29, 93; M. meeting with Narendra, 37; M. and the Master, 47, 54, 57, 100, 155, 157, 168, 235, 238, 259, 285, 304.
Madness of Love, 168.
Mahima, 171, 223, 233.
Mani and the married Man's Problem, 109.
Manomohan, 231.
Married man, 109, 218.
Mathoor, 4, 13, 97, 149.
Maya, 61, 67, 156; and Brahman 82.
Mayavada and Parinamavada, 82.
Mujumdar, 171.
Meditation, 14 how to meditate 106.
Men, divided into four classes, 43.
Message from the Beyond, 307.
Message of Hope for the Householder, 235.
Misfortune, 158.
Monastic Life, strict discipline of, 279.
Money and Riches, 36.
Mother, the Omnipotent, 73; and Karma, 79; the Spider and Her Web, 120; Divine Mother and the Liberated Soul, 121; Divine Mother and Her Relation to Sri Ramakrishna, 132; Divine Mother and Her Manifestation, 140; Her Special Manifestations, 145; all Power comes from Her, 152; gives Brahmajnan 152; She alone can Bless, 153; Her Presence in every Home, 154; Divine Mother, 119, 122; Divine Mother and God the Absolute, 144; Her Special Manifestations (N a r e n d r a, Rakhal and others), 145.
Motherhood of God and Brahmo-Samaj, 148.
Mukta (liberated), 43.
Mumukshu, 43.

N

Naba Gopal 7.
Narayan, 7, 223, 213, 244, 249, 253.
Narendra (Vivekananda) 213, 227, 234, 248; meets M. 37; how to deal with bad men, 38; doctrine of non-resistance, 39; the Ever-perfect, 46; on School Discipline, 100, and the One thing Needful, 104, and the Master, 93, 135, 159; a Pure Soul; 145. and the World, 235; God-in-man, 263; the Special Manifestation of the Mother, 145; and M. 37; and Girish, 256; and Dr. Sirkar, 299; and Renunciation, 309; and His Heroic Spirit 310.
Narendra (Junior), 240.
New Philosophy, 76, 77-85.
Newspapers, 255.
Nirakara, 219.
Nitya (ever-free), 43.
Nityasiddhas, Narendra, Rakhal, and Bhabanath, 166.
Non-attachment and Divine Wisdom, 206.
Non-dualist, 115.

O

Om, 26.
Omnipotent Energy, 144.
One and Many, 63, 72, 144; one God with different Names, 115.
Oneness of God, 115, 117.

P

Paltu, 7, 244.

Panchavati, 18, 107, 212; place of Sadhan (practice) *vide* illustration.
Parables—Elephant and a Disciple, 39; Snake and the Holy Man, 40, A Devotee Crossing the Ocean 45; Homa Bird, 46; Ants and the Mountain of Sugar, 63; Salt Doll, 63 the Vedic Father and his Two Sons, 64; the Rich Man and a Steward, 86; Vibhishan and a Bhakta, 87; Man Sinking a Well, 133; the Calf and its Fortunes, 172; The Woodcutter and the Sannyasin: Go on Ahead 176; the Poor Man and his Hut, 179; Pandit and the King, 229; Akbar and the Fakeer, 231; Flies and the Basin of Syrup, 189; Maid-servant in Master's House, 35, 181; Ramachandra and Hanuman, 87; a Girl and her Friend, 290; the Mango Orchard, 292; the Dyer, 268; Chameleon, 268; Newspaper readers, 276; Ice and Water, 75.
Path of Knowledge and Love both lead to God, 75, 272, 273, 309; Path of Work and the Path of Devotion, 136, 273.
Perception, of the Seer, 146; Perception of the Infinite, 232.
Perfect Man, 59.
Personal and Impersonal, 69; one and the same, 70, 81, 89; Personal God, proof of, 73; a necessity, 77; can He give the Knowledge of the Absolute, 79.
Physical Science, 276.
Pilgrimage, the value of 97, 194.
Power of the Mind, 124.
Powharibaba, 114.
Practice (Sadhan), 186, 298.
Prahlad 225, 271; his Love of God, 280.
Praise and Censure, 254.
Pratab (Majumdar), 171.
Prayer, 103; its efficacy, 83; Lord's Prayer, 103, 151, 153; How to Pray, 207, 252, 295.
Pre-arrangement, 205.
Preceptor, 298.
Problem for this Age solved 175.
Pure and Selfless Love, 280.
Purity, 169, 196; the pure in hearts (See God), 85.
Purna, 7, 244.

Q

Quarrels condemned, 131.

R

Raja-Yoga, or Ashtanga-Yoga, 190.
Rakhal (Brahmananda,) 7, 93,98, 141, 142, 184, 203, 218, 231, 241,; at Syampukur 283, Nityasiddha, 166.
Rama (Datta) 223, 237, 253, 256.
Rama Kumar, His brother, 3.
Ramachandra, 87, 207, 295.
Ramakrishna — in *Samadhi*, 28, 48, 57, 73, 111, 113, 141, 159, 167, 183, 186, 205, 251, 253, 261, 286; and the Mother of the Universe, 132, and Brahmo Samaj, 128, 147, 148, 177; and Christianity, 9, 125, 202; and Jesus, 9, 119; and Islam, 9, 119; and female devotees, 10; and Chaitanya, 60, 110, 210, 224; His acceptance of all religions, 119, 138; His love for the Disciples, 214, 221; 305; and the End of Life, 135, 215, 278, 293; and the ideal for *Sannyasin* (Renunciation) 227, 228-30; and the Tantras, 119; and science, 276; and Vedanta (*vide* Vedanta); and Jnana-yoga, 61, 190, 192; and Bhaktiyoga, 85, 190, 192, 193; and Karma-yoga, 174, 181, 190; and lectures, 32, 107, 187, 188; and Social reforms, 107; and married men, 109; and purity, 169, 196; and Immortality of the Soul, 143; and Realisation, 65, 77, 84, 185, 208, 288; and mere Book-learning, 273; and how to Pray, 252; and Sin and Man's Responsibility, 293; and yoga, 190; and Theosophy, 297 His child-like simplicity, 50; with M. and Narendra, 52, 305; His story as told by himself, 93,

a hint, 200, 208, 217; no respector of person, 96; His chiding Rani Rashmoni, 97; His relation to the Divine Mother, 132; talking, with the Mother, 141; His love for a disciple, 170, 221; teaches how to pray, 252; is everybody's disciple, 284; the Ideal Teacher, 187; and Vidyasagar, 57; and Keshab Sen, 111, 140; and Girish 241; and Rakhal, 306, 307; and Narendra, 93, 159, 223, and Balaram, 241; and M. (*vide* M.); and Dr. Sarkar, 266; and Surendra, 167: and Sasadhar, 183; and Visvanath Upadhyaya, 159; Ramakrishna and the sins of men, 300; His state after God-vision, 95; teaches Narendra Bhakti and and Jnana, 304; God-vision by Him, 305; incarnated for the sake of humanity, 302; anxious to awaken souls even while suffering, 303.

Ramakrishnanda (See Sasi).

Ramanuja and his Visishtadwita, 258.

Rani Rashmoni, 3, 11, 97.

Reasoning; Ratiocination Futile, 74, 75, 81, 163, Realisation, 65, 84, 262; by the path of Knowledge and the path of Love 75; six steps leading to it, 209; after Realisation all is Brahman, 225; of the absolute, 288; company of holy men essential to, 291.

Reconciliation of all religions, 68, 82, 119, 192.

Reforms, social, 107.

Religion, all religions lead to the same Goal, 138, 192.

Religious awakening and time factor 144, 206.

Religious teachers, three classes, 195.

Renunciation, or Sannyasa, 26, 51, 178, 182, 220, 240, 309.

Revelation Vs. Reason, 69, 74,

Revelations of the Master, 73.

Master's Revelation, 311.

S

Samadhi, 69, 85.

Sambu (Mullik), 8, 135, 275.

Samsara, a fact, 273

Sandhya, 26.

Sankara, His philosophy, 67, 309.

Sannyasa (Renunciation), strict discipline in 281; and Narendra, 227, 233.

Saptabhumi (seven planes), 199.

Sarat, 7, 284.

Sarkar and Girish, 275, 300; and Vivekananda, 301.

Saroda (Trigunatita) 7.

Saradamani Devi, His wife and disciple, 4, 302.

Sasadhar, 186.

Sasi, 7, 284, 303, 304.

Schisms, condemned, 177.

Science, Physicial, 276.

Seers of God, their number limited, 206.

Self, the Higher Self knoweth the Higher Self, 67; the True Self Formless,95; Self after God-vision, 173.

Self-surrender, 147.

Sermon at the Temple by the Master, 205.

Serve only God, 169; service of the world, 170, 231.

Service, curse of, 170, 231.

Shad Chakta, (six wheels,) 199.

Shyness, contempt and fear, 288.

Siddhas and Incarnations, 307, 308.

Sikh soldiers, 196.

Sin, the sense of, 125; saying 'I am a sinner is degrading 156; the doctrine of sin and worship from fear, 202; and responsibility, 292.

Solitude—the value of, 34; contemplation in solitude, 35.

Songs for worldly objects, 196.

Songs— 46, 49, 51, 98, 101, 106, 160, 203, 204, 205, 233, 274, 311, 312, 313; the Sinner and the Power of God's Name, 45; Divine Mother, Omnipotent, Unknown, Unknowable, 71; Identity of the Personal and the Impersonal God, 89; Faith at the Root, 88; the name of God, 88: Identity of the Mother and God, the Absolute, 121, the Divine Mother and Her Children, 123; God's Sacred Name and its Power, 126; the world to a lover of God, 128; My Divine Mother and the Discipline of the Mind, 127; Yearning for the Lord, 130; Dive Deep, 180, 189; the Mother of the Universe and the Difficulty of Realisation, 204; the Love of God, 205; the Devotee and Her Ecstatic Love for Chaitanya, 203; Gouranga, God Incarnate, 246; Ecstatic Love of God, 246; the Great Mystery, the Impersonal-Personal, 250; the Mother and Her Weary Children, 250, Beloved Mother of the Universe, 249; God-vision, 264; the Lord my Husband, 286; the Mother of the Universe; 285; God and His Works, 285, the Science of God-vision, 289.

Soul and the Body, 114.

Soul, why is it imperfect? 122; its treatment, 150.

Spider and her Web, 120.

Spiritual Forms, 75.

Spiritual discipline and time factor, 210.

Stages of Spirituallty, 207.

Subodh, 7.

Subtle Body, 293.

Sukadeva, 25, 62.

Surendra, 167.

Suvankar and Sri Ramakrishna, 2.

Syam Babu, 296.

T

Tantras, 120.

Tarak (Shivananda), 7.

Teacher—the Divine Teacher, 108; the Commissioned Teacher, 133; should not make disciples without commandment, 133; Commissioned Teacher invincible, 187; Commissioned Teacher and Organization, 187; Teacher and Wisdom of Life, 187; must realise first, 188; Religious Teachers are of three classes, 195; Highest Teachers save men 200, 279; and Atonement, 300.

Tej-chandra, 7, 244.

Temple-garden, 11.

Theosophy, 296.

Think not of Morrow, 216.

Time-factor, 194.

Totapuri, His Guru, 5, 256.

Trailinga Swami, 7, 200.

Truth and Revelation 145.

U

"Unity of Everything" Sri Ramakrishna's favourite saying, 165.

Unity in Diversity, 72, 118.

Universe Unreal, 67, 269.

Unknown and Unknowable or Brahman 62.

V

Vaishnava Charan, 5.

Vaishnavism (see Ramanuja, Chaitanya Bhakti-yoga.)

Vanity, 291.

Variety, 47; is the law, 33.

Vedanta Philosophy, 61, as interpreted by Sankara, 67; by Ramanuja; 258; and Jnana-yoga, 61, 173, 190, 191; and the Problem of evil, 61; its goal, 63; and Realisation, 58, 68; and Maya, 67; and Revelation, 69, 73; and God, the Mother, 73, 79, 80; and the Bhakti-yoga, 75, 84, 175, 184, and the external world, 76; its conclusion, 269; and Bhakti (*vide* Bhakti-yoga); and Karma (*vide*-Karma yoga).

Vedanta Practical, *vide* work.

Vidyasagar, 57.

Vijnanins, 68.

Viswanath, Upadhyaya, 6, 160,

Vivekananda (See Narendra).

W

Ways to the Sea of Immortality infinite, 34, 190, 200.

Wheels six 199.

Wisdom, 206, 273.
Woman, two sorts, 31, as Mother 10, 103.
Work, (Karma), its renunciation for the Lord, 26; without attachment, 59, 123, 172; the Western idea of Work, 171; the path of work, 136; not the end of life, 175; giving up of 175; work *v.* faith, 194, 216; work unattached, 216; the path of work difficult, 191; *vide* Karma and Karma-yoga.
World—external world, what is it? 76; its pleasures abandoned for God, 280; a prison-house, 113; to a Lover of God, 128; world and Prema, 221; the curse of the service of the world, 170; can live in it without attachment, 218.
Worldly men, their nature, 184; like vultures, 194; worldly man and his hope, 208; not easily changed by Divine Grace, 211; and ochre coloured robe, 213; and Work without Attachment, 296.
Worship, many-sided, 305; of a Guru, 298.

Y

Yearning after the Lord, 129, 169, 240.
Yoga, 116, 190.